# BIBLE STUDY TOOL

Appendices to the
Updated American Standard Version

*Published by*

Christian
Publishing
House

# BIBLE STUDY TOOL

## Appendices to the Updated American Standard Version

Edward D. Andrews

First Edition

Christian Publishing House

Cambridge, Ohio

Unless otherwise stated, Scripture quotations are from Updated American Standard Version (UASV) Copyright © 2022 by Christian Publishing House

*BIBLE STUDY TOOL: Appendices to the Updated American Standard Version* by Edward D. Andrews

ISBN-13: **978-1949586602**

ISBN-10: **194958660X**

# Table of Contents

Edward D. Andrews

# Introduction To the Purpose and Use of This Book

The Scriptures were given in real human languages, within real historical settings, through inspired men who wrote with precision, intention, and clarity. Every word carried meaning for its first hearers, shaped by grammar, context, covenant, and the unfolding plan of redemption. For modern readers who desire to understand what each biblical author actually meant by the words he used, a reliable translation is essential. Yet translation alone is not enough. Readers also need the tools that allow them to grasp the depth of those words, to see the historical world from which they arose, and to evaluate the accuracy of the text that has been handed down through generations of careful copying and transmission. This book was created to meet that need.

The contents of this volume gather the most essential subjects required for a serious and faithful understanding of Scripture. Each appendix addresses a key area of biblical study that every Christian—whether a new believer, a developing teacher, or an experienced student of the Word— must understand in order to handle Scripture accurately. Taken together, these studies lay the groundwork for approaching the Bible with clarity, confidence, reverence, and skill. They guide the reader into the historical-grammatical method of interpretation, anchor understanding in the inspired text, and demonstrate how Jehovah has preserved His Word through the centuries.

This introduction explains why these subjects matter, how they work together, and how the reader should use this book to grow in knowledge and faithfulness.

## The Need for a Foundation in Biblical Understanding

The Bible was not given as a collection of isolated sayings, nor as a mystical code open to whatever meaning a reader chooses to impose upon it. Each book, each chapter, and each sentence was written by an author who selected particular words for particular reasons. To understand Scripture rightly, one must understand those words as they functioned in their own languages and settings. The historical-grammatical method of interpretation is built upon this principle. It seeks to uncover the intent of the inspired author by examining vocabulary, grammar, literary structure, cultural background, historical situation, and covenantal context. It refuses to read modern assumptions, later traditions, allegorical systems, or personal impressions into the text. Instead, it allows the text to speak for itself.

These appendices equip the reader to do exactly that. A reliable translation such as the Updated American Standard Version gives direct access to the inspired wording, but these studies explain the principles that guided its creation, the manuscript evidence that undergirds its accuracy, and the historical realities that shaped the biblical world. When readers grasp these matters, they are able to approach Scripture with a disciplined mind and a reverent heart, ready to receive what God caused His writers to record.

# The Relevance of These Studies for Every Christian

Every Christian is called to handle the Word with care, to test all teachings against Scripture, and to grow in knowledge. This responsibility falls on all believers, not merely pastors or scholars. The apostolic writings consistently urge Christians to pursue understanding, to guard against error, and to build their faith on the truth. The path of discipleship requires a mind shaped by the Word and a life molded by obedience to it.

For that reason, this book is designed not only for specialists but for all who desire a deeper grasp of the Scriptures. It assumes no advanced training. Instead, each appendix explains its subject with clarity and purpose, while maintaining the academic precision needed for serious study. The goal is to give readers the tools to understand Scripture for themselves, to evaluate teachings wisely, and to grow into mature, informed disciples of Christ.

# How These Appendices Work Together

Although each appendix treats a distinct subject, they form a unified whole. Together they answer four essential questions that stand at the center of biblical understanding.

The first question asks how the Bible should be translated. To know what an author meant, one must know what he actually wrote. Translation philosophy directly influences the clarity and accuracy of the text a reader encounters. This book explains why a formal, word-for-word approach best preserves the inspired wording and how the UASV reflects that commitment.

The second question concerns the reliability of the biblical text. Many Christians have never examined the manuscript evidence that preserves the Hebrew and Greek Scriptures, yet this evidence is one of the strongest testimonies to the trustworthiness of the Bible. These appendices explore how the text was transmitted, how early manuscripts confirm its stability, and why the modern critical text accurately reflects the original writings.

The third question addresses interpretation. Even with an accurate translation and well-established text, the reader must know how to interpret Scripture faithfully. Interpretation is not guesswork. It is a disciplined process shaped by linguistic, historical, and contextual analysis. The appendix on interpretation guides readers through these principles, showing how each passage must be understood according to the author's intended meaning.

The fourth question concerns background. The Scriptures assume knowledge of ancient cultures, geography, politics, religious practices, family structures, and covenantal expectations. Understanding these matters enriches one's grasp of the text and guards against misinterpretation. The background studies in this volume illuminate the world of the Old and New Testaments, enabling the reader to follow the biblical narrative with greater clarity.

These core subjects prepare the reader to engage confidently with the remaining appendices, which explore apologetics, evangelism, Bible difficulties, and the significance of the divine name. By progressing through them, the reader gains a complete study foundation that strengthens faith and deepens understanding.

## The Importance of Knowing What the Biblical Authors Meant

The heart of biblical study lies in uncovering authorial intent. Because the Scriptures are inspired, the meaning the author intended is exactly the meaning God intended. This truth places enormous importance on accuracy, clarity, and careful study. When a reader knows what an inspired author meant by the words he chose, he is able to grasp doctrine correctly, apply wisdom faithfully, and obey God with understanding rather than assumption.

Each appendix in this volume is crafted to support that goal. They do not offer speculation or impose later theological systems on the text. Instead, they bring the reader closer to the world of the biblical authors, to the words they used, and to the truths they communicated. Through these studies, the reader becomes better equipped to understand Scripture as it was given, rather than as it is often misinterpreted.

## Why These Subjects Are Essential for Serious Bible Study

Without a strong foundation in translation principles, manuscript reliability, historical background, interpretation, and apologetic clarity, biblical study remains shallow. Readers may rely on paraphrastic versions that obscure the original wording. They may encounter questions about manuscript differences or historical claims and lack the knowledge to respond. They may misinterpret passages by imposing modern categories or separating verses from their context. They may overlook the significance of covenantal development, the meaning of key terms, or the theological richness of Scripture.

These appendices address these needs directly. They provide the reader with essential tools that strengthen confidence in Scripture, illuminate its meaning, and build skill for lifelong study. They show that Jehovah has preserved His Word with precision and clarity and that the diligent reader can understand it with accuracy and reverence.

## How to Use This Book

This book can be read straight through, but it is also suitable for topical study. Readers may consult specific appendices when particular questions arise, or use the entire volume as a companion to their reading of Scripture. It can serve as a reference for personal study, a foundation for teaching, or a guide for discipleship. Because each appendix builds toward understanding what the biblical authors meant by the words they used, the reader will benefit most by reading them with Scripture open, examining the texts discussed, and applying the principles outlined.

This volume is designed to foster growth. Each subject has been selected because it helps the reader understand Scripture more accurately, apply it more faithfully, and defend it more confidently. The more familiar the reader becomes with these studies, the more clearly the Scriptures will unfold.

## The Value of a Disciplined Approach to Scripture

The Bible yields its meaning to those who approach it with humility, diligence, and discipline. It is not unlocked by emotional impressions, allegorical imagination, or speculative interpretation. It must be studied with a sound method, grounded in the inspired words themselves. These appendices provide that method. They train the mind to think carefully, to ask the right questions, to pay attention to language, context, and historical reality. They lead the reader away from subjective interpretation and toward a clear understanding of what God caused His authors to write.

Through this disciplined approach, the reader grows in wisdom, discernment, and faith. Scripture becomes not merely familiar but deeply understood. Difficult passages become clear. Apparent contradictions find resolution. The doctrines of Scripture rise steadily from the inspired text.

The path of obedience becomes more defined, and the reader becomes more firmly rooted in truth.

# A Resource for Lifelong Study

The contents of this book are not meant to be mastered in a single reading. They provide a foundation for a lifetime of study. As the reader continues to grow, these subjects will return again and again, each time offering new insight and deeper understanding. The Scriptures do not change, but the reader's capacity to understand them increases as knowledge is strengthened. This book exists to build that capacity. It invites the reader into a deeper engagement with the Word and equips him for faithful study throughout life.

# APPENDIX 1 Principles of Bible Translation for the Updated American Standard Version

## Introduction: Why Translation Principles Matter

The Bible was written in real human languages, in specific historical settings, by inspired men who chose particular words and constructions under the guidance of the Holy Spirit. The Old Testament was composed primarily in ancient Hebrew with some Aramaic, while the New Testament was written in Koine Greek, the common Greek of the first century C.E. Since very few Christians can read these languages with competence, the Scriptures must be translated into the contemporary languages of the world so that God's people can hear what He has actually said.

Because translation inevitably stands between the original text and the modern reader, the philosophy that governs the translator's work becomes crucial. A translator either aims to reproduce the words that God caused His authors to write, or he attempts to reproduce what he believes those words mean. These two aims are not identical. The Updated American Standard Version (UASV 2022) deliberately follows a formal, or essentially word-for-word, approach because its purpose is to give readers as direct an access as possible to the inspired wording itself. The task of determining the full meaning of that wording belongs first of all to the careful reader, teacher, and expositor.

This article explains the principles that govern the UASV. It distinguishes literal translation from interpretive rendering, clarifies the proper use of interlinear tools, addresses barriers that prevent a "perfect" translation, and illustrates why a disciplined literal method best honors the authority and precision of Scripture.

# Original Languages and The Necessity of Translation

The Hebrew and Greek Scriptures arose in concrete historical settings. Moses addressed Israel in Hebrew as they came out of Egypt. The prophets spoke in Hebrew or Aramaic to the covenant people across centuries. The apostles wrote in Koine Greek to assemblies scattered across the Roman world. A first-century believer who heard Paul's Letter to the Romans read aloud encountered it directly in the language Paul wrote.

Modern readers do not share that linguistic world. English, Spanish, Swahili, Korean, and thousands of other languages differ markedly in vocabulary, grammar, and idiom from Biblical Hebrew, Aramaic, and Koine Greek. Therefore, if people today are to hear "every word that proceeds out of the mouth of God," the original wording must be carried over into their tongue as faithfully as possible.

Translation is thus not a luxury but a necessity. The question is not whether the Bible should be translated, but how.

# Two Competing Translation Philosophies

### Dynamic Equivalence: Interpretive Translation

Dynamic equivalence, often called "thought-for-thought," deliberately prioritizes the translator's assessment of the meaning over the exact wording of the text. Versions such as the CEV, TEV or GNT, NLT, NIV, NRSV, and similar works do not simply reproduce what the original authors actually wrote. Instead, the translators analyze a passage, decide what they think the biblical writer intended to convey, and then write an English sentence that, in their judgment, communicates that intention in a natural, idiomatic way.

This approach may produce smooth, contemporary prose, but it builds interpretation into the translation itself. The rendering the reader receives is already a paraphrase of the original. The line between a translation and a running commentary becomes blurred. Where the translators are correct, the reader may be helped; where the translators misinterpret a construction, an allusion, or a theological nuance, their misunderstanding is quietly embedded into the "Bible" that the reader holds.

Dynamic equivalence advocates sometimes claim that word-for-word translation is impossible or even misleading, and that only a meaning-based approach genuinely communicates Scripture. That claim is exaggerated. Words carry meaning; God chose words. When translators replace those words with their own explanatory paraphrases, they inevitably insert their own theology and exegesis into the text.

## Formal Equivalence: Literal Translation

Formal equivalence, or essentially literal translation, seeks to preserve the lexical choices, grammatical structures, and even the word order of the original languages wherever intelligible English allows. Versions such as the ASV, RSV, NASB (especially the 1995 edition), and the UASV stand in this tradition. The ESV and CSB retain many literal features, though both self-consciously describe themselves as "essentially literal" or "optimal equivalence," signaling a greater willingness to depart from the form of the text when the translators deem it useful.

A genuinely literal translation does not mindlessly force Greek or Hebrew syntax onto English. It does, however, insist on maintaining as much of the form as possible, precisely because that form was chosen by the inspired author. When Paul writes a genitive construction, a participle, or a specific preposition, those choices are meaningful. The task of the formal-equivalence translator is to represent those choices transparently so that readers and teachers can wrestle with what God actually said.

Hence the guiding principle of the UASV: the translator's duty is to give readers what God said through His human authors, not what the translator thinks God meant. Determining meaning from the words belongs to the interpreter.

# Interlinear Tools Versus Literal Translations

## What an Interlinear Actually Is

An interlinear is not a translation but a study tool. Typically, the Greek or Hebrew text appears in one line, while beneath each word stands a simple lexical gloss, often drawn straight from a lexicon without regard to context, grammar, or idiom. In another column there may be a full English translation such as the ESV or NASB.

Because the glosses under the original words follow the original word order, and because they often use the most basic dictionary equivalent, the resulting English string is usually rough, choppy, and sometimes almost unintelligible. For example, an interlinear for Romans 3:22 may read something like: "righteousness but of God through faith of Jesus of Christ into all the believing not for there is distinction." No one would call this English. It is simply a mapping of Greek words to basic English glosses.

The interlinear is designed to help those who do not read Greek or Hebrew verify how a translation relates to the underlying text. It alerts the student when a version has added, omitted, or significantly paraphrased words. But an interlinear is not itself a model of good translation.

## Misrepresentation of Literal Translation

Advocates of dynamic equivalence sometimes treat interlinear strings as examples of "literal translation" and then declare such literalism to be impossible or useless. Authors such as Bill Mounce, J. Scott Duvall, and Daniel Hays have taken interlinear word sequences and presented them as if they represent what a genuine formal-equivalence translation aims to do. They then point out, quite correctly, that such English is hardly readable, and conclude that "literal translation" is a myth or "linguistic nonsense."

This argument trades on confusion. Literal translations such as the ASV, NASB 1995, RSV, and UASV do not attempt to reproduce interlinear-style glosses. They begin with the original words, but they also fully reckon with morphology, syntax, and the normal patterns of English.

Grammar is not ignored; it is carefully mapped. Thus Romans 3:22 in these versions reads along the lines of: "even the righteousness of God through faith in Jesus Christ for all those who believe; for there is no distinction." The form of Paul's sentence is preserved, but the result is clear, grammatical English.

| δικαιοσύνη | δὲ | θεοῦ | διὰ πίστεως |
|---|---|---|---|
| righteousness | but | of God | through faith |

| Ἰησοῦ | Χριστοῦ | | |
|---|---|---|---|
| of Jesus | of Christ | | |

| εἰς | πάντας | τοὺς | πιστεύοντας. |
|---|---|---|---|
| into | all | the | believing |

| οὐ | γάρ | ἐστιν | διαστολή |
|---|---|---|---|
| not | for | there is | distinction |

The same can be seen with Matthew 17:18. An interlinear might show "and rebuked it the Jesus and came out from him the demon and was healed the boy from the hour that." Yet the ASV, NASB 1995, UASV, RSV, ESV, and CSB render this as, "And Jesus rebuked him, and the demon came out of him, and the boy was healed from that hour," or with minor variations. Literal translations respect grammar and idiom; they are not bound to the wooden glosses of an interlinear study aid.

# Why Literal Translation Best Honors Inspiration

Translation is sometimes described, even by scholars, as "translating meaning, not words." In practice, this slogan often means that the translator feels free to re-express what he believes the text intends to say, with relatively little concern for preserving the actual wording. Yet words are precisely how meaning is encoded. When God inspired Scripture, He did not merely breathe out abstract "meanings"; He breathed out specific sentences, constructions, and expressions.

The literal translator therefore attends intently to every lexeme, particle, and syntactic relation. When Paul chooses the preposition "through" rather than "on account of," or when James uses a participle rather than a finite verb, those are not incidental. They participate in the meaning. If a translator discards them, the reader is prevented from seeing details that the Holy Spirit chose to include.

Literal translation does not guarantee correct interpretation. But it preserves the inspired data upon which sound interpretation depends. Dynamic equivalence, by contrast, tends to flatten and domesticate that data. When a committee converts a metaphor into a prosaic statement, weakens a theological term, or replaces a precise expression with a generalized paraphrase, the reader receives a filtered and sometimes distorted message.

The UASV recognizes that the meaning of Scripture is accessed by exegesis, preaching, and personal study, not by translators making interpretive decisions on behalf of the church. Therefore it privileges lexical and grammatical accuracy over smoothness and novelty.

# Barriers to a Perfect Translation

No translation in any language can be absolutely perfect. Several barriers stand in the way, even when translators are reverent and careful. Recognizing these limitations helps define realistic goals and highlights why a disciplined literal method is still the most trustworthy.

### Textual Barriers

The autographs—the original documents penned by Moses, David, Isaiah, Paul, and others—no longer exist. What we possess are thousands of handwritten copies preserved in various textual families: Alexandrian, Byzantine, Western, Caesarean, and others. For the New Testament alone, there are roughly 5,900 Greek manuscripts, as well as ancient versions in Latin, Syriac, Coptic, and more.

Because scribes occasionally made mistakes, the copies do not agree in every detail. For over a millennium of transmission, there were periods when scribes sometimes added marginal notes, harmonized parallel passages, or made other changes, whether accidental or intentional. Yet the overwhelming majority of differences are minor: spelling variations, word order shifts, or obvious slips of the pen.

From the nineteenth century onward, scholars worked to compare all available witnesses and reconstruct the earliest attainable text. The 1881 Westcott-Hort edition was a watershed. Later, the Nestle-Aland and United Bible Societies editions refined this work, drawing also on twentieth-century discoveries of early papyri, many within decades of the original writings. These papyri largely confirmed the Alexandrian-type text favored in critical editions.

Between Westcott-Hort and current Nestle-Aland editions, the difference is small, often estimated well above 99 percent. The remaining variants rarely affect any doctrine. For evangelical translators, the goal is not to reproduce a particular manuscript or textual tradition but to render the original wording. Using all the evidence, one can say with confidence that the Hebrew and Greek texts underlying modern critical editions reflect that wording with an accuracy of at least 99.9 percent.

The UASV draws primarily on the best critical texts—Westcott-Hort, Nestle-Aland, UBS, and the Biblia Hebraica series—while also consulting readings from the major textual families. When variants are exegetically significant, footnotes can inform the reader. This is far superior to simply following a late ecclesiastical text such as the Textus Receptus or preserving traditional but secondary readings for sentimental reasons.

### Language Barriers

A second barrier is the difference between ancient and modern languages. Hebrew, Aramaic, and Koine Greek have grammatical features with no direct equivalent in English. They use aspects, stems, and cases rather than the tense system of English. Their vocabulary clusters differently; a single Hebrew or Greek word can cover a wider range of meanings than any one English term.

Because of this, no single English word can fully capture every nuance of a given Hebrew or Greek lexeme. When translators choose an English equivalent, some flavor may be lost and some modern connotations may be unintentionally introduced. Yet this barrier is not insurmountable. English possesses a vast vocabulary, almost always allowing a reasonably close match. Where further precision is needed, footnotes and study tools can supplement the translation.

For example, the Hebrew word zeraʿ and its Greek counterpart sperma literally mean "seed" but commonly refer to offspring or descendants. In many contexts, rendering them as "offspring" or "descendant" communicates the sense more naturally in English, while a footnote can alert the reader that the underlying word is "seed" with its covenant and promise associations. Similarly, Jesus' parable of the sower can retain the literal "seed," since there the sowing imagery is central and He Himself explains that the seed pictures the word of God.

Another example is the word group around Hebrew qin'ah in Proverbs 6:34, often translated "jealousy." In many contexts English "jealousy" has primarily negative overtones, yet in the proverb the term describes a husband's righteous zeal for his marriage covenant when wronged by adultery. Literal translation preserves the lexical link, while explanation in footnotes or commentaries can unfold the righteous dimension of the jealousy in question. The related word chemah literally carries the image of heat or venom and can denote "rage," "wrath," or "fury." Translating it with a strong term such as "enrages" communicates the intensity of the emotion.

### Translation Barriers

The third barrier is the translator himself. No translator is free from limitations of knowledge, judgment, and theological bias. Even with a sound philosophy, a translation committee might sometimes choose a weaker English expression, overlook a grammatical detail, or unconsciously favor a reading that aligns with its doctrinal preferences.

Literal translation controls these tendencies by tethering the translator closely to the words on the page. When the method is consistently followed, there is less room to impose external theology onto the text. The translator chooses among lexical options allowed by the grammar and immediate context, but he resists stepping into commentary.

Dynamic equivalent versions largely abandon this restraint. When a committee believes that a literal rendering will be "confusing" or "misunderstood," they often recast the sentence in a way that imports their exegesis and closes off other legitimate readings. The result is not so much translation as running interpretation.

Perfection would require translators who are both sinless and infallible, who always choose the best available rendering out of many possibilities. That standard cannot be met in this age. Nevertheless, a disciplined formal-equivalence approach, combined with transparent notes and dependence on the most reliable textual evidence, can produce a translation highly trustworthy for study and teaching.

# Examples of Translation Decisions in the UASV

### Romans 3:22–23

Romans 3:22–23 provides an important test case. An interlinear gloss might give the reader: "righteousness but of God through faith of Jesus of Christ into all the believing for there is not distinction for all sinned and fall short of the glory of God." This string preserves Greek word order and offers basic dictionary equivalents, but it is not English.

The UASV renders Romans 3:22 as, "even the righteousness of God through faith in Jesus Christ for all those who believe; for there is no distinction." Verse 23 continues, "for all have sinned and fall short of the glory of God." Several features deserve notice.

First, the definite article and genitive construction "faith of Jesus Christ" are translated as "faith in Jesus Christ." Grammatically, the phrase could be understood as Christ's own faithfulness (an objective genitive) or as faith that has Him as its object. Context throughout Romans, where believers are called to believe in Christ, strongly favors the latter. A formal-equivalence translator must choose, but he chooses among grammatically viable options, not by importing an alien idea.

Second, the sequence "for there is no distinction, for all have sinned" is preserved. Paul's argument that Jews and Gentiles are equally guilty rests on that connection. A paraphrase that shortens or rearranges the structure might dull the force of his logic.

Third, the present tense "fall short" is retained rather than being flattened to a simple past. This encourages the reader to consider the ongoing effects of sin, not only a past event.

## Matthew 17:18

In Matthew 17:18, the UASV reads, "And Jesus rebuked him, and the demon came out of him and the boy was healed from that hour." Here the translation keeps the three coordinated clauses connected by "and," reflecting the Greek conjunctions that tie the narrative together. The demon is specified as the object of the rebuke in some versions, but the UASV follows a more direct rendering of the pronoun in context, while still yielding smooth English.

The interlinear's awkward "and rebuked it the Jesus and came out from him the demon and was healed the boy from the hour that" demonstrates again that literal translation is not the same as interlinear glossing. The UASV handles grammar and syntax while preserving the essential sequence and wording.

## James 3:6

James 3:6 provides a cluster of important decisions. The UASV translates, "And the tongue is a fire, the world of unrighteousness; the tongue is set among our members, staining the whole body, setting on fire the course of life, and is set on fire by Gehenna."

Older versions used "iniquity" for the Greek term adikia. Because "iniquity" has become dated and less transparent in modern English, the UASV uses "unrighteousness," which more clearly expresses the moral crookedness in view while still reflecting the lexical range. The participle that literally says "spotting the whole body" becomes "staining the whole body," which gives a more intelligible picture of defilement. The vivid but obscure phrase "wheel of birth" or "wheel of existence" is rendered "the course of life," with a footnote explaining the literal imagery. Most significantly, instead of translating Gehenna, the UASV simply transliterates it, forcing readers and teachers to investigate its background rather than silently importing traditional conceptions of "hell" that blend different biblical terms.

## Sleep as a Metaphor for Death

Both Testaments use the language of "sleep" for death. The Greek verb koimaō can refer to ordinary sleep, as in Matthew 28:13, where soldiers confess that "we were asleep." It can also describe believers who have died, as in Acts 7:60, 1 Corinthians 7:39, and 1 Thessalonians 4:13. Hebrew uses similar imagery; Psalm 13:3 warns, "lest I sleep in death," and 1 Kings 2:10 records, "Then David slept with his forefathers."

Dynamic equivalent versions often collapse these expressions into "died," erasing the comparison between physical sleep and the condition of the dead awaiting resurrection. The UASV retains "slept" or "fell asleep," and when necessary adds "in death" to clarify the figurative sense, as in "fell asleep in death." This preserves the metaphor preferred by the inspired writers and invites readers to ponder its implications, while still avoiding confusion with ordinary nighttime rest in contexts where that is not intended.

## Terms Such as "Elder," "Seed," and "Jehovah"

The Hebrew zaqen and Greek presbyteros can denote simply an older man, or they can refer to an office of leadership in Israel or in the congregation. The UASV usually translates these words as "elder," allowing context to determine whether the reference is to age or to office. This choice preserves the lexical connection across passages such as 1 Timothy 5:1–2, James 5:14, and the descriptions of elders in Revelation.

For zeraʿ and sperma, the UASV frequently uses "offspring" or "descendant," but keeps "seed" where theological or literary reasons commended by context justify it. Footnotes often indicate the underlying term. This approach respects both clarity and intertextual connections, particularly in covenant-promise passages.

Most significantly, the UASV retains the divine name Jehovah throughout the Old Testament where the Tetragrammaton (JHVH) appears, rather than replacing it with the title "LORD" in small capitals. Many modern versions suppress the personal name of the Father thousands of times, even though it appears in the Hebrew manuscripts. By restoring Jehovah, the UASV allows readers to see when the inspired authors used the covenant Name and to distinguish it from generic titles such as "God" and "Lord."

## Literal Rendering and When It Must Yield to Clarity

Literal translation does not mean slavishly reproducing every idiom even when the result would be gibberish in English. There are rare occasions where a strictly literal rendering would be misunderstood or would obscure rather than reveal the author's intention. In those cases, the UASV provides an accurate sense translation while often explaining the underlying literal expression in a note.

James 5:12 literally reads, "let your yes be yes and your no, no," with the infinitive "to be" implicit. Rendering this exactly is still quite comprehensible in English and so can be preserved. But the surrounding clause, literally "let yours be the yes yes and the no no," would puzzle readers; therefore it is expressed as, "but let your 'yes' be yes and your 'no' be no," which captures the point of straightforward truthfulness.

Romans 12:11 uses a participial phrase literally meaning "boiling in spirit," alongside "not slothful in zeal." English readers might incorrectly associate "boiling" with anger; the UASV therefore renders, "Do not be slothful in zeal, be fervent in spirit, serving the Lord," using "fervent" to convey intense spiritual energy without misleading connotations. A note may mention the literal imagery of boiling.

These carefully chosen departures from strict literalness are exceptions governed by the principle of faithfulness. When the literal wording would baffle or misdirect, the translator may render the underlying sense, but he does so sparingly, notes the choice whenever significant, and never uses this as a pretext to insert theology or speculation.

# The Divine Name Jehovah in Translation

One of the most consequential decisions in English Bible history has been the treatment of the Tetragrammaton, JHVH. Ancient Hebrew manuscripts contain the Name thousands of times. Yet many modern versions substitute the title "LORD" in small capitals. This convention arose from Jewish scribal practice, not from any instruction in Scripture itself. The result is that readers often cannot distinguish between texts that speak of Jehovah personally and those that speak of "my lord" or "the Lord" in a more general sense.

The UASV reverses this trend by restoring the Name as Jehovah wherever the Tetragrammaton occurs. This aligns with the 1901 ASV, which likewise used "Jehovah" consistently. The choice is both theologically and linguistically significant. It reminds readers that the God of Israel revealed His personal Name to Moses, that this Name is bound up with His covenant faithfulness, and that Scripture speaks of Jehovah not as an abstract deity but as the living God who enters into relationship with His people.

Literal translation requires that proper names be translated as names, not replaced with titles. Just as the UASV does not substitute "the Anointed One" every time the Greek Christos appears, but rather preserves "Christ" and lets teachers explain the term, so it does not hide Jehovah behind the generic "LORD."

# The Updated American Standard Version Within the Spectrum of English Bibles

Historically, English Bibles have ranged from highly literal to freely paraphrastic. At the explicit literal end stand versions such as the Young's Literal Translation and the 1901 American Standard Version, which, despite some archaic language and occasional infelicities, seek to stick very close to the Hebrew and Greek forms. The Revised Standard Version and its descendants, including the early NASB, maintained a strong formal-equivalence posture.

Over time, market pressures and changing translation theories led many committees to loosen their methods. The ESV labels itself "essentially literal," signaling that it will sometimes adopt more interpretive renderings for the sake of clarity or stylistic preference. The CSB calls its philosophy "optimal equivalence," an intentionally flexible term. The 2020 revision of the NASB moves noticeably toward thought-for-thought renderings in places, reflecting the influence of readers accustomed to smoother, less demanding versions.

Against this background, the UASV deliberately positions itself as a fully literal modern translation. It builds upon the ASV's rigorous treatment of the original text while removing archaic pronouns and forms, correcting known lexical and textual issues, and incorporating more than a century of advances in textual criticism and lexicography. Where the ASV used "iniquity," "thee," or "ye," the UASV updates to "unrighteousness," "you," and contemporary sentence structure, yet it resists the strong trend toward interpretive paraphrase.

Because the UASV is anchored in the best critical texts rather than in the Textus Receptus or ecclesiastical traditions, it is free to follow the earliest and most reliable readings. Because it is governed by the principle of formal equivalence, it allows readers to see where modern dynamic versions have significantly departed from the wording of Scripture.

# Methodology of the UASV

The methodology of the UASV can be summarized in several interrelated commitments.

First, it adheres to the historical-grammatical method of interpretation. The translators investigate how words and constructions functioned in the original languages, how they were used in comparable literature, and how they operate in context. This exegesis then informs the choice among legitimate English equivalents without importing allegorical or speculative meanings.

Second, it consistently distinguishes translation from commentary. The base text aims to be as transparent a representation of the Hebrew and Greek as English will allow. When additional explanation is helpful, such as clarifying that a metaphor refers to death or that an expression is literally "wheel of birth," that information appears in the margin or footnotes, not as part of the main text itself.

Third, it utilizes the best available textual evidence, giving careful attention to the Alexandrian witnesses, significant Byzantine readings, and early versions. Readings are weighed, not counted. When substantial variants bear on interpretation, the UASV alerts the reader rather than silently choosing one and obscuring the others.

Fourth, the UASV maintains consistent rendering of key theological and lexical terms wherever context permits. Words such as "righteousness," "justification," "sanctification," "soul," and "spirit" are translated with uniformity so that readers can trace themes across books. Where context demands a different rendering within the accepted semantic range, that choice is made deliberately and documented.

Fifth, it retains metaphors and figures of speech rather than prematurely collapsing them into abstract explanations. Sleep for death, walking for conduct, heart for inner person, flesh for human weakness, and similar expressions are preserved so that readers encounter Scripture's own imagery and can meditate on it.

Finally, the UASV recognizes that absolute perfection is unattainable in any human work, but that disciplined adherence to a coherent, reverent philosophy can produce a translation that is exceptionally accurate, stable, and useful for serious study, preaching, and personal reading.

By striving to give the church what God actually said through Moses, the prophets, Christ's apostles, and other inspired writers, the Updated American Standard Version seeks to uphold the authority, clarity, and sufficiency of Scripture in a world that often prefers ease to precision and interpretation to truth.

# APPENDIX 2 Bible Manuscripts and Versions – Why We Need to Know

## Manuscripts of the Hebrew Old Testament

The manuscripts of the Hebrew Old Testament form a continuous, traceable stream of transmission from Moses' day down to the present. That stream can be studied in its languages, its materials, its copyists, and its textual history in both Hebrew and early translations. When all of this data is examined together, the picture is one of remarkable stability and preservation rather than loss and corruption.

## Materials

The earliest Hebrew Scripture writings were not bound books but scrolls. The Law that Jehovah commanded Moses to write (for example, Exodus 24:4; Deuteronomy 31:9, 24–26) would have been written on a scroll, likely of prepared animal skin. By the time of the monarchy, references to the "Book of the Law" and other written prophetic collections indicate a growing library of written revelation preserved in the royal and temple archives.

In the ancient Near East, scribes used several materials: stone, clay tablets, papyrus, and leather or parchment. For the Hebrew Scriptures, the primary materials were:

1. Stone or other durable media for brief inscriptions (for example, the Ten Commandments written on stone tablets; shorter monumental inscriptions in Paleo-Hebrew).

2. Papyrus for some letters and documents, especially in later periods and in Egypt and the diaspora.

3. Leather or parchment for formal synagogue and temple scrolls, on which the bulk of Scripture text was preserved.

Leather scrolls, made from the skins of kosher animals, became the standard for biblical manuscripts. The scrolls were sewn together from multiple sheets, written in carefully arranged columns. Margins were left on all sides, and the number of lines per column was often regulated. Ink was usually carbon-based, made from soot and gum, which produced a deep black writing that adhered well to the prepared surface.

Over time parchment (a more carefully prepared animal skin) became more common, especially for codices (leaf-books) in the first millennium C.E. The great Masoretic codices, such as Aleppo and Leningrad, are parchment codices, representing the culmination of centuries of scribal refinement.

## Styles of Writing

The earliest Hebrew inscriptions and documents used an ancient script often called Paleo-Hebrew, a form of the old Canaanite alphabet. This script appears in early inscriptions from the monarchic period, such as the Siloam inscription, and likely reflects the script in which the earliest biblical books were originally written.

During and after the Babylonian Exile, Jewish scribes increasingly adopted the Aramaic "square" script, which eventually became the standard Hebrew script. By the time of Ezra and Nehemiah in the fifth century B.C.E., this shift was well underway. The square script, refined and standardized over the centuries, remains the basic form of Hebrew writing today.

Within the square script, various styles developed: formal book hands for Scripture; less formal documentary hands for contracts and letters; and ornamental scripts for special purposes. The Masoretic manuscripts exhibit a highly disciplined book hand, with carefully formed letters, consistent spacing, and standardized decorative flourishes for certain letters at the beginnings or ends of lines.

The Dead Sea Scrolls show both formal and semi-formal Hebrew hands. Some biblical scrolls are written in very elegant scripts, while others use more functional styles. Interestingly, a few Qumran manuscripts of the Torah are written in Paleo-Hebrew script, even though the language itself is standard Biblical Hebrew. This suggests a conscious archaism, perhaps to signal particular reverence for the Pentateuch.

## Copyists

The people who copied the Hebrew Scriptures were not merely professional penmen; they were guardians of a sacred text. In various periods they are referred to simply as "scribes" (sopherim in Hebrew) or, in later periods, as Masoretes. Even when not named directly, they are presupposed throughout Scripture wherever written revelation is read, corrected, or transmitted.

Before the Exile, scribes in the royal court and temple circles would have been responsible for copying and preserving Scripture. Men like Ezra, described as "a scribe skilled in the Law of Moses," stand at the head of a long tradition of scholars who not only copied but also taught and explained the text. From his time forward, scribal activity became more centralized and disciplined, especially concerning the Law and the prophetic writings.

The later Jewish scribes and Masoretes developed rigorous rules to ensure accurate copying. Traditional rabbinic sources describe practices such as counting letters and words, identifying the central letter of a book, and destroying faulty copies. Whether every detail of those later descriptions reflects earlier practice, the Masoretic manuscripts themselves show that the process of copying was extremely careful. Spelling is remarkably uniform. Marginal notes call attention to rare forms or potential errors. Parallel passages are cross-checked.

These copyists saw themselves as transmitters, not editors or authors. Their task was to reproduce exactly what they had received. When uncertainties arose, they noted them in the margins (for example, in the Masora), rather than silently altering the text. The result is a tradition that is not only faithful but also self-documenting.

## Manuscripts Preserved Down to Ezra's Day

By Ezra's time in the fifth century B.C.E., the Law of Moses and earlier historical books had already been preserved for centuries. The discovery of "the Book of the Law" in the days of King Josiah (2 Kings 22–23) shows that at least one authoritative scroll of the Torah was kept in the temple archives. That scroll was old enough by Josiah's reign (late seventh century B.C.E.) to be treated as an ancestral text, yet when it was read, its content was recognized as binding.

The events of the Exile, including the destruction of Jerusalem in 587 B.C.E., posed a serious threat to the physical library of Scripture texts. Yet the restoration under Zerubbabel and later under Ezra and Nehemiah shows that the Law and many of the prophetic writings were preserved and recognized. Ezra read "the Book of the Law of Moses" to the returned exiles

(Nehemiah 8), and the people understood that this was the same Mosaic revelation binding upon their fathers.

Given the ancient Near Eastern practice of maintaining archival copies and the reverence with which the Law was treated, it is reasonable to understand that carefully preserved scrolls, possibly including early or even original exemplars, were transmitted through priestly custodians and scribes down to Ezra's day. Ezra's ministry marked a fresh standardization and public affirmation of the Law and, by extension, the other inspired writings that had accumulated up to that point.

From the standpoint of textual history, Ezra sits at a critical junction. Before him, Scripture was already written, copied, and preserved; after him, Scripture would be increasingly studied, explained, and guarded by classes of scribes whose whole vocation centered on the written Word.

## From Ezra's Time Forward Copying of the Hebrew Scriptures

From Ezra's time forward, the copying of the Hebrew Scriptures took place within a growing network of scribal schools and synagogue communities. The Law and Prophets were regularly read in the synagogue. This repeated liturgical use required multiple copies and encouraged careful uniformity.

The post-exilic period saw the development of a more formal canon consciousness. The Jews recognized a fixed body of inspired writings, and that recognition naturally sharpened the concern to preserve those writings accurately. Books came to be grouped (Law, Prophets, Writings), and the entirety was referred to in summary expressions like "the Law and the Prophets."

During the Second Temple period, scribes produced multiple copies of the Hebrew Scriptures, as evidenced by the Dead Sea Scrolls, which range from the third century B.C.E. to the first century C.E. Some groups, such as the Qumran community, also created their own sectarian compositions, but these were clearly distinguished from the biblical texts they copied.

After the destruction of the Second Temple in 70 C.E. and the dispersion of the Jews, synagogue communities across the Mediterranean and the Near East still centered their life around Scripture. This dispersion has important textual implications. Once Jewish communities were scattered throughout many lands, no central authority could simply revise or replace the text everywhere. Any attempt to alter the text in one region would immediately be exposed by comparison with copies preserved elsewhere.

The scribes and later Masoretes of Tiberias and other centers did not invent a new text. They received a consonantal text that already exhibited a very high degree of stability, and they dedicated themselves to preserving and refining it down to the smallest detail of spelling, punctuation, and accent.

## What Were Genizahs, and How Were They Used?

A genizah was a storage place, usually associated with a synagogue, where worn or damaged sacred texts were deposited rather than casually discarded. The Hebrew Scriptures, containing the divine Name Jehovah, were treated with special reverence. When a scroll became too worn for liturgical use, it could not simply be thrown away. Instead, it was placed in a genizah or sometimes buried.

The most famous example is the Cairo Genizah of the Ben Ezra Synagogue in Old Cairo. Over many centuries, Jewish communities placed their worn manuscripts—biblical texts, commentaries, prayer books, legal documents, and everyday writings—into a storeroom rather than destroying them. In the late nineteenth and early twentieth centuries, scholars began to examine this hidden archive and discovered hundreds of thousands of fragments, including many Hebrew Bible pieces from the first millennium C.E.

Genizah material is invaluable for textual study. Because it preserves manuscripts that otherwise would have disappeared, it provides a cross-section of the text as used in diverse communities over many centuries. The Cairo Genizah fragments confirm that the Masoretic tradition was dominant and remarkably uniform. Minor variations in spelling or word order are documented, but there is no indication of a radically different text.

Thus, the genizah practice, motivated by reverence for Jehovah's Word, unintentionally created a time capsule of manuscript evidence that now confirms the careful transmission of the Hebrew Scriptures.

## How Many Hebrew Manuscripts Have Now Been Cataloged

While exact numbers vary depending on how one counts fragments versus complete manuscripts, thousands of Hebrew Bible manuscripts and fragments are now known and cataloged. These include complete codices, partial codices, scrolls, and single leaves or small fragments. The discovery of the Dead Sea Scrolls alone added over two hundred biblical manuscripts, many of them very early. The Cairo Genizah added several thousand fragments.

In the eighteenth century, Benjamin Kennicott cataloged and collated around 615 Hebrew manuscripts and numerous early printed editions. Shortly afterward, J. B. de Rossi added collations from more than 700 additional manuscripts. Already at that time, the number of known Hebrew copies approached or exceeded 1,300.

Since then, manuscript collections in Europe, the Middle East, and elsewhere have been systematically studied, and many more manuscripts have been identified. Large libraries and collections, such as those in St. Petersburg, London, Paris, Oxford, Rome, and Jerusalem, house extensive holdings of Hebrew biblical manuscripts.

When all complete and partial manuscripts are considered—Masoretic codices, medieval scrolls, Genizah fragments, Qumran texts—the total easily reaches into the many thousands. Counting every tiny fragment individually yields a high number; counting only complete or nearly complete codices yields a smaller number but still represents a robust textual base.

The important point is not the precise total but the pattern that emerges from these witnesses: they represent multiple geographical regions, many centuries, and diverse communities, yet they overwhelmingly agree in presenting the same consonantal text as the Masoretic tradition.

## Early History of the Hebrew Language

Hebrew belongs to the Northwest Semitic family and, according to Scripture's own chronology, descends from the language used by Shem's descendants and later by Abraham. Abraham, called from Ur and then Haran around the early second millennium B.C.E., spoke a language that drew from the pre-Babel linguistic stream but took a distinctive form among the Hebrews.

By Moses' day (fifteenth century B.C.E.), Hebrew was already a well-developed language with a rich vocabulary capable of legal, historical, and poetic expression. The Pentateuch reflects a coherent linguistic system, characteristic of early Biblical Hebrew. Subsequent books show normal development and variation:

Early Biblical Hebrew is characteristic of the Pentateuch and early historical books.

Classical Biblical Hebrew appears in much of the historical and poetic literature, including many Psalms and wisdom texts.

Late Biblical Hebrew is evident in books written closer to the Exile and afterward (for example, Chronicles, Ezra, Nehemiah), showing subtle shifts in vocabulary and syntax.

Throughout this history, Hebrew remained distinct from Aramaic, although bilingualism was common in later periods. Parts of Ezra and Daniel are written in Aramaic, but most of the Old Testament remains in Hebrew. The Dead Sea Scrolls, Apocryphal works, and the Mishnah demonstrate that Hebrew continued to function as a living, literate language well into the first centuries C.E.

After the destruction of Jerusalem in 70 C.E., Hebrew's everyday spoken use declined in some areas, but it was preserved as a literary and liturgical language in the synagogue, rabbinic writings, and biblical manuscripts. The Masoretes, working mainly between the sixth and tenth centuries C.E., inherited this living tradition of pronunciation and accentuation and encoded it in the system of vowel points and cantillation marks.

Thus, the Hebrew language did not vanish and later get "reconstructed" by scholars. It moved through identifiable historical stages, always anchored in the continuous reading of Scripture, and the Masoretic tradition represents a late but authentic phase of this continuous usage.

# Earliest Translated Versions

As Jews spread throughout the ancient world, translations of the Hebrew Scriptures into other languages became necessary for communities whose first language was not Hebrew. These early versions are important witnesses to the text. They do not stand above the Hebrew, but they confirm and illuminate its state at the time when they were produced.

### The Samaritan Pentateuch

The Samaritan community, centered around Mount Gerizim, preserved its own form of the Pentateuch. This Samaritan Pentateuch is written in a variant of Paleo-Hebrew script and contains a text of the five books of Moses with characteristic features.

Textually, the Samaritan Pentateuch is closely related to the proto-Masoretic tradition in many passages, but it also exhibits distinctive expansions and harmonizations. Some of these appear to smooth difficulties in the narrative or to align parallel passages in Exodus, Numbers, and Deuteronomy. A few readings serve clear sectarian interests, especially regarding the centrality of Mount Gerizim instead of Jerusalem.

Because of these intentional alterations and harmonizations, the Samaritan Pentateuch cannot serve as the primary standard for the Hebrew text. However, it is still valuable. In some places it supports readings also found in the Septuagint and in certain Dead Sea Scrolls. In those cases, it may preserve an ancient minority reading. Where it agrees with the Masoretic Text against other witnesses, it adds another line of converging support for the traditional consonantal text.

## The Aramaic Targums

As Aramaic became widely spoken among Jews, especially in the Persian and Hellenistic periods, there arose a need for explanations of Scripture in Aramaic. In synagogue readings, it became customary for a meturgeman (translator) to paraphrase the Hebrew reading orally into Aramaic. Over time these paraphrases were written down, giving rise to the Targums.

The best-known Targums include:

Targum Onkelos on the Pentateuch, which tends to be relatively literal, though still interpretive.

Targum Jonathan on the Former and Latter Prophets, which contains more paraphrase and expansion.

There are also Palestinian Targums, such as Neofiti and the Fragment Targums, which show even more interpretive elements.

As translations, the Targums reflect the Hebrew text in a mediated way. Their primary value lies in how they interpret and understand the underlying Hebrew. When the Targum gives a straightforward rendering of a Hebrew phrase, it confirms that the Hebrew text, as received at that time, matched the Masoretic tradition. When the Targum diverges, it often reflects interpretive theology more than a distinct underlying text.

Even so, occasional textual clues can be gleaned from the Targums. For example, where the Targum appears to presuppose a different consonantal reading, and where that reading is also supported by other early witnesses, it may indicate a genuine variant in the early transmission.

## The Greek Septuagint

The Septuagint (often abbreviated LXX) is the earliest substantial translation of the Hebrew Scriptures. It began with the Pentateuch, translated into Greek in Alexandria during the third century B.C.E., and over the next century or so, the rest of the books were translated.

The Septuagint's value lies partly in its antiquity: it reflects a Hebrew text at least several centuries earlier than the major Masoretic codices.

However, it is crucial to remember that the Septuagint is a translation, and its quality varies from book to book. Some books are translated quite literally; others are paraphrastic or interpretive. The translators sometimes rearranged material, smoothed chronology, or clarified perceived difficulties.

In many cases, the Septuagint supports the Masoretic Text and therefore confirms that the Hebrew text in use among Greek-speaking Jews in the Hellenistic period was essentially the same as the Masoretic consonantal text. In other cases, it diverges, sometimes clearly due to translation technique, sometimes due to a different underlying Hebrew Vorlage.

When the Septuagint agrees with other early witnesses—such as certain Dead Sea Scrolls or the Samaritan Pentateuch—against the Masoretic reading, textual critics carefully evaluate whether the non-Masoretic reading might preserve an authentic early variant. However, the Septuagint is never treated as automatically superior to the Hebrew. The Masoretic Text remains the base, and the Septuagint serves as one important line of evidence among others.

The New Testament writers occasionally quote Old Testament passages in forms that align closely with the Septuagint. This shows that the Septuagint was widely used among early Christians and that its overall rendering of the Hebrew was sufficiently faithful to convey the inspired message. It does not, however, overturn the primacy of the Hebrew text itself.

## The Latin Vulgate

The Latin Vulgate, produced primarily by Jerome in the late fourth and early fifth centuries C.E., is especially significant because Jerome translated most of the Old Testament directly from Hebrew rather than from the Greek Septuagint. He consulted Jewish scholars and had access to Hebrew manuscripts from his time.

Jerome's work confirms that the Hebrew text used in his day already closely matched the proto-Masoretic tradition. Where the Vulgate agrees with the Masoretic Text against variant readings in the Septuagint, it supports the conclusion that the Masoretic reading reflects the stable Hebrew tradition, while the Septuagint reflects a translation choice or a secondary textual tradition.

The Vulgate therefore stands as another early witness in the chain of evidence, demonstrating continuity between the Hebrew text preserved in late antiquity and the text now printed in critical editions of the Hebrew Bible.

# The Hebrew-Language Texts

The heart of the textual tradition is, of course, the Hebrew text itself. This includes the early consonantal text, the work of the Sopherim and Masoretes, and the physical manuscripts that carry their work.

### The Sopherim

The Hebrew term sopherim originally referred to scribes or learned men who dealt with the written Law. In a broad sense, it includes figures such as Ezra and those who followed him in teaching and transmitting Scripture. In a more technical sense, later Jewish tradition uses Sopherim to refer to early scribes who worked on the text before the Masoretic period.

One feature associated with the Sopherim is the group of so-called tiqqune sopherim, "corrections of the scribes." Rabbinic lists mention a limited number of places where earlier scribes are said to have adjusted the text, usually out of reverence for Jehovah or to avoid expressions that might be misunderstood as irreverent.

These "corrections" do not involve doctrinal alterations or major narrative changes. They are few in number, clearly identified in later tradition, and often involve minor adjustments of wording. Importantly, the Masoretic tradition, rather than hiding such places, calls attention to them. This openness allows textual scholars to evaluate each case.

The Sopherim, therefore, should not be pictured as secret editors rewriting Scripture. Their main role was the safeguarding and accurate transmission of the text, and the very fact that their limited interventions are documented argues against large-scale, undetectable alterations.

## The Masora Reveals Alterations

The Masora (or Masorah) consists of the marginal notes found in Masoretic manuscripts. The Masora Parva appears in the side margins, while the Masora Magna appears in the top and bottom margins. These notes record a vast array of information about the text: unusual spellings, occurrences of rare words, lists of verses where a particular form appears, and so on.

Among the data preserved in the Masora are notes about special readings, including some of the tiqqune sopherim and other curiosities. The Masora also marks Qere and Ketiv readings, where the written form (Ketiv) is one thing and the traditional reading aloud (Qere) is another.

The function of the Masora is fundamentally conservative. It protects the text by documenting every unusual feature so that a scribe does not "correct" it away. When the Masora notes that a form appears only once in the Bible, or that a word is spelled unusually, it does so to ensure that future copyists reproduce it exactly.

In this way, the Masora reveals alterations in the sense that it preserves the record of where earlier scribes or traditions recognized a special reading. But it does not encourage ongoing alteration. On the contrary, it freezes the text and encircles it with a protective fence of notes and statistics.

## The Consonantal Text

Originally, Hebrew was written without vowels, using only consonants and a few matres lectionis (consonant letters that sometimes represent vowels, such as waw and yod). The pronunciation of the words, including the vowels, was preserved orally through continuous reading and teaching.

The consonantal text—the sequence of Hebrew consonants—is the backbone of the Hebrew Bible. All early textual witnesses, including the Dead Sea Scrolls and the earliest Masoretic codices, essentially agree on this consonantal base, with only very minor variations. Spelling differences often involve whether a vowel is indicated by a mater lectionis or not (so-called "full" vs. "defective" spelling). These do not alter the meaning of the word.

By the early medieval period, the Masoretes in Tiberias and elsewhere developed a system of vocalization and accents that encoded the traditional pronunciation and cantillation. They placed small vowel signs around the consonants and added musical accent marks that also signal syntactic structure. This system does not change the consonantal text. It records, in written form, the pronunciation that had already been transmitted orally.

Modern printed Hebrew Bibles still reproduce the same consonantal text that the Masoretes received, and the vowel pointing reflects the traditional reading. This consonantal text is the foundation for all serious work in Old Testament exegesis and translation.

### The Masoretic Text

The Masoretic Text (MT) is the Hebrew Bible as transmitted and vocalized by the Masoretes, especially the Ben Asher school of Tiberias, between about the sixth and tenth centuries C.E. It includes the consonantal text, vowel points, accent marks, and the Masoretic notes.

The most important Masoretic manuscripts include:

The Aleppo Codex (c. 930 C.E.), originally containing the entire Hebrew Bible and representing a masterful Ben Asher text. Parts of the Torah were later lost, but the remaining sections are of the highest value. The Leningrad Codex B 19A (dated 1008/1009 C.E.), the oldest complete manuscript of the entire Hebrew Bible, also reflecting the Ben Asher tradition. This codex serves as the base text for most modern critical editions.

The Cairo Codex of the Prophets (895 C.E.), containing the Former and Latter Prophets.

These codices are not isolated oddities. They stand at the end of a long stream of carefully controlled copying. When compared with the Dead Sea Scrolls, which are more than a thousand years older, the stability of the text is striking. The Great Isaiah Scroll from Qumran, for example, though it shows some orthographic and minor textual differences, fundamentally agrees with the Masoretic Isaiah. The overall message, structure, and wording remain the same, demonstrating textual continuity across more than a millennium.

The Masoretic Text, therefore, is not a late invention but the mature form of a tradition that can be traced back at least to the second temple period and, in its essentials, to even earlier stages in Israel's history.

## Dead Sea Scrolls

The Dead Sea Scrolls, discovered in caves near Qumran beginning in 1947, revolutionized the study of the Hebrew Bible by providing manuscripts a thousand years older than the great Masoretic codices. Among the scrolls are portions of every book of the Old Testament except Esther, with some books represented by many copies.

These manuscripts range in date from about the third century B.C.E. to the first century C.E. They show that, even at this early period, multiple textual traditions existed side by side:

A large number of manuscripts belong to the proto-Masoretic type, closely agreeing with the text later preserved by the Masoretes. Some manuscripts resemble the Samaritan Pentateuch in their tendency toward harmonization and expansion.

Some manuscripts reflect readings similar to those found in the Septuagint.

The crucial point is that the proto-Masoretic type is strongly represented and already exhibits the same general form as the later Masoretic Text. The evidence from Qumran does not show a wildly fluid text that later solidified into something new. Instead, it shows that the Masoretic tradition was already well established and widely used in the last centuries before Christ.

Where the Dead Sea Scrolls offer different readings, textual scholars can compare those variants with the Masoretic Text, the Septuagint, the Samaritan Pentateuch, and other witnesses. Sometimes a Qumran reading may preserve an early alternative that helps clarify a difficult passage. More often, however, the Masoretic reading remains superior, both in its quality and in the broad support it receives from other witnesses.

In short, the Dead Sea Scrolls overwhelmingly confirm the reliability of the Masoretic Text, while also supplying valuable additional data for fine-grained textual analysis.

# The Critical Hebrew Text

Modern critical editions of the Hebrew Old Testament are not new "versions" of Scripture. They are scholarly presentations of the Masoretic Text, accompanied by an apparatus that lists variant readings from manuscripts and early versions. The goal is to present the best attainable text, based on all available evidence, while fully documenting areas where the witnesses differ.

Several key figures and editions have shaped this field.

### Jacob ben Chayyim

Jacob ben Chayyim ibn Adonijah, a Jewish scholar in the early sixteenth century, edited the Second Rabbinic Bible, printed by Daniel Bomberg in Venice (1524–1525). This edition became the standard Hebrew Bible for centuries.

Ben Chayyim's work was based on a collection of Masoretic manuscripts then available to him. He collated these, reproduced the consonantal text, and carefully incorporated the Masora in the margins. Although later scholarship would have access to even better manuscripts, especially in the Ben Asher line, Ben Chayyim's edition was remarkably accurate and deeply respectful of the received text.

For generations, translators and scholars used the Second Rabbinic Bible as their base text. Many early vernacular translations of the Old Testament (for example, the early Reformation translations) are ultimately indebted to Ben Chayyim's edition.

### Benjamin Kennicott

In the eighteenth century, Benjamin Kennicott, an Oxford scholar, undertook a massive project to collect and compare Hebrew manuscripts.

Between 1776 and 1780, he published a two-volume work listing variants from around 615 Hebrew manuscripts and numerous printed editions.

Kennicott's goal was to test the purity of the Hebrew text by seeing how widely manuscripts differed. The result was striking: he found many minor variants, particularly in spelling and orthography, but very few substantial differences. His work demonstrated that the Hebrew text had been transmitted with extraordinary fidelity.

Kennicott did not replace the Masoretic Text; he confirmed it. His collations gave later scholars a much clearer picture of where variations actually occur, and they showed that the vast majority of those variations do not affect translation or doctrine.

## J. B. de Rossi

Giovanni Bernardo de Rossi, an Italian scholar, extended Kennicott's work by examining additional manuscripts in continental libraries. Between 1784 and 1788, he published a four-volume collection of variants drawn from more than 700 manuscripts and various early printed editions.

De Rossi's findings were similar to Kennicott's. He documented more differences, but again, the overwhelming pattern pointed to a stable tradition. The variants he cataloged mostly involved minor differences in spelling, word division, and occasionally word choice. Only in a small number of cases did variants raise significant textual questions, and even then, they rarely affected interpretation in a major way.

Together, Kennicott and de Rossi provide detailed evidence from over 1,300 Hebrew manuscripts, showing that the Masoretic Text is not the product of a small number of late manuscripts but is supported by a wide array of independent witnesses.

## S. Baer

Seligmann Baer, a nineteenth-century Masoretic scholar, devoted himself to producing highly accurate editions of the Hebrew text, particularly for individual books and sections. He paid meticulous attention to vowel pointing, accents, and Masoretic notes.

Baer's work aimed to refine the printed text to match the best Ben Asher manuscripts available. He often collaborated with Franz Delitzsch, who provided introductions and sometimes theological commentary, while Baer concentrated on the textual and Masoretic details.

Baer's editions influenced later scholars by showing how careful analysis of the Masora and the best manuscripts could correct small errors that had crept into printed editions. His work anticipated the need for a more rigorous critical text based on the finest Masoretic witnesses.

## C. D. Ginsburg

Christian David Ginsburg, a British scholar of the nineteenth and early twentieth centuries, produced one of the most important critical editions of the Hebrew Bible. He began with an edition based on the Ben Chayyim text but later shifted focus toward the Ben Asher tradition, especially as represented by the great codices.

Ginsburg's edition, published in stages and finally in full in the early twentieth century, includes an extensive introduction discussing the history of the Hebrew text, the Masora, and the manuscripts. His textual apparatus gathers variants from manuscripts, early printed editions, and ancient versions.

Although later editions would adopt the Leningrad Codex more consistently as their base, Ginsburg's work laid foundations in collating and evaluating the Masoretic tradition. He showed that careful comparison of the best manuscripts can yield a very precise representation of the Ben Asher text.

### Rudolf Kittel

Rudolf Kittel, a German scholar, edited the Biblia Hebraica (BH), a critical edition of the Hebrew Old Testament. The first and second editions of BH used the Ben Chayyim text as their base, but the third edition (Biblia Hebraica, often called BHK) adopted the Leningrad Codex B 19A as the base text, aligning more directly with the Ben Asher tradition.

Kittel's editions emphasized a full apparatus of variants, not only from Hebrew manuscripts and early printed editions but also from the Septuagint, the Samaritan Pentateuch, the Vulgate, and other ancient versions. His work made it easier for scholars to see at a glance where ancient witnesses agree or differ.

The shift from Ben Chayyim to Leningrad did not produce a radically different Old Testament. It simply refined the printed text to match a slightly older and arguably better Masoretic exemplar. Differences between the Ben Chayyim and Ben Asher traditions are small, mostly in matters of orthography and pointing.

## Biblia Hebraica

The term Biblia Hebraica refers primarily to the sequence of critical editions beginning with Kittel's work. The first two editions used the Ben Chayyim text. The third edition (BHK, 1937) used Leningrad as the base and became widely accepted as the scholarly standard.

These editions present the Masoretic Text in the main body, with the Masora Parva in the inner margins and the Masora Magna often reproduced at the end of each book or in separate volumes. The critical apparatus at the bottom of the page lists alternative readings from other manuscripts and versions.

The goal of Biblia Hebraica is not to undermine the Masoretic Text but to document its history. The apparatus allows scholars to evaluate whether any variant reading offers a better explanation of the evidence. In the vast majority of cases, the Masoretic reading remains clearly superior. Only in a small number of places do editors suggest that a non-Masoretic reading might be adopted.

## Biblia Hebraica Stuttgartensia

Biblia Hebraica Stuttgartensia (BHS), published in fascicles from the 1960s and as a complete edition in 1977 (with later corrections), is a revision of BHK. It continues to use the Leningrad Codex B 19A as its base text. Its apparatus is more complete and more carefully organized than that of BHK.

BHS remains the standard scholarly edition used in many seminaries and universities. It presents the Masoretic Text with great precision, including minor orthographic features, and supplies an apparatus that draws on the Dead Sea Scrolls (where available), other Hebrew manuscripts, and the main ancient versions.

A newer project, Biblia Hebraica Quinta (BHQ), continues this tradition with even more detailed apparatus and commentary on textual decisions. Yet all these critical editions share the same fundamental base text: the Masoretic tradition as represented by Leningrad and related codices.

In other words, there is not a series of competing Old Testaments. There is one stable Masoretic Text presented in progressively refined scholarly forms, accompanied by ever more complete documentation of the variants known from manuscripts and versions.

# Manuscripts of Hebrew Scriptures

When all is surveyed together, the manuscripts of the Hebrew Scriptures form a rich and coherent corpus. Major codices like Aleppo, Leningrad, and Cairo stand as flagships of the Masoretic tradition. Numerous other codices and scrolls, scattered across collections worldwide, confirm their readings.

Earlier witnesses such as the Dead Sea Scrolls and the Samaritan Pentateuch show that, even centuries before the Masoretes, the basic consonantal text existed in a form very close to what the Masoretes transmitted. The presence of some minority textual traditions at Qumran does not undermine this; it simply shows that copies with small expansions, harmonizations, or alternative readings circulated alongside the more conservative proto-Masoretic text.

The genizah discoveries, especially in Cairo, reveal the Masoretic Text in actual use in medieval synagogue life. These fragments, though often small, match the great codices in spelling and phrasing to a remarkable degree.

Together, these Hebrew manuscripts testify that the Old Testament text has been transmitted through many centuries, across many lands, with a level of care and stability unmatched by any other ancient literature.

Edward D. Andrews

# What Assurance Is There That the Old Testament Has Not Been Changed?

The question of assurance is answered not by vague appeals to tradition but by concrete evidence. Several lines of data converge.

First, the internal scribal discipline is evident in the manuscripts themselves. The Masoretic notes, the counting of letters and words, and the careful marking of unusual forms all show that copyists were intent on preserving, not altering, the text. They did not edit silently; they annotated.

Second, the chronological spread of the witnesses shows stability over time. The Dead Sea Scrolls, written more than a thousand years before the Leningrad Codex, already reflect the same basic text. Differences exist, but they are minor and do not overturn the picture of continuity.

Third, the geographical spread of the witnesses prevents the possibility of a late, coordinated revision. Jewish communities in Palestine, Egypt, Mesopotamia, and later Europe all used Hebrew manuscripts that match one another in the vast majority of readings. No central authority could have altered all those copies in unison. Any attempt to do so would have been exposed by comparison with manuscripts in other regions.

Fourth, the early translations and secondary witnesses, such as the Septuagint, the Samaritan Pentateuch, the Targums, and the Vulgate, generally confirm the substance of the Masoretic Text. Where they diverge, the differences can be precisely documented and evaluated. No foundational doctrine of Scripture rests on a text that is uncertain.

Fifth, the work of textual critics from Kennicott and de Rossi to modern editors of Biblia Hebraica has not uncovered a hidden, radically different Old Testament. Instead, by collating more manuscripts and versions, scholars have been able to demonstrate that the Hebrew text as printed today reflects the original wording with extremely high accuracy. The remaining areas of uncertainty are small, localized, and fully documented in the apparatus. They do not touch the core of biblical theology.

Finally, the very fact that the manuscripts preserve their own history— that the Masora records unusual readings, that Qere and Ketiv are noted, that tiqqune sopherim are acknowledged—shows that the tradition is transparent. Alterations are not concealed; they are exposed to view. This transparency is itself strong evidence of integrity.

Taken together, the materials, writing styles, scribal practices, genizah deposits, early translations, Masoretic codices, and modern critical editions all point in the same direction: the Hebrew Old Testament has been transmitted with extraordinary fidelity. The text available today, represented in the Masoretic-based critical editions, reproduces the original writings of Moses, the Prophets, and the other inspired authors with a precision that justifies full confidence.

The Old Testament, as preserved in the Hebrew manuscripts, has not been lost or essentially changed. It stands as a stable, well-attested text, anchored in history and confirmed by evidence.

# Manuscripts of the Greek New Testament

The Greek New Testament stands at the center of Christian faith and doctrine. Yet believers are often confronted with the question of whether the text that exists today genuinely reflects what the inspired authors wrote in the first century. Behind every translation stands a long history of copying, transmission, and scholarly comparison involving thousands of manuscripts and other witnesses. Textual criticism examines these materials with the goal of recovering, as precisely as possible, the original wording of each book, not through speculation but through disciplined evaluation of the documentary evidence. The result of this work is not uncertainty but a remarkably high degree of confidence in the text. The early and abundant manuscript tradition, combined with careful scholarly method, shows that Jehovah has providentially preserved the New Testament, not through a single miracle of an untouchable printed text, but through a rich, checkable manuscript heritage.

To understand why the modern critical text of the Greek New Testament is trustworthy, one must first grasp the physical and historical context of the manuscripts: the materials on which they were written, the forms books took, and the hands that penned them. This is the domain of paleography. From there, one must consider the different types of sources that bear witness to the New Testament text: Greek manuscripts, ancient translations, and quotations found in Christian writers of the early centuries. These sources collectively document how the text was transmitted across languages, regions, and centuries.

The story then moves from the period of handwritten copying to the age of print. Early printed editions, especially the so-called Textus Receptus, were pioneers but were based on limited and late evidence. As additional manuscripts and versions were discovered and collated, the need for a thoroughly critical text became evident, leading to the great nineteenth-century efforts of scholars such as Lachmann, Tischendorf, Tregelles, and Westcott and Hort. Their work laid the groundwork for modern editions such as the Nestle-Aland and United Bible Societies Greek texts, which continue to be refined as new evidence is evaluated.

The following study surveys the main areas necessary to evaluate the reliability of the New Testament text: paleography, the sources of the text, the process of transmission, the rise of printed texts, and the age of the modern critical text. It culminates in answering the central question: What assurance is there that the New Testament has not been changed in a way that would alter Christian doctrine or misrepresent the inspired message that Jehovah gave through His apostles and prophets of the New Covenant?

# Paleography

Paleography is the study of ancient handwriting and writing materials. For New Testament textual criticism, paleography provides crucial help in dating manuscripts, understanding how scribes worked, and explaining certain types of copyist mistakes. It deals with the physical and visual aspects of texts rather than their meaning, but its contributions to our confidence in the text are profound. By comparing the scripts of biblical manuscripts with dated documentary texts, scholars can place undated manuscripts within relatively narrow chronological ranges. This allows one to trace the development of the text from the second century onward, with special attention to the earliest papyri that bring us remarkably close to the autographs.

Paleography also shows that the New Testament was never confined to a single center of copying. The diversity of hands, materials, and regional features demonstrates a text that rapidly spread throughout the Mediterranean world. This wide dissemination is one of the strongest safeguards against large-scale corruption, because no single scribe, church, or region could control the text everywhere. Instead, many streams of transmission developed, which, when compared, provide a powerful means of identifying secondary alterations and recovering the earliest form of the text.

## Materials for Receiving Writing

The earliest New Testament manuscripts are written on papyrus. Papyrus is made from the pith of the papyrus plant, which was pressed and glued into sheets. These were then joined side by side to form rolls or cut into leaves and folded into codices. Papyrus was relatively inexpensive and well suited to the warm, dry climates of Egypt, where many early Christian manuscripts survived. Important early New Testament papyri include P52 (fragment of John, dated about 125–150 C.E.), P46 (Pauline letters, about 100–150 C.E.), P66 (John, about 125–150 C.E.), and P75 (Luke and John, about 175–225 C.E.). These witnesses stand within a century or so of the original writings and show a text substantially in harmony with that preserved in the great fourth-century codices.

As Christianity expanded and moved into regions less favorable to papyrus preservation, parchment became the main material. Parchment is made from animal skins that are cleaned, stretched, and smoothed to form durable writing surfaces. Some high-quality parchments, often called vellum, allowed for very fine writing and elaborate codices. The major uncial codices, such as Codex Vaticanus (B, about 300–330 C.E.) and Codex Sinaiticus (‭א‬, about 330–360 C.E.), are written on parchment. These are large, prestigious manuscripts that exhibit careful copying and a text that, especially in the case of Vaticanus, closely reflects the earliest papyrus witnesses.

By the late Middle Ages, paper—introduced from the East—gradually supplanted parchment for many manuscripts, particularly in the minuscule tradition. Paper was cheaper and easier to produce, allowing for a further multiplication of copies. These later manuscripts are important for the history of the Byzantine text, although they are much farther removed from the autographs in time. Across all these materials, the diversity of physical witnesses ensures that the New Testament text was never dependent on any single medium or geographic area, which again supports the stability of the textual tradition.

## Writing Utensils

The writing utensils used in producing New Testament manuscripts also affected their appearance and, in certain cases, the types of errors made. In the papyrus era, scribes typically used reed pens cut to a point and dipped into ink. The ink was usually carbon-based, made from soot mixed with a binding agent and water. This type of ink lies on top of the writing surface and, when well preserved, remains dark and legible for centuries. The relatively broad strokes of reed pens contribute to the bold and somewhat angular appearance of early majuscule scripts.

As parchment became common, quill pens from bird feathers came into wider use, especially in later centuries. These could be sharpened to a finer point, enabling more compact and flowing scripts such as the medieval minuscules. Alongside the change in pen type, inks gradually shifted from purely carbon-based mixtures to iron-gall inks. Iron-gall ink, made from tannins and iron salts, penetrates the writing surface more deeply, which helps durability but can sometimes contribute to corrosion of the parchment over time.

Ink quality, pen control, and the physical condition of the writing materials sometimes affected legibility and led to copying mistakes. Smudged letters, faded lines, or cramped writing in the margins could cause omissions or misreadings in subsequent copies. Paleographers take such factors into account when evaluating a manuscript's reliability. The very existence of these physical imperfections, however, reminds the reader that the scribes were real workers handling real tools under varied conditions. Despite such challenges, the overall fidelity of the copying process, judged by comparing manuscripts of different centuries and regions, is strikingly high.

## Book Forms

At the time of the New Testament's composition, the standard literary format in the Greco-Roman world was the scroll. A scroll consisted of papyrus sheets glued together and rolled around a staff, with writing arranged in columns. Scrolls worked reasonably well but were limited in capacity and difficult to navigate. Evidence suggests that early Christians, however, very quickly adopted the codex form, in which sheets were stacked, folded, and bound along one edge, much like modern books. This early preference for the codex is one of the distinctive features of Christian book culture.

The codex offered clear practical advantages. It was more compact, stored more text in a smaller volume, and allowed for easier consultation and cross-referencing. A codex made it possible, for instance, to place multiple Gospel accounts or several Pauline letters in a single volume, which fostered a sense of canonical unity. The codex also facilitated rapid comparison of parallel passages because a reader could flip back and forth rather than unrolling and rerolling a scroll. These advantages help explain why so many early New Testament manuscripts are codices, both in papyrus and parchment.

Among the most famous codices are Codex Vaticanus and Codex Sinaiticus, both from the fourth century, which contain most or all of the Old and New Testaments in Greek. Codex Alexandrinus (A, about 400–450 C.E.) and Codex Washingtonianus (W, about 400 C.E.) are further examples. These large, multi-column codices were costly undertakings, requiring skilled scribes, high-quality parchment, and substantial resources. Their existence demonstrates the high value the early church placed on Scripture and underscores that the New Testament text did not remain scattered in small, informal copies. Instead, it was gathered into large, carefully produced volumes that provide a reliable anchor for textual criticism.

## Handwriting

The history of Greek handwriting in biblical manuscripts can be broadly divided into majuscule (or uncial) and minuscule scripts. Majuscule scripts are characterized by large, separate capital letters with relatively uniform height and width. Early New Testament manuscripts, especially those from the second to fourth centuries, typically use a book-hand majuscule written in continuous script without spaces between words (scriptio continua). This style emphasizes clarity and formality, suitable for literary works. Papyri such as P66 and P75, and codices like Vaticanus and Sinaiticus, exemplify this style, although each manuscript exhibits its own scribal idiosyncrasies.

From about the ninth century onward, minuscule scripts became dominant. Minuscule writing uses smaller, more rounded and connected letters, allowing for more text per page and faster writing. This change, combined with the introduction of paper in later centuries, helped multiply copies of the New Testament. The vast majority of surviving Greek New Testament manuscripts are minuscules. Many of these reflect the Byzantine text, which became the standard ecclesiastical text in the Greek-speaking church for centuries. While later in date, some minuscules preserve valuable non-Byzantine readings, especially when they independently align with earlier Alexandrian witnesses.

Paleographers date manuscripts by comparing their scripts with those of dated documents, such as official letters, legal contracts, and other archival materials. This comparison allows them to assign an approximate time frame, often within a range of fifty years. Although paleographic dating is not mechanically precise, the broad pattern of evidence is consistent: many of the earliest New Testament papyri and the fourth-century codices reflect a text that is recognizably Alexandrian and very close to what modern critical editions print. This continuity across several centuries of handwriting confirms that the essential text was preserved without radical alteration.

# The Sources of the New Testament Text

The text of the New Testament is known today not from a single continuous line of copies but from multiple, independent streams of evidence. These sources fall into three main categories: Greek manuscripts, early versions (translations into other languages), and quotations in Christian writers. Each category has its strengths and limitations. Greek manuscripts directly transmit the original language text; versions show how that text was understood and rendered in other tongues; patristic citations reveal what verses were known and used in preaching, doctrinal argument, and pastoral instruction.

When these sources are brought together, they provide mutual control. A variant that appears in a small cluster of Greek manuscripts but is absent from early versions and early writers is likely secondary. Conversely, a reading that appears in early papyri, in Old Latin and Syriac versions, and in second- or third-century writers carries great weight. Textual critics judge such patterns not by subjective preference but by applying consistent principles: greater weight is given to earlier, diverse, and independent witnesses that can reasonably be expected to preserve the more original form of the text.

## Greek Manuscripts

Greek manuscripts remain the primary witnesses to the New Testament text because they preserve its original language. These manuscripts are traditionally classified into four categories: papyri, majuscule (uncial) manuscripts on parchment, minuscule manuscripts, and lectionaries. Papyri represent the earliest surviving witnesses, often fragmentary but precious for their closeness in time to the autographs. Many of them, such as P46, P66, and P75, attest the Alexandrian text and confirm that its readings are not late scholarly inventions but belong to an early and widely used stream of tradition.

Majuscule manuscripts, written on parchment in capital letters, span roughly from the fourth to the ninth centuries. Codex Vaticanus (B) and Codex Sinaiticus (א) are especially significant. The text of B in particular aligns closely with P75 in Luke and John, indicating a stable Alexandrian tradition extending from the early third century to the early fourth. Other important uncials include Codex Alexandrinus (A), Codex Ephraemi Rescriptus (C), and Codex Bezae (D). Each has its own characteristics; for example, Bezae preserves a distinctive Western text in the Gospels and Acts, which is valuable as a witness to an early but more paraphrastic tradition.

Minuscules, written in a smaller, cursive script, number in the thousands and date mainly from the ninth century onward. Many of these continue the Byzantine text-type, which became the standard liturgical text in the Eastern Church. Although late as a group, the minuscule tradition is not ignored. Some minuscules preserve early readings, especially where they break from the Byzantine norm and agree independently with Alexandrian witnesses. Lectionaries, collections of Scripture readings arranged for worship, also contribute evidence, particularly for frequently read passages.

### Versions

Because Christianity quickly crossed linguistic boundaries, the New Testament was translated into other languages at an early date. These ancient translations—called versions—are important witnesses to the text. Among the oldest are the Old Latin translations, which predate Jerome's

Vulgate and reflect a variety of textual forms, including Western readings. The Latin Vulgate itself, completed in the late fourth and early fifth centuries, became the standard Bible of the Western Church. Although often influenced by earlier Latin tradition, the Vulgate sometimes supports Alexandrian readings and thus serves as a valuable secondary witness.

In the East, Syriac versions occupy a similar role. The Old Syriac witnesses, such as the Curetonian and the Sinaitic Syriac, preserve early forms of the text, often with distinctive readings. The Peshitta, which became the standard Syriac Bible, generally presents a more smoothed and ecclesiastically accepted text but still provides useful support and control. Coptic translations, especially in the Sahidic and Bohairic dialects of Egyptian Coptic, likewise reflect early Egyptian textual traditions and often align with Alexandrian Greek witnesses.

Other versions include Armenian, Georgian, Ethiopic, and Gothic. Each arose in specific historical and missionary contexts and often reflects the text available in that region at the time. Versions, as translations, cannot always decide between finely balanced Greek variants, especially where the difference is one of word order or synonyms that the target language does not distinguish clearly. Nevertheless, where a version clearly supports a particular reading, and especially where several unrelated versions agree with early Greek witnesses, their testimony strongly confirms the antiquity and authenticity of that reading.

### Patristic Quotations

Christian writers from the second century onward quoted the New Testament extensively in their sermons, treatises, and commentaries. Figures such as Justin Martyr, Irenaeus, Tertullian, Origen, Athanasius, Chrysostom, and Augustine provide a vast reservoir of citations. In many cases, the cumulative effect of these quotations is so extensive that one could reconstruct the entire New Testament text many times over, apart from a few verses, using patristic citations alone. These quotations are not copies of manuscripts in the strict sense, but they show what text was known and authoritative in particular times and places.

Patristic evidence must be evaluated carefully. Writers sometimes quote loosely from memory, harmonize parallel passages, or adapt wording for rhetorical purposes. Yet they also frequently quote verbatim, especially when drawing doctrinal conclusions or debating heresies. When a writer like Origen comments on specific variants, noting that some manuscripts read one thing and others another, he offers precious insight into the textual situation already in the third century. Likewise, when a father consistently cites a reading found in early Alexandrian manuscripts, this reinforces the conclusion that such a reading was broadly known and respected in the early church.

The combined testimony of Greek manuscripts, versions, and patristic citations forms a threefold cord. No single strand is sufficient in isolation, but together they provide overlapping, mutually correcting evidence. This network of witnesses, extending across geography and centuries, undermines any claim that the New Testament was fundamentally altered by later scribes or councils. Alterations leave traces, and the surviving documentary record gives the tools needed to detect and correct them.

# The Transmission of the Text

Transmission refers to the process by which the New Testament text passed from the autographs written in the first century into the multitude of copies that survive today. This process was not centralized or mechanized. It took place in homes, small churches, and, later, in more formal scriptoria. Copyists varied in their training and skill, and the conditions under which they worked ranged from ideal to hurried and difficult. Yet, despite these human factors, the essential stability of the text is demonstrated by the high degree of agreement among early and geographically diverse witnesses.

Transmission was both conservative and adaptive. Conservative, because Christians revered Scripture as inspired and generally aimed to copy it accurately. Adaptive, because as manuscripts wore out or became scarce, new copies were produced, variations occasionally arose, and certain local text-forms developed. Textual criticism studies these patterns, not to undermine confidence in Scripture, but to understand how Jehovah preserved His Word through ordinary historical processes. The abundance of early witnesses shows that the text was not free to drift unobserved; instead, it was constantly being read, used, and recopied in communities that valued doctrinal fidelity.

## History of the Handwritten Text

The original New Testament writings were produced between about 50 and 100 C.E. on papyrus, as standard writing material in the Roman world. The autographs themselves no longer exist, but the rapid spread of Christianity ensured that copies were made early and widely. By the second century, Christian communities in Egypt, Syria, Asia Minor, Greece, and Rome possessed New Testament writings. The papyri discovered in Egypt—many dated between 100 and 250 C.E.—confirm that Christians had collections of Gospels and Pauline letters and that these collections already had a relatively stable text.

As the church grew and persecution fluctuated, some manuscripts were destroyed while others were preserved, sometimes hidden away. The fourth century, especially after the Edict of Milan in 313 C.E., brought new opportunities. Large, luxurious codices were produced, such as Vaticanus and Sinaiticus, which likely drew upon earlier exemplar traditions now lost. These codices, together with other uncials, form the backbone of the Alexandrian tradition that the modern critical text largely follows. Parallel to this, the Western and Byzantine streams developed, reflecting different copying tendencies and regional preferences.

In the Byzantine Empire, from roughly the ninth century onward, the Byzantine text-type became dominant. This text often shows a smoother, fuller style, with harmonized parallels and clarifying additions. It is well represented in the bulk of minuscule manuscripts and in the standard lectionaries. In the Latin West, the Vulgate played a similar role as a standard text. Throughout these centuries, copying was performed both in monasteries and, later, in more organized scriptoria, where teams of scribes produced multiple copies. This handwritten era continued until the invention of printing in the fifteenth century, when the text entered a new phase of transmission through printed editions.

## Types of Variants

Because the New Testament was copied by hand for many centuries, differences between manuscripts are inevitable. These differences are called variants. They arise from a relatively small set of causes. Many variants are simple spelling differences or interchangeable forms of words, especially in a language like Greek where spelling conventions changed over time. These are often called itacisms and rarely affect meaning. Word order variants are also common, since Greek word order is flexible and different orders can express the same basic sense.

Other variants stem from accidental omissions or additions. A scribe's eye may skip from one occurrence of a word or phrase to another similar one later in the line or on the next line, leaving out the material between. This is known as homoioteleuton or homoiarchton, depending on whether the similar sequences occur at the ends or beginnings of lines. The opposite problem—accidental duplication—also occurs. Some variants reflect deliberate changes: a scribe may attempt to harmonize parallel accounts, clarify an apparent difficulty by adding an explanatory phrase, or adjust wording to conform to liturgical use or doctrinal preference. Intentional changes are rarer but can be more significant.

Estimates of total variants across all manuscripts run into the hundreds of thousands, but such figures are easily misunderstood. When one considers that nearly six thousand Greek manuscripts exist, along with thousands of versions and patristic citations, even a small difference across many witnesses multiplies numerically. The vast majority of variants are trivial and do not affect translation or doctrine. Only a small subset merits serious discussion, and in most of those cases the external evidence strongly favors one reading. In a tiny handful of places, the evidence remains finely balanced, but even there the alternative readings do not create or remove any core teaching of the New Testament.

# The Text in Print

The move from handwritten manuscripts to printed editions in the sixteenth century did not immediately produce a critically established text.

Instead, early editors worked with limited resources, often using only a small number of late manuscripts. Nevertheless, once a text was printed and widely distributed, it acquired authority simply by virtue of being accessible and stable. This was true of the Greek text that stood behind the Reformation-era translations and that later came to be known as the Textus Receptus, or "Received Text." While honored for its historical role, this text is not a miraculously preserved standard but a late form of the Byzantine tradition, often unsupported by earlier and better witnesses.

As more manuscripts were cataloged and studied, scholars began to recognize both the richness of the textual tradition and the need to move beyond uncritical reliance on the printed text of the sixteenth and seventeenth centuries. The work of collation, comparison, and evaluation unfolded over several centuries, culminating in the great nineteenth-century critical editions and, eventually, in the Nestle-Aland and United Bible Societies texts. These efforts did not overturn the faith but refined the text, removing later accretions and confirming, again and again, the essential stability of the New Testament's wording from the earliest period.

## The Establishment of the Corrupt "Received Text" (1516–1633)

The history of the Textus Receptus begins with Desiderius Erasmus, who produced the first printed Greek New Testament in 1516. Working under time pressure, Erasmus relied on a small handful of late Byzantine manuscripts, primarily from the twelfth century or later. For parts of Revelation, where his Greek exemplar was defective, he even translated the Latin Vulgate back into Greek to fill the gaps. This procedure created readings found in no known Greek manuscript. Subsequent editions of Erasmus (1519, 1522, 1527, 1535) incorporated some improvements, but they remained fundamentally tied to a narrow and late textual base.

Robert Estienne (Stephanus) in Paris and Theodore Beza in Geneva issued further editions of the Greek text in the sixteenth century, drawing on slightly more manuscript evidence but still largely confined to the Byzantine tradition. In 1633, the Elzevir printers published a Greek New Testament whose preface spoke of the reader now having "the text which is now received by all," giving rise to the term Textus Receptus. This language referred to its widespread use, not to a theological claim of perfect preservation, yet later defenders treated the Textus Receptus as if it possessed a special divine status.

The Textus Receptus is described as corrupt not because it is heretical but because, from the standpoint of documentary evidence, it incorporates readings that lack early support, omits early readings attested in ancient witnesses, and occasionally preserves readings for which its own late Greek base is mixed or defective. It fails to reflect the wealth of evidence now available from papyri, early uncials, and non-Byzantine traditions. While Jehovah used the Reformation era and its translations powerfully for the spread of truth, the Greek text upon which those translations rested requires correction in the light of the fuller manuscript tradition now known.

## The Accumulation of Textual Evidence (1633–1830)

From the mid-seventeenth to the early nineteenth century, scholars increasingly recognized that the printed Greek text needed to be checked against manuscript evidence. Brian Walton's London Polyglot (1657) assembled various versions and provided some collation data. John Fell and John Mill made significant contributions by cataloging and noting variants. Mill's edition, published in 1707 after thirty years of labor, listed tens of thousands of textual variants, drawn from about one hundred manuscripts and several versions. This shocked some who equated the Textus Receptus with the original text, but others saw it as evidence of the rich documentary basis for more careful textual work.

J. A. Bengel in the early eighteenth century began to classify manuscripts into families and to propose principles for evaluating readings. Johann Jakob Wettstein expanded the cataloging of manuscripts and refined systems of referencing them. Meanwhile, important manuscripts such as Codex Alexandrinus and Codex Bezae were analyzed more closely. This period did not yet produce a fully critical text, but it laid the foundations for one by gathering data, recognizing the inadequacy of the Textus

Receptus, and proposing that earlier and more diverse witnesses must carry greater weight than late, uniform ones.

By the beginning of the nineteenth century, scholars possessed far more information about manuscripts, versions, and patristic citations than the early printers had known. The stage was set for a decisive break with the Textus Receptus as a base text and for the construction of a Greek New Testament grounded in the best available evidence rather than in tradition. It was in this context that the major critical editors of the nineteenth century carried their work forward.

## The Struggle for a Critical Text (1830–82)

Karl Lachmann was among the first to make a conscious break with the Textus Receptus. In his 1831 edition, he resolved to reconstruct a text based on the oldest witnesses then available, aiming to restore the text as it existed in the fourth century, before the dominance of the Byzantine tradition. Lachmann's method, though less refined than later approaches, marked a turning point. He treated the Textus Receptus not as a standard but as a late, secondary form. His work highlighted the strong agreement among early uncials and demonstrated that they often stood against the readings preserved in the printed text.

Constantin von Tischendorf devoted his life to the collection and publication of manuscript evidence. He traveled widely, discovering and collating manuscripts, the most famous being Codex Sinaiticus, which he found in stages at the Monastery of Saint Catherine on Mount Sinai. Tischendorf's critical editions, especially his eighth edition, presented a vast apparatus of variants. He sometimes preferred readings that later scholars judged secondary, and his internal criteria were not always consistent, but his documentary work was monumental and remains foundational.

Samuel Prideaux Tregelles likewise devoted himself to a critical text based on careful collation of manuscripts, versions, and patristic citations. Working with limited resources, he produced a text that, like Lachmann's, deliberately departed from the Textus Receptus when the evidence warranted. Together, Lachmann, Tischendorf, and Tregelles showed that the earliest manuscripts consistently supported a text differing at many points from the Received Text. Their efforts culminated in the influential edition of Westcott and Hort, which in 1881 presented a text closely aligned with the Alexandrian witnesses and laid out a more systematic textual theory.

## The Age of the Critical Text

The publication of Westcott and Hort's Greek New Testament in 1881 marks the beginning of what may be called the age of the critical text. From that point on, responsible scholarship no longer treated the Textus Receptus as the default standard. Instead, the goal was to reconstruct the earliest attainable text on the basis of manuscript evidence and sound principles. This age has seen increasing refinement in the understanding of textual families, the discovery of early papyri, and the development of critical editions whose apparatuses enable informed readers to evaluate variants for themselves.

Critical texts do not rest on the authority of any one manuscript or theory. They are provisional in the best sense: open to refinement as new evidence becomes available, while already representing a text that agrees very closely with the earliest and best witnesses. The modern critical text differs from the Textus Receptus in a relatively small percentage of its wording, and most differences are minor. Where significant variants exist, they are transparently noted. This transparency and openness to evidence gives believers a solid, informed basis for confidence that the text now printed is substantially the same as that written by the inspired authors.

## The Work of J. J. Griesbach, Karl Lachmann, Constantin von Tischendorf, Samuel Prideaux Tregelles

Johann Jakob Griesbach (1745–1812) stands as a bridge between the accumulation of evidence and the fully critical texts of the nineteenth century. He developed a system of classifying manuscripts into text-types: Alexandrian, Western, and Byzantine. Griesbach recognized that the Byzantine text often combined readings from earlier traditions, while the Alexandrian and Western types preserved earlier, though sometimes divergent, forms of the text. His text-critical canons, such as favoring the reading that best explains the origin of others, influenced later editors, though his use of internal criteria sometimes overshadowed documentary evidence.

Karl Lachmann, as noted earlier, took the decisive step of abandoning the Textus Receptus as a base. His method focused on reconstructing the text that could be shown to exist in the early centuries, based primarily on uncial manuscripts and early versions. Although his editions predated the discovery of many papyri, his insistence on grounding the text in ancient evidence helped free textual criticism from traditional attachment to a late printed text. Lachmann's work, while not definitive in its specific readings, advanced the principle that the earliest witnesses deserve primary consideration.

Constantin von Tischendorf's contribution lies especially in his tireless search for manuscripts and his exhaustive collation. His discovery and publication of Codex Sinaiticus added a major early witness that often supported Vaticanus against the Textus Receptus. Tischendorf's eighth edition provided a rich apparatus that future scholars could mine for data. Samuel Prideaux Tregelles, laboring independently, collated manuscripts and versions and produced a text that gave substantial weight to Vaticanus and other early uncials. Collectively, these men shifted the focus of textual criticism to external evidence, emphasizing the priority of Alexandrian witnesses such as Vaticanus and, indirectly, preparing the way for the recognition of the significance of early papyri like P75.

## The Textual Theory of Westcott and Hort

Brooke Foss Westcott and Fenton John Anthony Hort published their critical edition and accompanying introduction in 1881. Their text leaned heavily on Codex Vaticanus and Codex Sinaiticus, which they considered to preserve a "Neutral" text—what modern scholars would describe as essentially Alexandrian. They argued that the Byzantine text was the result of a later revision, a process they called "Lucianic" recensional activity in the fourth century. While some details of their reconstruction have been questioned, the core insight that the Byzantine text is secondary and that

Vaticanus and related witnesses are earlier and more reliable remains well supported by the manuscript evidence.

Westcott and Hort also articulated a more systematic use of internal criteria, such as preferring the more difficult reading or the shorter reading when external evidence was roughly balanced. Their canons aimed to explain how scribes typically changed the text and to identify the reading from which others most naturally arose. Later scholarship has modified their canons, recognizing that the shorter reading is not always original and that scribes sometimes omitted material accidentally. Yet the combination of strong external support from early Alexandrian witnesses and cautious internal considerations remains a sound method when applied carefully and subordinated to the documentary evidence.

Importantly, the discovery of early papyri in the twentieth century has largely vindicated Westcott and Hort's judgment regarding the value of the Alexandrian tradition. Papyri such as P66 and P75 show that readings found in Vaticanus and Sinaiticus were already present in manuscripts from the second and early third centuries. This undercuts claims that the Alexandrian text is a late academic creation and confirms that it reflects a very ancient form of the New Testament text.

## The Failed Defense of the Textus Receptus

In response to the rise of the critical text, some nineteenth-century figures attempted to defend the Textus Receptus or the broader Byzantine tradition as the standard. John William Burgon, for example, argued vigorously for the superiority of the traditional text and against what he saw as the undue elevation of a handful of manuscripts like Vaticanus and Sinaiticus. Burgon criticized specific readings of Westcott and Hort and insisted that the sheer numerical majority of Byzantine manuscripts demonstrated the purity of their text. Others later extended such arguments into claims of special divine preservation for the Textus Receptus or for translations based on it.

These defenses fail for several reasons. First, numerical majority in later centuries does not outweigh the testimony of earlier and more diverse witnesses. If a particular text-form became standard in a given period, the majority of subsequent copies will naturally reflect it, regardless of whether it is closest to the original. Second, the Textus Receptus rests on a very small and late sample of Byzantine manuscripts, and it contains readings not even representative of the Byzantine tradition as a whole. Third, appeals to a doctrine of miraculous preservation for a particular printed edition lack biblical and historical foundation. Scripture itself emphasizes that Jehovah entrusted His words to His people, who preserved them through ordinary means, not that He guaranteed an inerrant printer's text in the sixteenth century.

Furthermore, early papyri and uncials demonstrate that in many cases the Byzantine readings are secondary expansions, harmonizations, or stylistic smoothings. Alexandrian witnesses such as P75 and Vaticanus regularly present shorter, more difficult, and contextually coherent readings that explain how fuller Byzantine forms arose. The Western witnesses, though more paraphrastic, also attest many early readings that contradict the Textus Receptus. The combined external evidence shows that the Textus Receptus, while historically important, is not the most accurate representation of the apostolic writings.

## The Work of the Nestles, Alands, Metzger, and Others

Eberhard Nestle initiated a new phase in the history of the Greek text when he published an edition that compared readings from several nineteenth-century critical texts and generally adopted the reading supported by the majority among them. Over time, the Nestle text evolved into the Nestle-Aland series, as Kurt Aland and others introduced a more direct engagement with manuscript evidence and expanded the apparatus. The twenty-sixth, twenty-seventh, and twenty-eighth editions of Nestle-Aland (Novum Testamentum Graece) have become standard reference texts for scholars, pastors, and translators.

Parallel to Nestle-Aland, the United Bible Societies (UBS) produced editions designed especially for translators and scholars engaged in Bible versions. Bruce Metzger and his colleagues not only edited the text but also provided a textual commentary explaining why particular readings were preferred in places of significant variation. The UBS text and the Nestle-

Aland text are essentially identical in wording, differing mainly in the nature and scope of their apparatus. Together, they represent a mature critical text drawing on the best available Alexandrian witnesses, supplemented and checked by Western, Byzantine, and versional evidence.

Modern editors continue to refine the text and apparatus through projects such as the Editio Critica Maior, which offers exhaustive documentation for selected books, and through computer-assisted methods for tracing genealogical relationships between manuscripts. Yet these refinements operate within a framework where the basic text is already well established. Changes between successive critical editions are relatively few and minor, illustrating that the underlying text is stable. This stability rests not on institutional authority but on the sheer strength and coherence of the manuscript evidence.

## Current View of Local Texts

Earlier scholarship often spoke in terms of rigid text-types: Alexandrian, Western, and Byzantine, each with distinct readings and geographical centers. While these categories remain useful, modern research recognizes that manuscript relationships are more fluid. Textual streams overlap, and individual manuscripts can contain mixtures of readings from different traditions. Rather than sharply bounded text-types, it is more accurate to speak of textual clusters or local texts that developed in particular regions and periods and sometimes influenced one another.

Even with this more nuanced view, certain broad patterns stand. Alexandrian witnesses, especially P75, Vaticanus, and related manuscripts, consistently present readings that are earlier, more concise, and better explain the origin of others. Western witnesses, such as Codex Bezae and Old Latin versions, often exhibit paraphrastic tendencies and expansions yet sometimes preserve distinctive early readings. The Byzantine tradition, dominant in later centuries, frequently reflects a smoothing and conflation of earlier forms. Critical texts prioritize Alexandrian readings not because of preconceived theory but because, in case after case, they prove to have the strongest external support across early and diverse witnesses.

The concept of local texts underscores that the New Testament circulated in multiple centers of copying. No single church or bishop controlled the text across the Christian world. This decentralized transmission makes it highly unlikely that a systematic corruption of doctrine or large sections of Scripture could have been introduced and maintained without leaving traceable evidence in the manuscript tradition. Instead, we see the normal patterns of minor variation that arise in any large body of copied literature, with a clear core text that stands out amid the variants.

## Numeration of Greek Manuscripts [5,898]

As the number of known Greek New Testament manuscripts increased, scholars needed a standardized system for referring to them. The most widely used system today is the Gregory-Aland numbering. In this system, papyri are designated by the letter P followed by a superscript number (for example, P52, P46, P75). Majuscule manuscripts, originally denoted by capital letters (such as B for Vaticanus, ℵ for Sinaiticus, A for Alexandrinus), also receive numbers beginning with 0 (for example, 01 for Sinaiticus, 03 for Vaticanus). Minuscules are numbered sequentially without a prefix, and lectionaries are given an "l" prefix.

The number 5,989 reflects the approximate total of Greek New Testament manuscripts when one counts papyri, uncials, minuscules, and lectionaries. New discoveries and reclassifications occasionally adjust the total, but the general scale remains the same: several thousand Greek witnesses of varying size, date, and quality. Many are fragmentary; others are nearly complete New Testaments. Some are single-leaf scraps from the second or third century; others are large codices produced in medieval monasteries. Each manuscript, no matter how small, potentially contributes a piece of the textual puzzle.

This massive numerical base distinguishes the New Testament from virtually all other ancient works. Many classical texts survive in only a handful of manuscripts, often separated from the autographs by a millennium or more. By contrast, the New Testament has witnesses from within decades of the original composition and hundreds of manuscripts from the first five centuries alone. The Gregory-Aland system allows scholars worldwide to discuss these witnesses with precision, enabling detailed comparisons and collaborative research that further strengthen the text.

## 28th Edition of the Nestle-Aland Greek New Testament and the 5th Edition of the United Bible Societies Greek New Testament

The 28th edition of the Nestle-Aland Novum Testamentum Graece (NA28) and the 5th edition of the United Bible Societies Greek New Testament (UBS5) represent the current standard critical texts. NA28, building on previous editions, introduced changes mainly in the Catholic Epistles, reflecting the work of the Editio Critica Maior and a more refined assessment of manuscript relationships, including the use of the Coherence-Based Genealogical Method. These changes affect only a small number of passages but show the ongoing commitment to grounding the text in the best available evidence.

UBS5 presents essentially the same text as NA28 but with an apparatus tailored to the needs of translators. Instead of listing an exhaustive set of variants, UBS5 highlights those that have significant implications for translation or exegesis. It also provides evaluations of the relative certainty of each adopted reading. This approach assists translators in making informed decisions and helps pastors and teachers understand where genuine textual questions remain and how they bear on interpretation.

Both NA28 and UBS5 embody the principle of providential preservation through evidence. They do not claim to offer an inspired edition in themselves but to present, with extremely high confidence, the original wording of the New Testament in almost every verse. Where doubt remains, it is openly indicated, and the variants are recorded for scrutiny. For the believer, this transparency should strengthen, not weaken, confidence. Jehovah has not left His people dependent on a hidden or inaccessible text but has allowed the New Testament to be preserved in a way that can be examined, verified, and, where necessary, finely adjusted.

# What Assurance Is There That the New Testament Has Not Been Changed?

The question of assurance concerns both historical facts and theological conviction. Historically, assurance rests on the sheer quantity, quality, and spread of the evidence. The New Testament is supported by nearly six thousand Greek manuscripts, thousands more in ancient versions, and a vast body of quotations in Christian writers. Among these witnesses are early papyri dating to within a century of the autographs and major codices from the fourth century that present a text already very close to modern critical editions. This documentary wealth makes the New Testament text the best attested work of antiquity by a wide margin.

Because the manuscripts are numerous and geographically diverse, they do not present a picture of uncontrolled evolution or doctrinal manipulation. Instead, they reveal a stable core text with variations mostly in minor details. When variants are cataloged and compared, the vast majority are immediately recognized as trivial: spelling differences, word-order changes that do not affect meaning, obvious slips of the pen, or stylistic differences that leave doctrine untouched. Where more substantial variants exist, such as the longer ending of Mark or the story of the woman taken in adultery, the evidence is clear enough that modern editions can mark them as later additions, allowing readers and translators to handle them responsibly.

From a theological standpoint, assurance does not depend on a theory of miraculous preservation attached to a particular late printed edition. Scripture itself teaches that Jehovah entrusted His words to His covenant people, who were responsible to copy, read, and obey them. The New Testament bears witness that "all Scripture is inspired of God and beneficial" and that the sacred writings are able to make one "wise for salvation through faith in Christ Jesus" (2 Timothy 3:15–16). The process by which these writings have been transmitted fits with Jehovah's normal way of working in history: through providential oversight of ordinary means. The existence of variants does not negate inspiration; rather, the ability to identify and correct secondary readings underscores that the original, inspired text is still accessible.

Modern critical editions such as NA28 and UBS5 express this assurance in practical form. They embody decades of careful work by scholars who respect Scripture and apply rigorous criteria to the evidence. The text they print is overwhelmingly supported by the earliest and best manuscripts. In those relatively few places where genuine uncertainty remains, the possible readings are known and documented, and none introduces or removes any core Christian doctrine. A believer who reads a reliable translation based on the modern critical text may therefore trust that he or she is hearing the same inspired message that Jehovah gave through His apostles and evangelists in the first century.

Assurance does not require the absence of all questions; rather, it rests on the recognition that the questions are limited, well defined, and addressable with the tools of textual criticism. The vast convergence of early witnesses, the alignment between papyri and major codices, the confirming testimony of ancient versions and patristic citations, and the openness of modern editions together provide a strong rational basis for confidence. Jehovah, in His wisdom, has preserved the New Testament not by shielding it from the ordinary realities of copying but by giving His people an abundance of evidence through which the original text can be recognized, restored where necessary, and faithfully proclaimed.

# APPENDIX 3 The Earliest Translated Versions of the Hebrew Text – Why We Need to Know

The Old Testament was given in Hebrew (with small portions in Aramaic), and that Hebrew text stands at the center of all serious biblical study. As Israel's Scriptures spread across different lands and languages, translations arose so that non-Hebrew readers could hear and understand the Word of God. These translations do not replace the Hebrew text. Instead, they function as witnesses to it, reflecting how Jews and later Christians received, interpreted, and transmitted the Scriptures.

Among the earliest and most important witnesses are four distinct traditions: the Samaritan Pentateuch, the Aramaic Targums, the Greek Septuagint, and the Latin Vulgate. The Samaritan Pentateuch is not a translation into another language but a separate Hebrew textual tradition of the Pentateuch. The other three are genuine translations into Aramaic, Greek, and Latin.

Each of these witnesses arose in a specific historical setting. Each reflects particular linguistic, theological, and textual characteristics. When handled properly, they confirm the extraordinary stability of the Hebrew Scriptures and occasionally shed light on local details where a scribe or translator adjusted wording. None of them overturns the Hebrew Old Testament preserved in the Masoretic tradition. Rather, they show how faithfully that text was preserved and how broadly it was received.

What follows is a detailed examination of these four early witnesses: their origin, their character, and their value for understanding the Hebrew Old Testament.

# The Samaritan Pentateuch

The Samaritan Pentateuch is a Hebrew form of the five books of Moses preserved by the Samaritan community. The Samaritans accept only the Pentateuch as Scripture. For them, Genesis through Deuteronomy constitute the entire biblical canon. Their Bible is therefore not larger than the Jewish Old Testament but smaller, limited to the Torah alone.

Historically, the Samaritans trace their origins to the northern kingdom of Israel and to the region around Shechem and Mount Gerizim. After the Assyrian exile and subsequent resettlements, a distinct community formed that combined elements of Israelite ancestry with populations brought into the land. Over time this community developed its own identity and sanctuary on Mount Gerizim, in deliberate contrast to the temple in Jerusalem.

The Samaritan Pentateuch is written in a distinctive script often called Samaritan script. This script derives from the older Paleo-Hebrew script that Israel used before adopting the square Aramaic script in which the Masoretic Text is written. The script alone reminds us that Samaritan Torah copying stands in a long Hebrew tradition that precedes the medieval Masoretes.

## Historical And Textual Character

The Samaritan Pentateuch as a manuscript tradition appears in copies that are mostly medieval and later, but its textual character clearly reaches back into the Second Temple period. Hebrew manuscripts at Qumran show a "pre-Samaritan" type of text in which harmonizing and explanatory tendencies resemble what later becomes characteristic of the Samaritan Pentateuch. This means the Samaritans did not create an alternate Pentateuch from nothing. They inherited a Hebrew text family that already circulated among some Jewish groups before the time of Jesus.

When compared to the Masoretic Text, the Samaritan Pentateuch differs in thousands of details. This sounds dramatic, but the vast majority of those differences are minor: spelling variants, small grammatical adjustments, and harmonizations where parallel passages are made to match more closely. Only a smaller group of readings express distinct Samaritan theology.

A hallmark of the Samaritan Pentateuch is harmonization. Where the Masoretic Text preserves slightly different wording in repeated laws or narratives, the Samaritan scribes frequently brought those passages into greater agreement. For example, legal material that appears both in Exodus and Deuteronomy often shows small differences in Masoretic Hebrew. The Samaritan text tends to smooth those differences so that the parallel passages are nearly identical. This reflects a scribal desire for internal consistency, but it also shows that the Masoretic tradition scrupulously preserved the differing wordings that Moses originally wrote.

Another feature of the Samaritan Pentateuch is the occasional expansion of chronological or explanatory details. Genealogies or time statements may receive additional words that make the meaning more explicit for later readers. These expansions do not overthrow the basic narrative, but they reveal a willingness to clarify and sometimes to simplify.

## Sectarian Theological Alterations

The most theologically significant differences appear where Samaritan doctrine directly touches the text. The central issue is the place Jehovah chose for His sanctuary. The Samaritans insisted that Mount Gerizim, not Jerusalem, is the divinely chosen place. Predictably, some key passages are altered to support this claim.

One classic example appears in Deuteronomy 27. The Masoretic Text instructs Israel to build an altar on Mount Ebal. In the Samaritan Pentateuch, the command refers instead to Mount Gerizim. Certain passages referring to "the place that Jehovah will choose" are sharpened or connected explicitly with Gerizim. This is not a mere variant driven by scribal accident. It is an intentional sectarian reading that relocates the authorized center of worship away from Jerusalem.

These doctrinally charged readings are important because they show what happens when a community subjects the text to its theology, rather than submitting its theology to the text. At the same time, their very specificity allows textual criticism to identify them clearly and prevent them from gaining undue authority.

## Value For Textual Criticism

Because it is still Hebrew, the Samaritan Pentateuch occupies a special place among the witnesses to the Pentateuch. It stands below the Masoretic Text in authority but above all translations, since translations inevitably add another layer of interpretation.

Its sectarian and harmonizing tendencies mean that unique Samaritan readings are rarely preferred when reconstructing the original text. However, the Samaritan Pentateuch becomes very significant when its readings align with other independent witnesses. When a Samaritan reading agrees with the Greek Septuagint and with Hebrew fragments from Qumran against the Masoretic Text, that agreement can signal a genuine ancient variant.

Even in such cases, the original reading is not decided mechanically. One must consider which reading best explains the origin of the others, which fits the author's style and theology, and which is most in line with normal scribal behavior. Often the Masoretic reading remains clearly superior. In a few places, however, the Samaritan Pentateuch may preserve traces of early textual development that help us understand how the Pentateuch was transmitted.

Most importantly, the Samaritan Pentateuch overwhelmingly confirms the Masoretic Pentateuch. The vast agreement between these two independent Hebrew traditions demonstrates that the text of Genesis through Deuteronomy was remarkably stable across centuries, locations, and communities. The Samaritan differences draw attention precisely because the shared base is so large.

# The Aramaic Targums

The Aramaic Targums are translations or interpretive renderings of the Hebrew Scriptures into Aramaic. The word "targum" simply means "translation," but these works are more than bare translations. They combine a usually close rendering of the Hebrew text with built-in explanations, expansions, and applications that reflect synagogue teaching.

After the Babylonian exile, Aramaic functioned as a widely used language in the Near East. Many Jews, especially those in the Diaspora and in later generations, were more fluent in Aramaic than in Hebrew. Hebrew remained the language of Scripture, but ordinary hearers needed help to grasp what they were hearing. This gave rise to the practice of reading the Hebrew in the synagogue and then giving an oral Aramaic rendering to explain it.

Over time, these oral renderings took on stable forms and were written down. What began as spoken explanation eventually became literary Targums: fixed texts that could be copied, studied, and used in public worship.

## Historical Development and Major Traditions

The roots of the Targumic tradition likely reach back to the fifth century B.C.E. or earlier, when the post-exilic community gathered to hear the reading of the Torah. In Nehemiah 8, Levites read from the book of the Law of God and "gave the sense, so that they understood the reading." That passage reflects the same kind of explanatory ministry that later characterized the Targums, even if written Targums did not yet exist.

By the time of the Dead Sea Scrolls, Aramaic translations of parts of Scripture already circulated. Fragments of Aramaic renderings of Leviticus and Job show that Jews were translating Scripture into Aramaic centuries before the full literary Targums of later Judaism.

As the Targum tradition matured, two main families developed. One arose in the land of Israel and is associated with Jewish Palestinian Aramaic. This family includes Targum Neofiti, Targum Pseudo-Jonathan on the Pentateuch, and the Fragment Targums. These texts are often expansive, richly interpretive, and full of midrashic material.

The other family took shape in Babylonia and is associated with Jewish Babylonian Aramaic. Its main representatives are Targum Onqelos on the Pentateuch and Targum Jonathan on the Former and Latter Prophets. These Babylonian Targums are more restrained, especially Onqelos, which follows the Hebrew text quite closely and was treated almost like an official Aramaic version in some rabbinic circles.

Most of the Targums reached their final literary form between the third and fifth centuries C.E., though they preserve older traditions. Their final redaction is later than the Septuagint but earlier than the major medieval Masoretic codices.

## Translation Technique and Theological Interpretation

The Targums demonstrate a fascinating blend of literal translation and interpretive paraphrase. At the base level, they typically mirror the structure and sequence of the Hebrew text. A reader familiar with Hebrew can often align the Targum phrase by phrase with its source.

Overlaying that literal base, however, are interpretive elements. These include narrative expansions, doctrinal clarifications, and legal updates.

First, narrative expansions fill in gaps or spell out motives. Where the Hebrew text states that one character spoke to another, the Targum may supply the content of that conversation, turning a brief statement into a fully developed dialogue. These expansions are not arbitrary. They often reflect traditional Jewish explanations of why certain events occurred and what they meant.

Second, doctrinal clarifications are especially evident where the Hebrew text uses anthropomorphic language about Jehovah. When Scripture speaks of God "coming down," "repenting," or "remembering," the Targums frequently rephrase such expressions to avoid suggesting that God is changeable or limited like humans. They preserve the meaning of the event while protecting the truth of His unchanging character.

Third, halakhic adjustments appear in the rendering of laws. The Targumika often bring the Torah into closer alignment with later rabbinic practice. Where the Hebrew commandment is concise and leaves much implicit, the Aramaic rendering may insert the developed legal interpretation. This gives the congregation both the word of the Law and its expected application in one continuous text.

Finally, there are occasional geographical or cultural explanations. Obscure place names or ancient institutions may be clarified so that hearers in later centuries understand what the text refers to.

## The Targums as Textual Witnesses

For textual criticism of the Old Testament, the Targums are both valuable and complex. Because they are translations, they belong to a secondary tier of evidence below the Hebrew manuscripts themselves. The interpretive nature of the Targums requires careful distinction between genuine textual indications and mere paraphrase.

Targum Onqelos and Targum Jonathan are especially important because they typically follow a Hebrew base very close to the Masoretic Text. When their wording corresponds closely to the Masoretic Hebrew, they confirm the stability of that text as it was read and explained in late antiquity.

When a Targum differs from the Masoretic Text, one must first ask whether the difference can be explained as interpretation. If the Aramaic simply clarifies a theological point, expands a narrative, or incorporates later halakhic detail, that tells us much about Jewish exegesis but little about the original Hebrew wording.

However, there are instances where the Targum's rendering best fits a slightly different underlying Hebrew text. For example, if a Targum consistently implies the presence of a particular word or phrase that is absent from the Masoretic Text and this difference cannot be accounted for by interpretation, this can suggest that the translator had a divergent Hebrew reading before him. Such cases are not extremely frequent, but they exist.

Even then, the Targum by itself rarely overturns the Masoretic Text. Its greatest strength lies in convergence. When a Targum agrees with the Septuagint and with a Qumran Hebrew manuscript against the Masoretic reading, that combined testimony deserves serious attention. The Targum, standing between the Hebrew consonants and synagogue application, illustrates how deeply the Hebrew text was embedded in the life of God's people.

# The Greek Septuagint

The Greek Septuagint, commonly abbreviated LXX, is the earliest complete translation of the Hebrew Scriptures into another language. It arose in the Hellenistic period when many Jews lived outside the land of Israel and spoke Greek as their primary language. For those communities, a Greek translation of Scripture was essential for worship and instruction.

The traditional story of the Septuagint's origin is preserved in the Letter of Aristeas and later Jewish and Christian sources. According to that account, the Pentateuch was translated in Alexandria, Egypt, by a group of Jewish scholars who worked at the request of Ptolemy II Philadelphus for his royal library. While the details of this story are strongly embellished, its core aligns with historical reality: a Greek Torah was translated in the third century B.C.E. for Greek-speaking Jews in Egypt.

Most scholars date the translation of the Pentateuch to the third century B.C.E. The other books of the Hebrew Bible were translated over the next century or so, with the full Greek Old Testament taking shape by the second century B.C.E. This places the Septuagint more than a thousand years earlier than our complete medieval Hebrew codices and makes it a crucial witness to the text as it existed during the Second Temple period.

## Manuscripts And Textual History

The Septuagint survives in thousands of manuscripts and fragments. These range from early papyrus fragments containing portions of individual books to large parchment codices that contain much or all of the Greek Old Testament. Famous Christian codices such as Vaticanus, Sinaiticus, and Alexandrinus are key witnesses to the Septuagint tradition.

The Septuagint is not a monolithic text. Different books show different translation styles. Some underwent later revisions as copyists attempted to bring the Greek more closely into line with the Hebrew text used in their own day. As a result, the Septuagint tradition includes both early, freer translations and later, more literal revisions.

The history of the Septuagint also includes later Greek translations produced by Aquila, Symmachus, and Theodotion. These were not parts of the original Septuagint but were produced to offer alternatives that adhered more closely to the Hebrew text. Origen's great work, the Hexapla, placed these Greek versions in parallel columns with the Hebrew text and a revised Septuagint, attempting to clarify where the Greek did or did not correspond to the Hebrew.

## Translation Styles and Textual Forms

The Septuagint does not exhibit a single uniform translation technique. Some books, especially in the Pentateuch and historical books, are quite literal. They often preserve Hebrew word order, reflect Hebrew syntax closely, and attempt to render terms consistently. These literal books serve as very sensitive witnesses to the underlying Hebrew.

Other books are more idiomatic or interpretive. Wisdom literature, portions of Isaiah, and other poetic or prophetic texts sometimes show freer renderings that reorganize phrases, summarize ideas, or employ explanatory paraphrase. These renderings still follow genuine Hebrew sources, but they cannot be treated as simple word-for-word equivalents.

The relationship between the Septuagint and the Masoretic Text is complex. In many places, the Septuagint reflects a Hebrew text essentially identical to the Masoretic consonants. In other places, especially in books like Jeremiah and Job, the Greek corresponds to a Hebrew edition that differs in length and order. This shows that, for certain books, more than one Hebrew edition circulated in ancient Judaism.

Even here, however, the Septuagint does not overthrow the Masoretic Text. The Masoretic edition represents the form recognized and transmitted in the mainstream Jewish tradition. The Septuagint reveals that alternate editions existed, but it does not annul the authority of the Masoretic form. Instead, it helps us understand how Scripture was edited and arranged in the centuries leading up to the time of Christ.

Another significant element is the handling of the divine Name. Early Septuagint manuscripts often preserve the Tetragrammaton in Hebrew letters or as a special Greek transliteration embedded within the Greek text. Later manuscripts, especially in Christian circles, frequently replace the Name with the Greek word for "Lord." Even in those cases the translation presupposes the underlying Hebrew Name Jehovah in the original text.

## Use In Judaism and the Early Church

Originally, the Septuagint was a Jewish project for Jewish communities. It was widely used in synagogues throughout the Greek-speaking world. As Christianity spread, Greek-speaking Christians naturally adopted the Septuagint as their Old Testament. Many Old Testament quotations in the New Testament follow Septuagint wording, although the New Testament writers also show awareness of the underlying Hebrew.

Over time, as Christians used the Septuagint to argue that Jesus fulfilled the Old Testament, many Jews in the Greek-speaking world distanced themselves from it and favored more strictly literal Greek translations. This separation further sharpened the distinction between the Hebrew text maintained by Jewish scribes and the Greek text preserved in Christian communities.

Despite that later divergence, the Septuagint confirms that long before the Masoretic accents and vowel points were added, there already existed a stable Hebrew consonantal text that could be translated into Greek and used across the Mediterranean world. Where the Septuagint closely tracks the Masoretic Text, it offers powerful confirmation of the reliability of the Hebrew Old Testament.

### Textual-Critical Significance

For Old Testament textual criticism, the Septuagint is the most important of all the ancient versions. Its age, its widespread manuscript base, and its many close agreements with pre-Masoretic Hebrew make it indispensable.

At the same time, the Septuagint must always be treated as a translation. Differences from the Masoretic Text can arise for several reasons. Some reflect a genuinely different Hebrew parent. Others reflect interpretive translation choices. Still others result from Greek scribal errors or later recensional activity.

When using the Septuagint critically, one asks whether a given Greek divergence is best explained as a translation decision or as evidence of another Hebrew reading. If the divergence can easily be explained as the translator simplifying, clarifying, or interpreting, then it has limited weight as textual evidence. If the divergence cannot be accounted for by normal translation behavior and the Greek implies a different Hebrew phrase or clause, then it may indicate a variant in the Hebrew tradition.

The strongest cases occur where the Septuagint's reading aligns with independent Hebrew manuscripts from the Dead Sea region and sometimes also with the Samaritan Pentateuch or Targums. In such situations, the Septuagint stands as one member of a broader chorus of witnesses that must be weighed together. Even then, the Masoretic Text remains the base, and decisions are made by evaluating which reading best explains the rise of the others and fits the overall pattern of Scripture.

# The Latin Vulgate

The Latin Vulgate is the standard Latin translation of the Bible associated with Jerome in the late fourth and early fifth centuries C.E. Before the Vulgate, Christians in the Latin-speaking West used a collection of Old Latin translations that had been made from the Greek Septuagint. These Old Latin texts varied in quality and consistency and produced a rather uneven textual landscape.

Jerome was commissioned by Bishop Damasus of Rome to revise the Latin Gospels. As he worked and studied, his project expanded to a comprehensive revision and translation of the entire Bible. Jerome's crucial decision for the Old Testament was to translate from the Hebrew text rather than from the Greek Septuagint. He called this commitment the pursuit of the "Hebrew truth," meaning that the Hebrew text preserved in Jewish communities was the proper base for translating the Old Testament.

## Jerome's Training and Approach

Jerome received a thorough education in classical Latin literature, Greek, and rhetoric. He then devoted himself to biblical studies and learned Hebrew, studying with Jewish teachers in Palestine. He spent extended years in Bethlehem, where he had direct access to Hebrew manuscripts and Jewish interpretive traditions.

For the canonical books of the Old Testament, Jerome translated directly from the Hebrew. He consulted the Septuagint and other Greek translations, but he treated the Hebrew text as decisive. His Latin style is generally more literal than the Old Latin, aligning more closely with the structure and wording of the Hebrew while still aiming for intelligible Latin.

Jerome's prefaces make clear that he regarded the Hebrew text preserved in the synagogue as the authoritative standard. That Hebrew tradition corresponds in substance to what later emerges in full Masoretic form. Jerome's work therefore links the Jewish Hebrew tradition directly to the Latin theological and liturgical tradition.

Regarding books not found in the Jewish Hebrew canon (such as Tobit, Judith, Wisdom of Solomon, and others), Jerome distinguished them from the Hebrew Scriptures. He either declined to translate them from Hebrew, used existing Greek or Old Latin forms, or explicitly stated that they lacked the same authority as the canonical Hebrew books. This distinction demonstrates Jerome's awareness of the boundaries of the Hebrew canon.

## Reception and Impact

Jerome's Hebrew-based translation initially met with some resistance, particularly from those accustomed to the wording of the Old Latin. Over time, however, the superiority of a more consistent, Hebrew-aligned Latin text became evident, and the Vulgate gained broader acceptance.

Through centuries of copying and use, the Vulgate became the Bible of Western Christianity. It shaped the exegesis, theology, worship, and devotional life of the Latin West for over a millennium. While copyists introduced their own variations over time, the core of Jerome's translation remained and was reinforced in later standardized editions.

For many medieval theologians, the Latin Vulgate functioned practically as the authoritative form of Scripture. Yet at its base, Jerome's work stood upon the Hebrew text preserved among the Jews. The Vulgate thus serves as a powerful historical testimony to the stability and authority of that Hebrew text.

## Textual-Critical Significance

In Old Testament textual criticism, the Latin Vulgate occupies a supporting role. Because Jerome translated from a Hebrew text closely aligned with the Masoretic tradition, the Vulgate usually confirms the Masoretic consonants. Where the Vulgate differs, the variance often arises from Jerome's translation choices, Latin idiom, or later scribal changes rather than from a different Hebrew Vorlage.

There are, however, layers within the Latin tradition that can sometimes yield additional information. The earlier Old Latin translations, which often reflect the Septuagint more directly, sometimes preserve older readings. When those Old Latin readings can be recovered and are found to agree with the Septuagint and other witnesses against the Masoretic Text, they provide further evidence that a particular non-Masoretic reading has ancient roots.

Even so, neither the Vulgate nor the Old Latin forms are primary authorities for the Old Testament text. They are secondary witnesses whose main value lies in confirming the Hebrew and illustrating how it was understood by Latin-speaking Christians.

# How These Versions Relate to the Masoretic Text

All four of these early witnesses stand in a subordinate yet significant relationship to the Masoretic Text of the Hebrew Bible. The Masoretic tradition, especially as preserved in codices such as Aleppo and Leningrad, represents the culmination of a careful scribal transmission that preserved the consonantal text of the Old Testament with extraordinary precision. The Masoretes did not invent the text. They inherited it, guarded it, and supplemented it with vowel pointing, accents, and marginal notes.

The Samaritan Pentateuch demonstrates how a sectarian community could adjust the text to support its own theology while still preserving the vast bulk of the Pentateuch unchanged. Its harmonizations and doctrinal alterations underscore how restrained mainstream Jewish scribes were by comparison. The Masoretic Pentateuch preserves diverse wordings, difficult expressions, and theologically challenging statements without "correction," which testifies to its fidelity to what Moses originally wrote.

The Aramaic Targums show how Scripture functioned in the life of the synagogue. They reveal the interpretive traditions, theological concerns, and legal applications that surrounded the Hebrew text in late Second Temple and rabbinic Judaism. At the same time, their base translations generally presuppose a Hebrew text essentially identical to the Masoretic Text. Where they diverge due to interpretation, they showcase exegesis rather than an alternate canon.

The Greek Septuagint provides a window into the Hebrew Scriptures as they stood in the third and second centuries B.C.E. It confirms that the basic content and wording of the Old Testament were already established long before Christ. In books where the Septuagint reflects an alternate edition, it reminds us that certain compositions went through stages of arrangement and transmission. Yet even here, the Masoretic form stands as the recognized standard within the Jewish community from which Jesus and the apostles sprang.

The Latin Vulgate links the Hebrew text with the Western church. Jerome's deliberate return to the Hebrew establishes a clear chain of transmission from the synagogue scrolls to the Latin Bible that shaped Western theology. His translation work, grounded in the Hebrew, demonstrates that as of the fourth and fifth centuries C.E. the Hebrew Old Testament existed in a stable and authoritative form.

Taken together, these versions do not undermine confidence in the Hebrew Old Testament. They enhance it. They show that as the Scriptures passed into new languages and cultures, faithful Jews and Christians recognized the Hebrew text as the standard and sought to translate it accurately. Deviations that arose were limited, traceable, and subject to correction by comparison with the Hebrew base.

Through all these witnesses, one consistent picture emerges: Jehovah has preserved His written revelation through the ordinary, careful labor of scribes, translators, and teachers. The Samaritan Pentateuch, the Aramaic Targums, the Greek Septuagint, and the Latin Vulgate stand as distinct yet converging testimonies to the stability, clarity, and enduring authority of the Hebrew Old Testament.

# APPENDIX 4 The Earliest Translated Versions of the Greek Text – Why We Need to Know

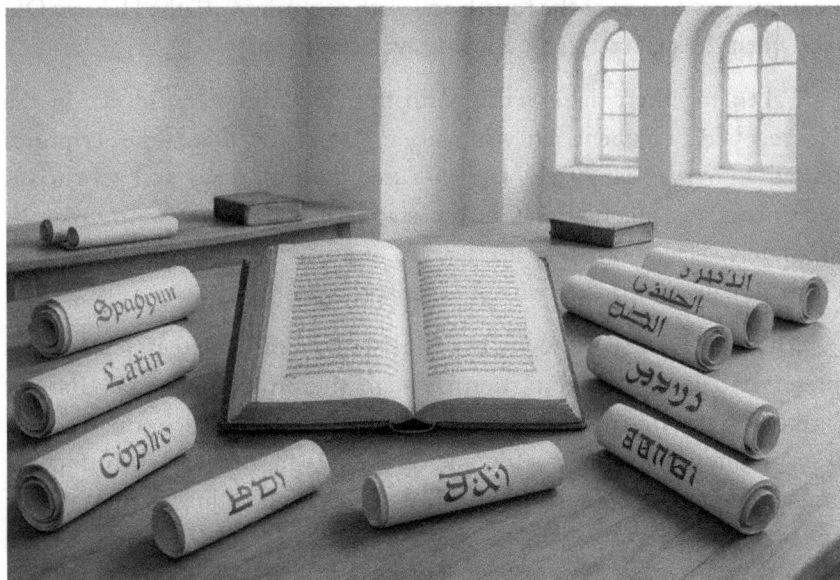

The earliest translated versions of the Greek New Testament form one of the major pillars of textual criticism. The inspired New Testament writings were originally composed in Koine Greek between about 50 and 96 C.E. As the Gospel spread, congregations of believers increasingly lived in regions where Greek was not the primary spoken language. Pastors and teachers still read the Greek text and preached from it, but ordinary worshipers needed Scripture in their own tongues. From that historical and pastoral need, a series of early translations arose in Syriac, Latin, Coptic, Gothic, Armenian, Georgian, Ethiopic, Arabic, Sogdian, Old Church Slavonic, and Nubian.

These versions are secondary in relation to the Greek text. Inspiration applied to the original writings of the apostles and their associates, not to later translations. At the same time, these translations are a crucial part of

Jehovah's providential preservation of the New Testament. Each version reflects a Greek Vorlage, that is, the Greek manuscripts that translators had in front of them. When we study these versions carefully and relate them to the Greek manuscript tradition, we gain additional data about which readings were known, accepted, and transmitted in different regions of the ancient world.

From the standpoint of the documentary method in textual criticism, versions are external witnesses. Greek papyri and majuscules remain central; P75 and Codex Vaticanus (B), for example, carry enormous weight because of their age and textual quality. Early versions cannot override such witnesses. They can, however, confirm that the type of text represented in early Alexandrian manuscripts was already widespread, or they can reveal that a particular secondary reading had a broad regional influence. The versions show that there never was a time when a radically different, "lost" New Testament existed; rather, the same basic text circulated in multiple languages, with variations that textual criticism can evaluate and resolve.

# Methodological Considerations in Using Versions

Because versions are translations, they require a distinct kind of analysis. The textual critic must ask several questions. The first question concerns date. The earlier a version arises, the closer its Greek Vorlage stands to the time of the original autographs. The second question concerns the quality and character of that Greek Vorlage. Some versions were translated from Greek texts that were largely Alexandrian in character, others from Western, Caesarean, or Byzantine forms, and some from mixed texts.

A third key question concerns translation technique. A very literal translation, which follows Greek word order, reproduces Greek particles, and tries to render Greek morphology as transparently as possible into the receptor language, allows more confident retroversion into Greek. A freer, idiomatic, or paraphrastic translation may still give strong testimony to major variants but offers less certainty about finer details. A fourth question concerns later revision. Several versions underwent systematic revision toward a different Greek standard. That process must be factored in, so that the critic distinguishes earlier layers from later ecclesiastical adjustments.

Because of these factors, the versions do not stand on the same level as Greek manuscripts. They do not occupy a higher authority, and they never silence strong Alexandrian evidence. Yet they are far from marginal. When the Old Latin, the Sahidic Coptic, and the Peshitta Syriac all attest a given reading that also appears in P75 and B, the external case for that reading becomes extremely strong. By contrast, when a reading is confined to a narrow stream of one version, unsupported by independent early Greek witnesses, that reading must usually yield to the more widely attested form.

With these methodological principles in place, it is possible to survey the major early versions and explain how each contributes to the restoration of the original Greek text.

## The Syriac Versions

Syriac is a dialect of Aramaic that became the chief literary and ecclesiastical language of Christians in Edessa and the wider Mesopotamian region. Because the earliest Christians in this area were bilingual or even trilingual, Greek Scripture and Syriac preaching coexisted for some time. As congregations matured and more people knew Syriac far better than Greek, the need for Syriac Scripture became urgent. The result was a layered Syriac tradition: Old Syriac, Peshitta, and later Philoxenian and Harklean revisions.

The Old Syriac represents the earliest stage of Gospel translation into Syriac. It is preserved chiefly in two manuscripts: the Curetonian Gospels and the Syriac Sinaiticus. These manuscripts date from about the fourth to fifth centuries, but their underlying translation reflects work that already existed by the late second or third century. The Old Syriac Gospels present a freer, more idiomatic translation style. The translators aimed at making the narrative flow naturally in Syriac, sometimes reshaping word order, smoothing roughness, or harmonizing parallel accounts. Textually, the Old Syriac often reflects a Western type of text. Its agreements with Codex Bezae (D) are numerous, especially in the Gospels. It shares the Western tendency toward expansions, paraphrases, and harmonizations, yet it also preserves shorter or more difficult readings that agree with early Alexandrian witnesses.

For the textual critic, the Old Syriac is valuable but must be handled carefully. Because of its idiomatic character, retroversion into Greek demands familiarity with both Greek and Syriac syntax. When Old Syriac supports a reading that also appears in P75 and B, particularly where that reading is shorter and more difficult, the combined testimony of Alexandrian Greek and Old Syriac strongly points toward originality. When Old Syriac stands alone in supporting an expansion or harmonized reading, its Western character indicates that such readings are secondary, even if they had some early circulation.

The Peshitta Syriac became the standard Bible of the Syriac-speaking churches. Its New Testament, in its early form, lacked 2 Peter, 2 and 3 John, Jude, and Revelation. These books were added from the sixth century onward. The Peshitta New Testament arose in its core form by about the late fourth or early fifth century, probably as the result of a deliberate revision and standardization process. Its translation style is more literal than that of the Old Syriac, often following Greek word order and preserving Greek particles. Yet it still reads naturally as Syriac and shows sensitivity to Syriac idiom.

Textually, the Peshitta presents a relatively conservative text. In the Gospels and Acts it frequently aligns with the later Byzantine tradition, though not in a slavish way. In the Pauline and Catholic Epistles, its text sometimes agrees with Alexandrian witnesses against Byzantine expansions. This mixed character makes sense historically. By the time the Peshitta emerged as a standard, Greek texts in the East were already moving toward a more unified form that would eventually dominate in the Byzantine Empire. The Peshitta, therefore, often reflects readings that had already gained broad acceptance. It is extremely helpful for tracing which readings had achieved "ecclesiastical" status by the early fifth century.

Later Syriac revisions illustrate a different kind of value. The Philoxenian version, associated with Bishop Philoxenus of Mabbug in the early sixth century, and especially the Harklean version, completed by Thomas of Harkel in 616 C.E., pursued a more exact equivalence to Greek.

The Harklean translator worked from a predominantly Byzantine Greek text, but he accompanied his main text with a rich marginal apparatus. In those margins he recorded alternative readings from other Greek manuscripts. In practice, the Harklean New Testament functions like a mini critical edition.

For textual criticism, the Harklean apparatus is extremely significant. Where the main Harklean text is purely Byzantine, its value for earliest text reconstruction is limited. However, the marginal readings sometimes preserve evidence of non-Byzantine readings, including Alexandrian or Western forms, that had not entirely disappeared by the seventh century. Because Thomas of Harkel copied these readings from Greek manuscripts he had in front of him, they effectively extend our knowledge of the Greek tradition that was still accessible in his day.

Taken together, the Syriac versions offer a chronological and textual cross-section of the Greek text's reception in the Syriac-speaking East. Old Syriac points to an early Western flavor; Peshitta reflects a more stable ecclesiastical text with significant Byzantine influence; and Harklean documents in its margins the diversity still present in Greek manuscripts of the early seventh century.

## The Latin Versions

In the western half of the Roman Empire, Latin increasingly displaced Greek as the language of law, administration, and everyday life. Congregations in North Africa, Italy, and Gaul quickly reached a point where Greek preaching alone no longer met pastoral needs. From at least the late second century, portions of the New Testament were circulating in Latin, forming what is now called the Vetus Latina, or Old Latin.

The Old Latin is not a single, unified version but a family of related translations. Different communities produced translations at different times, in different regions, and from Greek exemplars that were not identical. As a result, Old Latin manuscripts exhibit a wide spectrum of readings and translation styles. Some witnesses show a very literal rendering of the Greek, while others paraphrase freely. Textually, the Old Latin often reflects a Western type of text. It shares many features with Codex Bezae, including expanded readings, harmonizations, and narrative embellishments in the Gospels and Acts.

Despite these secondary features, the Old Latin tradition provides evidence of immense value. Its very existence in the second and third centuries shows how early the New Testament was already functioning as Scripture in the Latin West. For textual criticism, the Old Latin is especially useful where it preserves a reading that is shorter and more difficult, aligns with early Alexandrian witnesses, and stands against later Byzantine expansions. In those instances, the agreement of Old Latin and Alexandrian Greek demonstrates that the original reading was accepted across widely separated regions.

The Latin tradition entered a new phase with Jerome's work in the late fourth century. Commissioned by Bishop Damasus of Rome, Jerome undertook a revision of the Latin Gospels, and later other parts of the Bible, aiming to correct the text in line with Greek manuscripts available to him. This revision, together with later work, produced what became known as the Vulgate. Jerome's Greek base was not purely Alexandrian, yet he deliberately moved away from the more expansive Western readings. Where Old Latin had harmonized or embellished, Jerome tended to prune back to a more restrained text in closer accord with the Greek exemplars he trusted.

Over the following centuries, the Vulgate itself underwent copying, local revision, and partial assimilation to Byzantine readings. Careful study of the earliest Vulgate witnesses, however, allows textual critics to distinguish Jerome's initial work from later medieval adjustments. As a witness to the state of the Greek text used in Rome and the Latin West around 400 C.E., the earliest Vulgate carries considerable weight. When its readings coincide with Alexandrian manuscripts against Western or Byzantine alternatives, that agreement further anchors the original text.

The Latin versions also play an important role in demonstrating how deeply the New Testament text had penetrated the life of the church. By the time of Augustine, Latin Scripture was already central in preaching, catechesis, and doctrinal controversy. The text could not be radically altered without immediate notice. Even where Old Latin and Vulgate preserve secondary readings, their very stability shows that copyists worked with a high degree of respect for the text they had received. The Latin evidence thus complements the Greek manuscript tradition and confirms that the New Testament text was not subject to uncontrolled, creative rewriting over the centuries.

## The Coptic Versions

Coptic is the last stage of the Egyptian language, written using a largely Greek alphabet with additional characters to represent native Egyptian sounds. In Roman and Byzantine Egypt, Greek remained the language of administration and of much theological writing, especially in Alexandria. Yet large portions of the population spoke Egyptian dialects as their primary language. From the third century onward, as Christianity gained deep roots in Egypt, believers needed Scripture in Egyptian, and this need gave rise to the Coptic versions.

The most important Coptic dialects, from a textual perspective, are Sahidic and Bohairic. Sahidic was spoken in Upper Egypt and seems to be the earliest dialect into which the New Testament was translated. Fragments of Sahidic New Testament manuscripts date from the third and fourth centuries. Bohairic, associated with Lower Egypt and especially the Nile Delta, became the dominant liturgical dialect of the Coptic church in the medieval period. Other dialects, such as Fayyumic, Middle Egyptian, and Akhmimic, are also attested, though more fragmentarily.

The Sahidic Coptic version holds a central place in textual criticism. Its translation technique is generally quite literal. Translators tended to follow Greek word order, preserve conjunctions and particles, and mirror Greek clause structure as much as Egyptian grammar allowed. This literal character often permits a relatively precise retroversion into Greek, especially for major variants. Textually, Sahidic agrees most frequently with the Alexandrian text-type. Its agreements with P66, P75, Vaticanus, and Sinaiticus, especially where the Alexandrian text stands against a fuller Byzantine form, confirm the antiquity and widespread use of the Alexandrian text in Egypt.

At the same time, Sahidic sometimes reflects Western or unique readings. These show that Egyptian Christianity did not live in a textual vacuum. The presence of some Western forms demonstrates that the circulation of Western readings extended even into regions where Alexandrian manuscripts ultimately prevailed. In those cases, the Coptic evidence helps map the degree of textual diversity within Egypt itself.

The Bohairic Coptic tradition is later in its origin and more complicated in its transmission. The earliest Bohairic witnesses date from about the fourth to fifth centuries, but the majority of surviving manuscripts are medieval. Textually, Bohairic shows more influence from the Byzantine tradition than Sahidic does, especially in the Gospels. Nevertheless, its base text remains closer to an Alexandrian form in many books, and the translation is still predominantly literal. For the textual critic, Bohairic often confirms readings that are already well supported by Alexandrian Greek witnesses.

Other Coptic dialects, though more fragmentary, supply important corroborative data. For example, certain Fayyumic manuscripts of Acts reflect a text with strong Western affinities, demonstrating that Western readings had a real foothold in some Egyptian communities. Middle Egyptian and Akhmimic fragments likewise point to pockets of textual diversity. Collectively, these Coptic witnesses show that the Greek text in Egypt was not monolithic, but it was anchored by a strong Alexandrian core that matches the text recovered from early papyri and major codices.

The Coptic versions demonstrate that the Alexandrian text did not arise as a late scholarly revision, but was already widely used among ordinary believers. The convergence of Sahidic and Bohairic with P75 and Vaticanus testifies that the core Alexandrian text lies very close to the original, and the Coptic versions preserve that text in a vernacular dress that can still be traced back to its Greek source.

## The Gothic Version

The Gothic version introduces an entirely different linguistic and missionary context. Gothic is an East Germanic language spoken by the Goths, who, during the fourth century, came into significant contact with the Roman Empire. Christian missionaries, some influenced by Arian theology, evangelized the Goths and saw the need for Scripture in their own tongue.

According to strong early tradition, Ulfilas (or Wulfila), a Gothic bishop active in the mid-fourth century, created a Gothic alphabet and translated much of the Bible into Gothic. While not every detail of this tradition can be verified in full, the extant Gothic manuscripts reflect a translation project of considerable scope and care. Portions of all four Gospels survive, along with parts of Paul's letters.

The Gothic translation is notably literal. Ulfilas and his associates often rendered Greek words with consistent Gothic equivalents and maintained Greek word order more than many later vernacular translations would. This literal approach supports relatively secure retroversion into Greek. For example, if a Gothic verse shows a word order that matches one Greek reading and conflicts with another, the Gothic evidence helps decide between the Greek options.

Textually, the Gothic New Testament reflects a form of the text that stands closer to the early Byzantine tradition, though it is not identical with the later Majority Text. In many places it agrees with the text of fourth- and fifth-century Byzantine Greek manuscripts and with the text that later influenced the Greek Received Text. In other places, however, Gothic agrees with Alexandrian or other non-Byzantine witnesses, suggesting that the Greek exemplars available on the empire's northern frontier preserved a mix of readings.

Because the surviving Gothic manuscripts are later copies of Ulfilas' original work, some level of revision or assimilation may have taken place. Even so, the Gothic version demonstrates that by the fourth century a Greek text very similar to what would become the Byzantine tradition was already in use among mission churches outside the empire's linguistic centers. This confirms that the Byzantine form did not arise suddenly in the medieval period, but that its core had taken shape much earlier, even if it underwent further smoothing and harmonization in later centuries.

## The Armenian Version

Armenia's conversion to Christianity early in the fourth century led naturally to the desire for Scripture in the Armenian language. A crucial step was the creation of the Armenian alphabet, traditionally associated with Mesrop Mashtots around 405 C.E. Once a distinct alphabet and literary language were in place, church leaders undertook the translation of the Bible.

The Armenian New Testament has a complex history. The earliest phase of translation was probably made from Syriac exemplars, since Armenia had close ecclesiastical ties with Syriac-speaking regions. Some evidence of this survives in a limited number of readings and stylistic features. However, very soon after this initial stage, Armenian church leaders supervised a thorough revision based on Greek. The goal was to align the Armenian Bible more closely with the Greek text used in the broader church.

Textually, the Armenian New Testament exhibits a mixed character. In the Gospels, many Armenian manuscripts reflect a text that is broadly Byzantine. They share many readings with the Byzantine Greek tradition and with later Greek minuscules. At the same time, certain Armenian Gospel manuscripts, and specific readings within them, align with what has been called the Caesarean text-type, a group of witnesses that share features of both Alexandrian and Western texts, especially in the Gospels. In Acts and the Epistles, Armenian sometimes supports Alexandrian readings against Byzantine expansions, particularly in passages where the Alexandrian text is more concise or rugged.

The translation style of Armenian is moderately literal. Translators often followed Greek word order and strove for lexical consistency, yet they also adapted idioms and sentence structures to Armenian norms. This balance means that retroversion into Greek for major variants is normally secure. For more subtle variants that depend on word order or particles, caution is required, but the version remains highly useful.

From a documentary standpoint, Armenian evidence is especially important when it converges with early Greek witnesses that are geographically distant. For example, when Armenian supports a reading also found in Vaticanus or in an early papyrus, against a broadly attested Byzantine alternative, that agreement carries considerable weight. It indicates that such a reading was carried not only in Greek manuscripts but also into the Armenian-speaking world during the early centuries of Christian Armenia.

## The Georgian Version

The Georgian churches of the Caucasus region also pursued Scripture translation early in their Christian history. Christianity reached Iberia (eastern Georgia) in the fourth century, and over time a distinctive Georgian script and literary culture developed. As in Armenia, the formation of a written language and the translation of Scripture were closely linked.

The Georgian New Testament appears to have gone through several stages. Early translations seem to have been influenced by Armenian and possibly Syriac models, which the translators used alongside Greek. Later, there was a conscious effort to revise the Georgian text more directly on the basis of Greek manuscripts. As a result, different Georgian manuscripts reflect different stages of this process, and the textual critic must distinguish older from younger layers.

In the Gospels, early Georgian witnesses often show affinities with the so-called Caesarean text. They share distinctive readings with a circle of Greek manuscripts associated with Caesarea and with certain Armenian witnesses that also carry Caesarean features. These readings sometimes stand between the pure Alexandrian and the full Byzantine forms, preserving an intermediate text that reflects a different line of descent. In Acts and the Epistles, Georgian sometimes follows a more Alexandrian pattern, while in later revisions the text moves toward a clearer Byzantine profile.

The translation technique in Georgian is more idiomatic than that of Syriac Harklean or Coptic Sahidic, yet it still respects the Greek base. Narratives in particular read smoothly as Georgian, with natural word order and vocabulary. For textual criticism, this idiomatic character means that major variants are often clearly reflected, but the exact shape of more subtle Greek features is not always recoverable.

Even so, Georgian plays an important corroborative role. When Georgian preserves a distinctive reading that also appears in Armenian and in a certain group of Greek manuscripts, this threefold alignment shows that the reading had a real historical existence and was not a late scribal innovation in a single language. Conversely, when Georgian joins the Byzantine tradition against an isolated reading in one or two Greek manuscripts, the weight of evidence favors the Byzantine form. In either case, Georgian helps to map the spread of textual forms into the Caucasus and indicates which Greek readings were accepted in that region by the early medieval period.

## The Ethiopic Version

The Ethiopic (Ge'ez) version of the New Testament reflects the spread of Christianity to the kingdom of Aksum and surrounding regions in the Horn of Africa. Ge'ez is a Semitic language, written with its own distinctive script. Christian influence in Aksum dates to the fourth century, and by the fifth or sixth century significant portions of the Bible had been translated into Ge'ez.

The transmission history of the Ethiopic New Testament is complex. The earliest translations probably drew on Greek, possibly through intermediary languages such as Syriac or Coptic in some books. Over time, the text underwent local revision and expansion, and later manuscripts often differ among themselves. The majority of extant Ethiopic manuscripts are medieval or later, but the underlying version goes back much earlier.

Textually, the Ethiopic New Testament displays a strongly mixed character. Some books show clear affinities with the Alexandrian text-type. In such passages, Ethiopic aligns with early Egyptian Greek witnesses and with Sahidic Coptic, especially where the Alexandrian text is shorter or more difficult. Other portions of the Ethiopic New Testament reflect a Byzantine influence, especially where later revisions harmonized the text with readings widely used in other churches. In still other places, Ethiopic agrees with Western readings or preserves distinctive forms not easily classified.

The translation style of the Ethiopic version is more idiomatic and expansive than that of the hyper-literal versions. Translators often rendered the sense rather than the precise form of the Greek, choosing Ge'ez expressions that conveyed the meaning to local hearers. Narrative expansions and stylistic elaborations appear in some sections, making it harder to reconstruct a precise Greek Vorlage for every verse.

Because of these features, Ethiopic evidence is most valuable when it supports readings already found in early Alexandrian or other strong Greek witnesses. In such cases, Ethiopic demonstrates that these readings had spread as far as Ethiopia by the early medieval period. It shows that the same core text known in Greek and Coptic circles was also accepted in African churches outside Egypt. On the other hand, distinctive Ethiopic expansions or paraphrastic renderings, especially where unsupported by Greek manuscripts, must be treated as later developments within that version's transmission.

Even in its more secondary aspects, the Ethiopic version remains an important witness to the reception of the New Testament text in yet another linguistic and cultural setting. It displays both the stability of the core text and the variety of local adaptations that arose as Scripture was translated into new languages.

## The Arabic Versions

Arabic versions of the New Testament emerged when Christian communities in the Near East, North Africa, and parts of the Mediterranean shifted to Arabic as their primary spoken language. After Arabic became dominant in public life, Christians who had long used Greek, Coptic, or Syriac required Scripture in Arabic for preaching and catechesis.

The Arabic New Testament is not a single unitary version. Rather, several translation streams developed. Some Arabic New Testaments were translated directly from Greek, especially in regions where Greek churches continued to function. Others were translated from the Syriac Peshitta, from the Coptic versions, or from the Latin Vulgate. In some cases, translators combined more than one source, using Syriac for the Epistles and Coptic for the Gospels, for example.

As a result, the textual character of Arabic New Testament manuscripts varies considerably. Where the underlying source is Byzantine Greek, the Arabic text typically reflects the Byzantine tradition. Where the source is Peshitta Syriac, the Arabic aligns with the Peshitta's blend of Byzantine and non-Byzantine readings. Where Coptic serves as a base, Arabic inherits the Alexandrian tendencies of the Coptic text, particularly in Sahidic-influenced traditions.

Translation style in Arabic ranges from quite literal to markedly paraphrastic. Some translators tried to mirror the earlier language closely, reproducing word order and vocabulary, while others focused on clarity and theological explanation for Arabic-speaking congregations. Because most Arabic versions are relatively late and because of the layered nature of their sources, their direct value for reconstructing the earliest form of the Greek text is more limited than that of Syriac or Coptic.

Nevertheless, Arabic versions remain important for at least two reasons. First, they map the later reception of the New Testament in the Arabic-speaking world, showing which Greek or Syriac readings were accepted and disseminated after the rise of Islam. Second, when an Arabic manuscript can be tied clearly to a particular Greek or Syriac exemplar that no longer survives, it can indirectly extend the textual evidence for that exemplar. For example, if an Arabic translation demonstrably depends on a specific form of the Harklean Syriac text, it may preserve details of that form in places where surviving Harklean manuscripts are damaged or scarce.

In short, Arabic versions primarily illuminate the later stages of the text's transmission and the adaptation of Scripture to an Arabic-speaking Christian environment. They belong more to the history of interpretation and reception, but they occasionally provide meaningful support for earlier versions and Greek witnesses.

## The Sogdian Version

The Sogdian version represents the expansion of the New Testament text into Central Asia. Sogdian was an Eastern Iranian language spoken along key trade routes of the Silk Road. Christian communities, often associated with the Church of the East, established themselves in Sogdian-speaking regions. These believers required Scripture in their own language, and so portions of the New Testament were translated into Sogdian.

The surviving Sogdian New Testament is fragmentary. Manuscripts discovered in Central Asia preserve portions of the Gospels and some other books, often in a damaged state. Despite this, these fragments give valuable insight into how Scripture functioned on the eastern fringes of the Christian world.

Textually, the Sogdian New Testament was translated from Syriac. The Peshitta stands behind much of the text, and in some instances other Syriac recensions may also have influenced the translation. This dependence on Syriac means that Sogdian is at least two steps removed from the Greek originals. The Greek text shaped the Syriac, and the Syriac text then shaped the Sogdian. The translation style tends to be reasonably literal with respect to Syriac, maintaining the structure of Syriac clauses and preserving key terms.

From a textual-critical perspective, the Sogdian version has a derivative but still useful role. When Sogdian agrees with the Peshitta against other Syriac witnesses, it confirms that the Peshitta reading had been carried along the Silk Road and embraced by Central Asian Christians. When Sogdian appears to preserve a reading that diverges from the Peshitta, one must ask whether that reading reflects a different Syriac Vorlage or a translational adjustment into Sogdian. In either case, Sogdian evidence remains subordinate to the Syriac and Greek manuscripts themselves, yet it enriches our view of the geographical reach of certain readings.

Most importantly, the Sogdian fragments demonstrate that by the early medieval period the New Testament text had reached far beyond the Mediterranean world, translated for traders and settlers in distant lands. The same basic text, transmitted in Syriac and then rendered into Sogdian, accompanied believers who lived thousands of kilometers from the regions where the New Testament was first penned.

## The Old Church Slavonic Version

The Old Church Slavonic version stands at the beginning of Slavic Christian literature. In the ninth century, Byzantine missionaries Cyril and Methodius undertook work among Slavic peoples in Central Europe. They created a script suitable for writing the Slavic language and produced translations of the Scriptures and liturgical texts. This work laid the foundation for later Slavic Christian cultures, including those using the Cyrillic script.

The Old Church Slavonic New Testament was translated from Greek. Cyril and Methodius and their associates worked from the Greek text that circulated in the Byzantine Empire of their time. By the ninth century, this Greek text was thoroughly Byzantine in character, though not yet in the fully standardized medieval form that appears in late minuscules.

Textually, Old Church Slavonic gives powerful testimony to the dominance of the Byzantine text in the Greek-speaking church by that stage. In the Gospels, Acts, and Epistles, the Slavonic version aligns closely with the Byzantine readings later found in the Majority Text and in the Greek text underlying many traditional printed editions. The presence of such a text in the early Slavic missions shows that the Byzantine form was already the standard ecclesiastical text for missionary work sent out from Constantinople.

The translation style in Old Church Slavonic is relatively literal. Greek syntactic structures and vocabulary often shine through the Slavic rendering. The translators intended their work to be used in liturgical reading and doctrinal teaching, so they preserved theological terminology with care. Because of this literalism, retroversion from Old Church Slavonic back into Greek is usually straightforward for major variants.

For textual criticism, the primary importance of Old Church Slavonic lies in confirming the stability and wide diffusion of the Byzantine text in the later first millennium. When Old Church Slavonic supports a Byzantine reading that is also well attested in Greek minuscules, this alignment confirms that the reading was not a late local innovation but a broadly accepted form across Greek and Slavic churches. When Old Church Slavonic diverges from the Byzantine Greek tradition in isolated instances, those divergences invite closer examination of both the Greek and the Slavic transmission histories.

The Slavonic tradition thus illustrates how a particular form of the Greek text gained liturgical dominance and was carried into new linguistic fields as the Gospel reached the Slavs. It shows that the Byzantine text, while later than the Alexandrian, was nevertheless deeply rooted and consistent over large areas of the Christian world.

## The Nubian Version

The Nubian version reflects the spread of Christianity into the Nile Valley south of Egypt, in the region of modern northern Sudan and southern Egypt. From about the sixth century onward, Christian kingdoms in Nubia received strong influence from both the Coptic church of Egypt and the Byzantine world. In this context, Scripture came to be translated into local Nubian languages written in a script derived largely from Greek, with additional characters from Coptic and other sources.

Our knowledge of the Nubian New Testament comes from scattered Old Nubian manuscripts and fragments discovered in archaeological excavations. These manuscripts contain portions of the Gospels, Acts, Epistles, and possibly other books, but the evidence is far from complete. Even so, they demonstrate that Nubian Christians had access to the New Testament in their own tongue and used it in worship and teaching.

Textually, the Nubian New Testament depends on Greek exemplars and, in some cases, on Coptic intermediaries. Because Nubian Christianity stood in close contact with the Coptic church, it is not surprising that its New Testament reflects a strongly Byzantine text, similar to the text used in Egypt during the medieval period. The readings in Nubian fragments generally align with the Byzantine tradition in the Gospels and Epistles.

The translation style is moderately literal but adjusted to Old Nubian grammar and idiom. Translators preserved key terms and doctrinal vocabulary but expressed them in ways that fit Nubian sentence structure. As with Ethiopic, retroversion into Greek is more secure for major variants than for minor ones.

In terms of textual criticism, Nubian evidence occupies a supporting role. It does not reach back close to the time of the autographs, nor does it typically preserve readings independent of the Byzantine stream. However, it is an important witness to the later geographic spread and stability of the New Testament text, showing that the same basic Byzantine form found in Greek and Coptic manuscripts was also translated and used in Nubian churches. The Nubian version confirms that the Greek New Testament had become a stable, widely recognized text across diverse African cultures, long before the advent of modern printing.

The Nubian fragments also remind textual critics that the New Testament was not the property of one linguistic group. Greek, Coptic, Nubian, and other languages all shared in transmitting the same message. Although the Nubian data do not usually decide between rival readings, they contribute to the overall picture of a New Testament text that remained remarkably consistent as it crossed linguistic and cultural boundaries.

# Comparative Value of the Early Versions

When viewed together, the earliest translated versions of the Greek New Testament offer a rich, multi-layered picture of the text's history. Syriac, Latin, and Coptic give direct windows into the first few centuries after the autographs, each reflecting a different geographical context: the Syriac-speaking East, the Latin West, and Greek-speaking Egypt with its Egyptian vernaculars. Gothic, Armenian, and Georgian show how the text functioned on the northern and eastern frontiers of the Christian world, while Ethiopic, Arabic, Sogdian, Old Church Slavonic, and Nubian trace its expansion into Africa, Central Asia, the Slavic lands, and the Nile south of Egypt.

Some versions, such as the Sahidic Coptic and the Old Latin, often align with the Alexandrian text-type and help confirm that the Alexandrian form reflects the original wording. Others, such as the Peshitta and the Gothic, reveal how the text crystallized into more standardized forms without losing its essential content. Still others, such as Sogdian and Nubian, primarily illustrate the geographical reach and ecclesiastical stability of the text by the early medieval period.

From the perspective of the documentary method, the versions never displace the primary Greek witnesses, especially the early papyri and the great Alexandrian codices. Instead, they stand alongside them as additional lines of documentary evidence. Where strong Greek evidence exists, versions tend to confirm it. Where Greek evidence is sparse or divided, versions sometimes tip the scales by showing which readings gained real traction beyond the Greek-speaking churches.

Taken as a whole, the earliest translations of the Greek New Testament demonstrate that the text Jehovah inspired through the apostles was not lost, nor radically corrupted, nor re-created in later centuries. Rather, it was faithfully copied, translated, and transmitted across languages and continents. The versions reveal some secondary accretions, expansions, and harmonizations, especially in Western and later Byzantine traditions, but these are identifiable precisely because the documentary evidence is so abundant and diverse. Through careful, disciplined textual criticism that prioritizes the best Greek evidence and uses the versions in a responsible way, the modern reader gains access to a Greek New Testament that stands in overwhelmingly close agreement with the original writings.

# APPENDIX 5 How to Interpret the Bible

## The Goal of Biblical Interpretation

The Bible is not a book to be reshaped by human opinion. It is the inspired, inerrant, infallible Word of God, given through human authors so that His people would know His will, believe His promises, and obey His commands. The task of interpretation is therefore not to discover what Scripture "means to me," but what Jehovah meant by what He caused the human authors to write, and how that meaning rightly applies to us today.

Every passage has one intended meaning, rooted in the intention of the inspired author, as understood by the original audience. Applications and implications can be many, but the meaning is one. Sound interpretation is the disciplined pursuit of that single, God-given meaning.

# Hermeneutics, Exegesis, And Eisegesis

The classical Greek verb *hermēneuō* means "to explain, to interpret." From this comes "hermeneutics": the study of principles and rules of interpretation. When you study how to interpret the Bible, you are studying hermeneutics.

"Exegesis" comes from *exēgeomai* – "to lead out." Exegesis is drawing meaning *out of* the text. The interpreter carefully observes words, grammar, literary structure, historical background, and context, to discover what the author actually said and meant.

"Eisegesis" comes from *eis* ("into"). It is reading meaning *into* the text—imposing your ideas, traditions, or emotions on Scripture instead of submitting to what God actually said. Eisegesis asks, "What do I want this text to say?" Exegesis asks, "What did Jehovah cause this author to say, and what did He intend those words to mean?"

The faithful Christian always aims at exegesis. Hermeneutics provides the rules. Exegesis is the practice of those rules.

## The Absolute Priority of Context

Context is not a suggestion; it is a command. Words have meaning only in sentences, sentences in paragraphs, paragraphs in sections, sections in whole books, and books in the whole canon and covenantal storyline.

You must consider:

- The immediate context: the verses and paragraphs right before and after your passage.

- The remote context: the flow of thought in the chapter, section, and book.

- The canonical context: how the passage fits in the whole Bible.

- The covenantal context: which covenantal era is in view (patriarchal, Mosaic, New Covenant, etc.).

- The historical-cultural context: the time, place, customs, and circumstances of writer and readers.

Authors often signal their purpose (scope) explicitly. Luke writes so that Theophilus "may know the certainty" of what he has been taught (Luke 1:1–4). John states that he wrote his Gospel "so that you may believe that Jesus is the Christ, the Son of God, and that believing you may have life in his name" (John 20:31, UASV). That scope must govern how you read individual episodes in those books.

Even the structure of books is often woven into the text itself. Genesis is divided by recurring formulas: "These are the generations of..." (Gen. 2:4; 5:1; 6:9; 10:1, etc.). This is God's way, through Moses, of organizing early history—from creation and flood to patriarchs—in ordered "histories." You only see this when you read whole books, not isolated verses.

# Historical-Grammatical Method Versus Historical-Critical Method

There are two fundamentally different approaches to Scripture in the modern world.

### The Historical-Grammatical Method

The historical-grammatical method asks:

- What did the inspired author mean by the words he used?

- How would his original audience, in their language, culture, and situation, have understood those words?

"Grammatical" means we take words, syntax, and literary forms seriously. "Historical" means we take the real setting in history seriously: author, audience, geography, politics, and culture. This method assumes that language works, that human authors are capable—especially under the Spirit's moving (2 Pet. 1:21)—of communicating clearly, and that God is not playing games with His people.

This is an *objective* method. It seeks meaning outside ourselves, located in the text as given by God through human authors, not in our inner impressions.

## Textual Criticism ("Lower Criticism")

Textual criticism is sometimes called "lower criticism." It compares Hebrew and Greek manuscripts, early versions, and patristic citations to recover the original wording of the text. Done reverently and carefully, it is constructive, not destructive. The result is that the Hebrew Old Testament and Greek New Testament as found in reliable critical editions reflect the original autographs with extraordinary accuracy—well beyond 99.9%.

## Historical-Critical Method ("Higher Criticism")

"Higher criticism" or the historical-critical method is a cluster of speculative approaches (source criticism, form criticism, redaction criticism, various postmodern "criticisms," and more). It treats Scripture as a human religious product to be dissected, corrected, and sometimes contradicted by the critic, instead of as the inerrant Word of God.

Typical outcomes include claims such as:

- Moses did not write the Pentateuch.

- Isaiah was written by multiple anonymous authors centuries apart.

- Daniel is a late second-century fiction, not a sixth-century prophet.

- Gospel accounts contain large amounts of legend; sayings are invented or reshaped by the church.

These ideas rest on conjecture, not verifiable evidence, and they consistently erode confidence in divine inspiration and inerrancy. When men place their theories above God's Word, the Bible becomes "the word of man," chopped up and rearranged according to academic fashion.

The only faithful approach for a conservative, Bible-believing Christian is the historical-grammatical method, grounded in the full truthfulness of Scripture as God's written Word.

# Dangerous Misuses of Scripture

## Proof-Texting

"Proof-texting" is not simply quoting verses to support doctrine. All sound theology must be grounded in passages of Scripture. The error is *stringing together* isolated phrases without regard for context to force Scripture to say what we already want.

Acts 2:38 is often misused this way:

"Repent and be baptized every one of you in the name of Jesus Christ for the forgiveness of your sins; and you will receive the gift of the Holy Spirit." (UASV)

Some immediately declare:

1. You must be baptized to be saved.

2. Baptism itself removes sins.

3. One must be baptized only "in Jesus' name" as a formula.

But Peter's first imperative is "Repent." Repentance—turning from sin to God—is the inner turning that brings forgiveness. Baptism is the public, symbolic expression of this inward repentance and faith, not a magical ritual that removes guilt. To wrench the verse from its context in Acts and the whole New Testament is to mishandle Scripture.

Proof-texting happens whenever people ignore context, genre, and authorial purpose and treat the Bible as a box of clips to support their system rather than as the Lord's voice to which all systems must bow.

## Allegorical Interpretation

Allegory treats historical persons, places, and events as if their "real" meaning is something else—hidden and symbolic—often unrelated to what the text itself presents.

Philo, a Jewish philosopher, treated the "garments of skin" in Genesis 3:21 as symbolic of the human body, turning a simple historical statement into speculative philosophy. He also allegorized the four rivers of Eden as four virtues. This is not exegesis; it is imagination.

Biblical authors sometimes *use* symbol or speak "allegorically" in a controlled, inspired way. Paul writes in Galatians 4:24–26 that the story of Hagar and Sarah is spoken "allegorically" (or "illustratively"), applying the historical narrative to make a doctrinal point about the covenants. That allegorical *application* is authoritative precisely because it is given by an inspired apostle.

We are not apostles. We are not inspired. We have no right to invent allegorical meanings and then treat them as Scripture. Our task is to receive *their* inspired meaning by historical-grammatical exegesis. If Scripture itself declares, "this is allegorical" or "this stands for," we gladly accept it. Otherwise, we interpret narratives, laws, psalms, and prophecies according to their plain historical and literary character.

## Typological Interpretation

Typology traces divinely designed patterns in history—persons, institutions, or events that foreshadow later realities. For example, the New Testament itself presents Adam as a "type" of Christ (Rom. 5:14), the Passover lamb as fulfilled in Christ's sacrifice (1 Cor. 5:7), and the temple as fulfilled in Christ and His people (John 2:19–21; 1 Cor. 3:16).

Again, when Scripture itself identifies a type and antitype, we accept it. But modern interpreters are not free to hunt for new "types" everywhere, turning almost every detail into a hidden symbol. That becomes subjective and arbitrary. The safe rule is simple:

- Recognize and teach typology where the New Testament clearly identifies it.

- For all other passages, use normal grammatical-historical interpretation, and treat any broader "patterns" as implications or illustrations, not new inspired meanings.

### Author, Text, And Reader

Every act of communication involves three realities: author, text, and reader. Modern relativism often claims that meaning resides in the reader's response ("reader-response" criticism): each person brings their own meaning, and all are equally valid. If twenty people give conflicting "readings" of a text, this view treats them all as correct.

That destroys the authority of Scripture. God inspired human authors to convey *His* meaning. The text is the fixed record of that meaning. The reader's duty is not to create meaning but to discover, submit to, and apply the meaning that God gave through the human writer.

## Objection: "We Can't Get into the Author's Mind"

We do not need to crawl into Paul's head and relive his experiences. When you read any book today, you do not know the writer's whole psychology, yet you understand what is written. The author chose words to communicate, not to hide. Under inspiration, the biblical authors did this infallibly in the original manuscripts.

## Objection: "We Are Too Far Removed In Time And Culture"

We are separated by thousands of years, languages, and customs. That certainly creates difficulty, but not impossibility. Even in biblical times, some things were "hard to understand" (2 Pet. 3:16), yet the original readers could understand because it was their world, language, and idioms.

Our responsibility is to bridge the gap with faithful study. We use good translations, word dictionaries, Bible dictionaries, background resources, maps, and careful observation. We ask: Who wrote this? To whom? When? Under what circumstances? What did the words mean in their language at that time?

### Meaning and Implications

Meaning is what the author intended by his words. But within that meaning there are implications—applications and extensions that fit the pattern of the author's teaching, even if he did not foresee every later circumstance.

Paul lists "the works of the flesh" in Galatians 5:19–21 and ends with "and things like these." That phrase explicitly invites the reader to discern further behaviors that fit the same pattern. Likewise, when he commands, "Do not get drunk with wine" (Eph. 5:18), the prohibition obviously extends to any intoxicant used in the same way—beer, whiskey, modern drugs—that impair the mind and foster sinful living. This is not a new meaning; it is the faithful extension of his original meaning into new situations.

The rule is:

- One meaning, fixed and stable.

- Many implications, as long as they remain truly consistent with that original meaning and pattern.

# The Role of the Holy Spirit in Interpretation

The Holy Spirit's work in relation to Scripture has two distinct aspects.

1. **Inspiration (past, complete)** – The Spirit moved the biblical authors so that what they wrote is truly God's Word (2 Tim. 3:16; 2 Pet. 1:21). This work is finished. He does not inspire new Scripture today.

2. **Illumination (present, ongoing)** – The Spirit enables believers to recognize the glory, significance, and demands of the Word He previously inspired. He does not give secret extra meanings, but He softens hearts, removes moral blindness, and strengthens faith and obedience.

Unbelievers can understand the *content* of Scripture at an intellectual level. That is clear because we are commanded to preach the gospel to them; it would be pointless if they literally could not grasp the message.

1 Corinthians 2:14 says the "natural man does not accept the things of the Spirit of God, for they are foolishness to him." The key is "does not accept." The problem is not that he cannot parse sentences or follow arguments, but that he rejects their value and authority. In the same letter,

Paul says that God regards "the wisdom of the world" as "foolishness" (1 Cor. 3:19), yet God fully understands it. Likewise, unbelievers may understand Scripture but despise it or treat it as irrelevant.

2 Corinthians 4:3–4 explains that "the god of this world has blinded the minds of the unbelievers" so they do not see the light of the gospel. This is moral and spiritual blindness, not an inability to read. Jehovah is just; He does not command people to repent of a message that they literally cannot comprehend. He holds them responsible because they *do* understand at some level and refuse to bow.

At the same time, believers can grieve the Spirit (Eph. 4:30) and dull their own understanding through sin, pride, tradition, or laziness. Preunderstanding—our prior beliefs, experiences, theological systems, and prejudices—can choke the Word if we refuse to let Scripture correct us.

So:

- The Spirit does not bypass the mind or give private revelations of meaning.

- He uses the Word He inspired, working through ordinary study, meditation, and obedience.

- He convicts, comforts, and clarifies the *significance* of the text, especially for those whose hearts are humble and submissive.

The Bereans are the model: they "received the word with all readiness of mind, examining the Scriptures daily to see whether these things were so" (Acts 17:11, UASV). They used their minds, searched the text, and yet did so with eager receptivity.

# Genre Awareness in Biblical Interpretation

God did not give the Bible as a flat textbook. He used many genres: narrative, law, poetry, wisdom, prophecy, apocalypse, parable, epistle, proverb, riddle, and more. Each has its own "rules of the game" that the original readers knew instinctively.

You cannot interpret Proverbs as if it were case law, nor read the Psalms as if they were historical annals, nor treat apocalyptic visions as plain newspaper language. The meaning is always real and anchored in history, but the *mode of expression* varies. Recognizing genre prevents both wooden literalism and uncontrolled speculation.

# Interpreting Riddles and Wisdom Sayings

Hebrew *chidah* refers to a riddle, puzzling saying, or dark saying. It is designed to provoke thought, to conceal from the lazy and reveal to the wise.

Jehovah told Israel that He spoke with Moses "mouth to mouth, clearly, and not in riddles" (Num. 12:8, UASV), emphasizing the clarity and privilege Moses enjoyed. But wisdom literature uses riddles to train discernment.

Proverbs 30:18–19 lists four "too wonderful" things:

- The way of an eagle in the sky.
- The way of a serpent on a rock.
- The way of a ship on the high seas.
- The way of a man with a young woman.

The first three share something: their path leaves no visible trail. This analogy then illuminates "the way of a man with a young woman"—the subtle, often hidden dynamics of seduction. Riddles like this require the reader to ponder and see the connection.

Proverbs 1:5–6 says that wisdom equips a person "to understand a proverb and a saying, the words of the wise and their riddles" (UASV). Riddles are not arbitrary puzzles; they are training tools for spiritual insight.

# Interpreting Proverbs

A proverb is a compact, memorable saying that expresses a general truth and often implies counsel. Hebrew *mashal* probably arises from a root meaning "to compare," which suits the fact that many proverbs are comparisons or analogies.

Crucial principles for interpreting proverbs:

1. **Proverbs are generalizations, not ironclad guarantees.** Proverbs 22:6 says, "Train up a child in the way he should go; and when he is old, he will not depart from it" (UASV). This is not a mechanical promise that faithful parents *cannot* have wayward children. It expresses a general pattern: wise, consistent training normally shapes a child's life enduringly.

2. **Proverbs operate within a fallen world.** Proverbs 3:9–10 says that honoring Jehovah with your wealth results in abundance. That is generally true, but godly believers can still experience poverty, persecution, or hardship because of Satan's world and human wickedness. Proverbial wisdom must be balanced with awareness of suffering and eschatology.

3. **Proverbs use poetic parallelism.** The second line often clarifies, sharpens, or contrasts with the first. For example, "The wicked borrows but does not pay back, but the righteous is gracious and gives" (Prov. 37:21, UASV). The contrast clarifies the moral point.

Proverbs are meant to govern our daily choices. They are not optional slogans but God-given patterns for wise living, interpreted "generally speaking," not as rigid mathematical formulas.

# Interpreting Figurative Language and Word Pictures

Scripture is rich with figures of speech. This does not make it less true; it makes the truth more vivid. The rule is simple:

Identify the figure accurately, then take the *meaning* of the figure literally.

You do not take the imagery literally, but you do take the truth it expresses literally.

## Simile And Metaphor

A simile explicitly compares using "like" or "as":

- "He is like a tree planted by streams of water" (Ps. 1:3, UASV).

A metaphor declares that one thing *is* another:

- "You are the light of the world" (Matt. 5:14, UASV).

In both cases, the interpreter asks: what is the point of similarity in this context? Psalm 1 pictures a righteous person as a well-rooted, well-watered tree: stable, fruitful, enduring.

## Hypocatastasis

Hypocatastasis is an implied comparison where only one element is named. Saying, "You are a beast" is metaphor; simply shouting, "Beast!" is hypocatastasis. Scripture uses this intensified form to shock and awaken.

## Metonymy And Synecdoche

Metonymy substitutes a related term:

- "You prepare a table before me" (Ps. 23:5) uses "table" for the full provision of a feast.
- "As for me and my house, we will serve Jehovah" (Josh. 24:15, UASV) uses "house" for family.

Synecdoche uses a part for the whole or vice versa:

- "Their feet run to evil" (Prov. 1:16) uses "feet" to represent the whole person rushing into sin.

## Merism, Hendiadys, Personification

- Merism uses two extremes to indicate the whole, as "heaven and earth" for all creation.
- Hendiadys uses "and" to express a single idea ("ministry and apostleship" = apostolic ministry).

- Personification attributes human traits to creation: "the trees of the field shall clap their hands" (Isa. 55:12, UASV).

Creation does not literally clap, but nature is portrayed as rejoicing in Jehovah's saving work.

## Anthropomorphism, Anthropopathism, Zoomorphism

- Anthropomorphism gives God human features—eyes, hands, arms—to communicate His knowledge, power, and activity in ways we can grasp.

- Anthropopathism attributes human emotions to God—jealousy, grief—to reveal His holy moral responses.

- Zoomorphism uses animal imagery, as when Job feels that God is like a predator tearing him (Job 16:9).

These figures do not mean God has a physical body or sinful passions. They are accommodations to our limited understanding, given by God Himself.

## Apostrophe And Euphemism

- Apostrophe addresses inanimate or absent things directly: "Hear, O earth" (Mic. 1:2).

- Euphemism softens harsh realities. Scripture uses many euphemisms for death ("sleep"), sexual relations, and judgment. Recognizing them prevents misinterpretation.

### Interpreting Idioms

Idioms are fixed expressions whose meaning cannot be deduced from individual words. English has many: "kick the bucket," "between a rock and a hard place," "spill the beans."

Biblical languages have their own idioms. For example:

- "Break the arm of the wicked" (Ps. 10:15) means to destroy their power, not literally fracture bones.

- "Noah found favor in the eyes of Jehovah" (Gen. 6:8, UASV) means Jehovah looked on Noah with grace.

- "I lift up my soul" (Ps. 25:1, UASV) is an idiom for entrusting oneself to God.

Translators must decide whether to preserve the original idiom and explain it, or to express its meaning in an equivalent idiom in the receptor language. Interpreters must never press idioms literally.

One common idiom is "a land flowing with milk and honey" (Deut. 6:3). This does not describe literal rivers of dairy and honey but a fertile, abundant land. The vivid picture deepens the promise.

Another example: "The fathers have eaten sour grapes, and the children's teeth are set on edge" (Jer. 31:29, UASV) was a proverb shifting blame from the current generation to their ancestors. God rejects that abuse and insists that each person is judged for his own sin (Ezek. 18). Understanding the idiom guards against distorted theology about inherited guilt.

## Poetry And Parallelism

Hebrew poetry rarely uses rhyme. Its primary features are parallelism, compact lines, and vivid imagery. Around a third of the Old Testament is poetry (Job, Psalms, Proverbs, major portions of the Prophets, and more).

Types of parallelism include:

- **Synonymous:** second line restates the first in different words. "The earth is Jehovah's, and the fullness thereof; the world, and those who dwell therein" (Ps. 24:1, UASV).

- **Antithetic:** second line contrasts with the first, sharpening the point.
  "The wicked borrows and does not pay back, but the righteous is gracious and gives" (Ps. 37:21, UASV).

- **Synthetic:** second line completes or expands the first. "The law of Jehovah is perfect, restoring the soul; the testimony of Jehovah is sure, making wise the simple" (Ps. 19:7, UASV).

- **Emblematic:** one line is a picture, the other its meaning. "As far as the east is from the west, so far has he removed our transgressions from us" (Ps. 103:12, UASV).

Poetry is not less true than prose; it is more intense. It aims to stir the heart and imagination. You do not treat it as scientific description, but neither do you empty it of content.

Compare Judges 4 (prose narrative of Deborah and Barak) with Judges 5 (poetic song about the same events). The song uses heightened imagery—stars fighting, torrents sweeping away enemies—to celebrate the same historical victory. Recognizing poetry prevents you from forcing poetic hyperbole into wooden literalism.

# Historical And Cultural Background

The Bible arose in real places, among real peoples. Archaeology, geography, and historical study help us see what the original readers took for granted.

For example, Judges 16:2–3 says that Samson took hold of the doors of the city gate of Gaza, pulled them up with the posts, and carried them "to the top of the hill that is in front of Hebron." When you learn what ancient city gates weighed (hundreds, possibly well over a thousand pounds), how far Gaza is from Hebron (roughly 37 miles), and the elevation of Hebron (about 3,000 feet above sea level), Samson's God-given strength becomes even more astonishing.

Background does not create new meanings, but it clarifies and enriches the meaning already in the text. The danger is to read our modern assumptions into the ancient world instead of letting the ancient world inform our reading.

# Interpreting Words: Lexical And Semantic Issues

Words have a semantic range: a set of possible meanings. The actual meaning in any given verse is determined by context, not by etymology or by piling every possible sense into one usage.

Key principles:

1. **Meaning is use, not origin.** The original root of a word does not control its later meaning. English "nice" once meant "ignorant." "Let" in 1611 English meant "hinder"; now it generally means "allow."

2. **Avoid the etymological fallacy.** Do not derive meaning from the pieces of a compound word if usage contradicts that. "Pineapple" is not a "pine" plus an "apple." Likewise, a Greek compound does not always equal the sum of its parts.

3. **Avoid illegitimate totality transfer.** A word may have several senses in a lexicon. You may not import all of them into every occurrence. The immediate context restricts which meaning fits.

4. **Use concordances and lexicons wisely.** Study how the same author uses the word in similar contexts, then how the New Testament uses it more broadly, and finally how the Septuagint may use it, always letting nearer contexts have priority.

These principles matter deeply in doctrinally loaded terms: *soul, spirit, Sheol, Hades, Gehenna, flesh, justify, sanctify.* For example, "soul" in Scripture refers to the whole living person, not an immortal immaterial entity; "Gehenna" refers to final destruction, not conscious torment; "flesh" often denotes human mortality and weakness, not an ontologically evil substance. Only careful contextual and lexical study guards doctrine from tradition-driven distortions.

# Interpreting Prophecy

"Prophecy" in Scripture includes both forth-telling (proclaiming God's message of warning, comfort, or instruction) and foretelling (predicting future events). Both are anchored in God's covenant dealings.

## Conditional Judgment Prophecies

Deuteronomy 18:20–22 says that if a prophet speaks in Jehovah's name and the word does not come to pass, that prophet has spoken presumptuously. Some raise Jonah as a problem:

"Yet forty days, and Nineveh shall be overthrown!" (Jonah 3:4, UASV)

Nineveh repented, and God did not overthrow the city at that time (Jonah 3:10). Was Jonah false? No. Jeremiah 18:7–10 states a principle the original audience knew:

- If God announces judgment on a nation, and that nation turns from its evil, He relents from the announced calamity.

- If He announces blessing, and that nation turns to evil, He withdraws the blessing.

Ezekiel 33:13–16 repeats the same moral logic for individuals. Judgment prophecies of this sort are implicitly conditional, even when not explicitly worded that way. Jonah himself knew this and resented God's mercy (Jonah 4:1–2).

Micah 3:12 foretold that "Zion shall be plowed as a field; Jerusalem shall become a heap of ruins" (UASV). In Jeremiah 26:18–19, elders recall Micah's prediction and explain that Hezekiah humbled himself, Jehovah relented, and the judgment was delayed. Later generations returned to wickedness, and the destruction came under Babylon. The prophecy was not false; it operated under the revealed principle of conditional judgment.

## Prophetic And Cosmic Language

Prophets frequently use cosmic imagery to depict God's decisive interventions in history:

- "The sun will be darkened, and the moon will not give its light, and the stars will fall from heaven" (Matt. 24:29, UASV).

- Joel, quoted in Acts 2:17–21, speaks of wonders in heaven, blood, fire, pillars of smoke, the sun turned to darkness, and the moon to blood.

Such language signals that God is shaking earthly powers and advancing His kingdom, not necessarily that astronomical bodies literally collapse. At Pentecost, Peter applies Joel's prophecy to the outpouring of the Spirit and the dawning of the last days, even though no literal celestial catastrophe occurred.

We still interpret these passages historically and grammatically. We ask: What historical or eschatological event is being described? What Old Testament background shapes the imagery? How did inspired writers apply similar language? We affirm Christ's literal future return and premillennial reign, while acknowledging that some prophetic descriptions use poetic and symbolic idioms.

## Interpreting Narrative

Narratives are God's inspired accounts of what He has done in history, especially with Israel and through Christ. They are not bare chronicles; they are theological history, selected and arranged to teach doctrine and godly living.

Romans 15:4 says, "Whatever things were written beforehand were written for our instruction, that through endurance and through the encouragement of the Scriptures we might have hope" (UASV). 1 Corinthians 10:6, 11 says that Old Testament events "happened to them as examples" and "were written for our instruction."

Principles for narrative interpretation:

- **Distinguish descriptive from prescriptive.** Not everything described is approved. David's sins, Samson's compromises, Peter's failures—these are warnings, not models.

- **Look at the larger narrative context.** Individual episodes fit into big story arcs: the exodus, conquest, monarchy, exile, return, the ministry of Jesus, the spread of the gospel in Acts. Understand smaller scenes in light of the big storyline.

- **Attend to authorial signals.** Repetitions, evaluative comments, and structures show what the inspired author emphasizes.

Mark's Gospel, for example, opens with "The beginning of the gospel of Jesus Christ, the Son of God" (Mark 1:1, UASV). John the Baptist appears, but only to point beyond himself: "the one stronger than I is coming after me" (1:7). The entire narrative then unfolds who Jesus is—His authority, His rejection, His death and resurrection. John is an important character, but not the focus. The author's stated aim keeps us from turning side characters into the main point.

# Interpreting Parables

A parable is a brief story or comparison drawn from everyday life to convey spiritual truth. Jesus often taught in parables (Matt. 13:34). Parables:

- Capture attention.

- Engage the mind and conscience.

- Reveal truth to the humble and conceal it from the hardened (Matt. 13:10–17).

- Expose hypocrisy and invite repentance, as Nathan's parable did with David (2 Sam. 12:1–7).

Key principles:

- Look at the context. Why does Jesus tell this parable here? What question or situation is He addressing?

- Identify the main point (or a small cluster of closely related points).

- Do not allegorize every detail unless Jesus Himself assigns symbolic meaning.

The parable of the prodigal son, for example, focuses on the Father's gracious welcome to repentant sinners and the older brother's hard-heartedness, not on arbitrary meanings for every robe or ring.

## Interpreting Epistles

The New Testament letters are Spirit-inspired apostolic instruction, often written to address specific situations in churches or individuals. They typically have:

- An opening (author, recipients, greeting, thanksgiving, prayer).

- A doctrinal section (teaching, argument, exposition).

- A practical section (commands, exhortations, specific instructions).

- A closing (final appeals, greetings, blessing).

Because epistles directly explain doctrine and ethics, they are central for shaping Christian belief and practice. They must be read as whole letters, not chopped into isolated verses. You ask:

- What problem or question is being addressed?

- How does the argument develop from beginning to end?

- How do individual verses fit into the logical flow?

Instructions about church leadership, gender roles, discipline, spiritual gifts, marriage, and government must be handled by close grammatical-historical exegesis. For example, when Paul restricts the teaching and governing office of the church to qualified men (1 Tim. 2:12–3:7; Titus 1:5–9), he grounds it not in local culture but in creation order and the fall. Those passages remain binding; sound interpretation does not explain them away to fit modern egalitarian pressures.

## Interpreting Laws and the Covenants

The Law of Moses, including the Ten Commandments, was given as a covenant to Israel, not to the nations generally (Deut. 5:1–3; Ps. 147:19–20). Its purposes included:

- Exposing sin and showing Israel's need for atonement (Rom. 3:20; Gal. 3:19).

- Guarding and setting Israel apart until the promised Seed came (Gal. 3:23–25).

- Providing a temporary theocratic constitution for the nation.

Christ fulfilled the Law. The Mosaic covenant, as a covenant, has ended. Believers are not "under law but under grace" (Rom. 6:14). The veil has been lifted in Christ (2 Cor. 3:7–11).

However, many commands in the Mosaic Law express God's unchanging moral character. These are repeated and reinforced in the New Testament: worship of the one true God, prohibition of idolatry, prohibition of murder, adultery, theft, coveting, and lying, and the obligation to honor parents. The moral law is not abolished but taken up into the "law of Christ" (Gal. 6:2).

The Sabbath command, as a sign of the Mosaic covenant with Israel, is not imposed on the church as a weekly legal requirement (Col. 2:16–17). Yet the principle of regular rest and devoted worship remains wise and beneficial. The New Covenant internalizes God's law: He writes His laws on the hearts and minds of His people (Heb. 8:10–11).

So, when interpreting Old Testament laws, you ask:

- What covenantal context is this law in?

- What purpose did it serve for Israel under the Mosaic covenant?

- Is this command repeated, transformed, or fulfilled in the New Testament?

- What abiding moral principle is revealed about Jehovah's character?

All Scripture remains "profitable for teaching, for reproof, for correction, and for training in righteousness" (2 Tim. 3:16, UASV), even where the specific legal form no longer binds us.

# Interpreting Hyperbole

Hyperbole is deliberate exaggeration for emphasis. Scripture uses it extensively. Recognizing it prevents absurd literalism.

Jesus said:

- "Why do you look at the speck that is in your brother's eye, but do not notice the log that is in your own eye?" (Matt. 7:3, UASV).

- "Blind guides, who strain out the gnat but swallow the camel!" (Matt. 23:24, UASV).

- "It is easier for a camel to go through the eye of a needle than for a rich man to enter the kingdom of God" (Matt. 19:24, UASV).

In each case, the imagery is intentionally impossible. No one imagines an actual log in a human eye or a camel literally going through a sewing needle. The point is to shock us into seeing hypocrisy, misplaced priorities, or the danger of trusting riches.

Hyperbole can often be recognized when:

- The statement is literally impossible.

- It conflicts with Scripture elsewhere if understood literally (for example, total hatred of parents vs. the command to honor them).

- It is clearly designed to arrest attention.

The meaning expressed through hyperbole is literal and serious. Jesus truly condemns hypocritical judgment, external religiosity, and love of money; the extreme language highlights how serious these sins are.

# Putting It All Together in Practice

Faithful interpretation is both art and discipline. A practical pattern for handling any passage is:

1. **Pray humbly.** Ask Jehovah to guard you from pride, laziness, and tradition, and to give you a teachable spirit.

2. **Read repeatedly.** Read the passage several times, then the whole section or book to see the flow.

3. **Observe carefully.** Note key words, repeated phrases, logical connectors, and structural markers.

4. **Clarify context.** Where are you in the book? What comes before and after? How does this fit the author's stated purpose?

5. **Identify genre and figures.** Is this law, narrative, poetry, wisdom, prophecy, epistle? Are there similes, metaphors, idioms, hyperbole?

6. **Use original-language tools through reliable resources.** Study key words with good lexicons and concordances, not merely popular word studies.

7. **Consider historical-cultural background.** Use reliable conservative works on archaeology, customs, geography, and ancient history.

8. **Compare Scripture with Scripture.** Let clearer passages illuminate more complex ones. Stay within the same author and testament first, then within the whole canon.

9. **Formulate the author's single intended meaning.** Express it in your own words, anchored in the text, not in your feelings.

10. **Draw implications and applications.** Ask how this meaning speaks to doctrine, worship, ethics, family, church, and mission today, always staying within the pattern of the author's intent.

For deeper training in hermeneutics, it is wise to study careful works by conservative scholars who defend historical-grammatical interpretation and reject higher criticism. Sound resources include works on basic Bible interpretation, Protestant hermeneutics, and classic grammatico-historical exposition. These sharpen your skills and protect you from dangerous interpretive fashions.

Finally, interpretation is never merely academic. We are not neutral observers dissecting a religious artifact. We stand before the living Word of the living God. Our task is to understand what He has spoken, to believe it, and to obey it—submitting our minds, desires, traditions, and culture to Scripture, never Scripture to them.

When God tells us not to get drunk with wine (Eph. 5:18), He also condemns abusing any intoxicant that clouds the mind. When He forbids adultery (Ex. 20:14), He also condemns lust in the heart (Matt. 5:28). When He reveals that eternal life is His gift through Christ, He exposes the lie of human autonomy and the myth of an immortal soul that lives on by nature.

To interpret the Bible rightly is to stand under its authority, to hear Jehovah's voice through the words He inspired, and to walk in the light that He gives through Christ until the day He returns to reign.

# APPENDIX 6 Bible Backgrounds of the Old and New Testaments

## Why Bible Backgrounds Matter for Understanding Scripture

The Bible is a record of real events in real places, involving real men and women who lived under social structures, laws, customs, and conditions very unlike those of the modern Western world. God inspired His Word within that concrete historical and cultural framework. If readers ignore that framework and read Scripture as though it were written yesterday in their own culture, they will repeatedly misread the text, import modern assumptions, and miss much of what Jehovah intended to communicate.

The Bible was written by more than forty human authors over roughly sixteen hundred years. We are now about two to three and a half millennia removed from the setting of most Old Testament books, and nearly two millennia from the New Testament. Those authors wrote in Hebrew, Aramaic, and Greek, in geographical zones stretching from Egypt to Mesopotamia, from Asia Minor to Rome. They addressed covenant people living under patriarchal clan structures, tribal confederations, monarchies, foreign empires, and Roman occupation.

Because Jehovah chose to reveal Himself through history, geography, and culture, those features become part of the "grammar" of revelation. Historical and cultural backgrounds never override the inspired text, but they clarify its sense and deepen our grasp of the author's intended meaning. This is the heart of the historical-grammatical method: we ask what the text meant in its original linguistic, historical, and covenantal setting so we can rightly apply it today.

# The Contribution of Biblical Archaeology

Biblical archaeology is a disciplined, scientific study of ancient cultures through their material remains. Archaeologists carefully excavate layers of earth in Bible lands—Palestine, Egypt, Assyria, Babylonia, Persia, Asia Minor, Greece, and Rome—exposing city walls, streets, gates, houses, tombs, tools, weapons, pottery, inscriptions, and coins. These artifacts provide an independent stream of data that helps illuminate the world in which God's people lived and in which His Word was written.

As the soil is peeled back layer by layer, archaeologists can reconstruct the layout of cities, the construction of fortifications, the style of domestic housing, the types of weapons carried in warfare, the trade contacts between regions, and the level of technology at different times. Inscriptions in Hebrew, Aramaic, Akkadian, Egyptian, Greek, and Latin shed light on names, titles, laws, treaties, weights and measures, and even phrasing similar to biblical expressions.

This work has shed particular light on the era from the Flood in 2348 B.C.E. to the close of the apostolic age at the end of the first century C.E. It has enriched our understanding of life in patriarchal tents, in Canaanite city-states, in Assyrian and Babylonian imperial systems, and in Hellenistic and Roman urban centers. Although faith ultimately rests on God's Word, not on the spade, archaeology repeatedly confirms that the Bible fits the historical and geographical realities of the ancient Near East and the Mediterranean world.

# Historical-Cultural World of the Old Testament

The Old Testament unfolds across a broad spectrum of historical settings: from nomadic patriarchs traveling between wells and pastures, to Israel as a tribal confederation, to a centralized monarchy, to exiles in foreign empires. Each stage carries its own cultural assumptions.

Explains clan structures, oaths, inheritance, nomadic movement, hospitality, and the social world of Abraham, Isaac, and Jacob—vital for understanding Genesis and covenant origins.

Patriarchal narratives reflect clan-based society, where family loyalty, inheritance, and oaths carry enormous weight. Later, during the monarchy, fortified cities, royal bureaucracy, and international diplomacy dominate the scene. Under foreign empires, Jews must live as a distinct people scattered among Gentile nations, wrestling with loyalty to Jehovah while under pagan authority.

One example that gains vividness from historical background is the account of Samson in Gaza. Judges 16 describes how the Gazites learned that Samson had entered their city and lay in ambush, planning to kill him at dawn. Instead, Samson rose at midnight, seized "the doors of the gate of the city and the two posts," lifted them out of their sockets, and carried them to a hill "in front of Hebron."

City gates in the Iron Age were not small garden gates; they were massive, reinforced structures securing the main entrance through a defensive wall. The doors would be heavy wooden leaves bound with metal, hung on thick posts set deep into stone. Conservative estimates place such gate leaves and posts at hundreds of pounds in weight; some reconstructions suggest well over a thousand. Gaza lies at sea level on the coastal plain, while Hebron stands roughly 3,000 feet higher in the hill country of Judah, about sixty kilometers away. To carry that load uphill over that distance in the dead of night magnifies the supernatural nature of Samson's Spirit-given strength and the terror this act would have instilled in the Philistines.

This illuminates events like Samson taking Gaza's gate or the fall of Jericho. Seeing how cities were built and defended is essential for many Old Testament accounts.

Another Old Testament narrative transformed by archaeological and architectural data is the fall of Jericho in Joshua 6. Excavations at the ancient tell of Jericho show that the city was defended by a stone retaining wall at the base of an embankment, about 3.5 to 4.5 meters high. On top of this stood a mudbrick wall roughly 2 meters thick and 6 to 8 meters high. At the crest of the earthen rampart stood another mudbrick wall surrounding the upper city. From the level of the outer approach, the combined height of retaining wall, rampart, and upper wall would have been imposing, humanly unassailable.

The archaeological evidence also indicates that dwellings were built on the lower slope between the outer and inner walls. This matches the description that Rahab "lived in the wall" and could let the spies down through a window. The total fortified system encompassed roughly nine acres. Using the common rule of thumb of about one hundred inhabitants per acre, and accounting for refugees from surrounding villages who would have sought shelter behind the walls, several thousand people may well have been inside Jericho at the time of Joshua's siege. When the walls collapsed under Jehovah's judgment, Israel did not overcome a small open settlement, but a tightly fortified stronghold entirely beyond their military capacity.

Such background data do not create the truth of the narrative, but they help modern readers visualize the scale of events and the human impossibility of victories that Jehovah granted to His covenant people.

# Dwellings and Domestic Life in Bible Lands

Old and New Testament references to houses, streets, and domestic space assume building methods and living patterns very different from modern suburban life.

In many regions of Palestine, quality cut stone was scarce or expensive, so ordinary homes were often constructed of sun-dried mudbrick, sometimes kiln-fired for added strength. These bricks retained warmth and provided inexpensive insulation, but they were vulnerable to erosion and to small animals. The prophet Amos uses this reality in a striking picture: a man escapes a lion, then a bear, and finally relaxes at home, placing his hand on the wall, only to be bitten by a serpent (Amos 5:19). Snakes could nest in crevices of mudbrick walls, warmed by the sun. The proverb's force rests on a typical house type, not a modern concrete structure.

This category clarifies countless passages—from digging through roofs (Mark 2) to dwelling in city walls (Joshua 2) to flat rooftops and mudbrick construction. Visualizing domestic space is foundational for understanding both Old and New Testament narratives.

City planning in fortified towns often placed houses directly against or even into the city wall. Joshua 2 explains that Rahab's house was "in the wall," with a window overlooking the exterior, from which she could lower the spies by a rope. In some double-walled systems, the space between the outer and inner walls was filled with packed earth, or in some cases built up with cheaper dwellings for the

135

poor. The wall was not a thin vertical barrier but part of a complex defensive and residential system.

Roofs were normally flat. Large wooden beams spanned from wall to wall, with smaller rafters laid across them. Over this framework, builders spread branches and reeds, then compacted a thick layer of earth, which could be coated with clay or lime plaster and periodically rolled to keep it tight. Such roofs served as workspaces, storage areas, and places to rest or sleep when the weather permitted. They had outside stairways or ladders for access.

This construction method stands behind the account in Mark 2. When four men could not reach Jesus because of the packed crowd inside the house, they went up onto the roof, removed part of the roofing material, and lowered the paralyzed man on his mat. They did not saw through rafters and cut asphalt shingles; they dug through compacted earth and branches between support beams, something entirely feasible with effort. The background detail shows not recklessness but determination and faith, and it explains why the disruption, though dramatic, did not permanently ruin the house.

By the first century, wealthier homes in Jerusalem's Herodian quarter could be quite large, with multiple stories and spacious upper rooms. Acts 1:13 describes the apostles gathering in an "upper room" in Jerusalem. Archaeological finds from that district include houses with rooms measuring roughly thirty-plus feet by twenty-plus feet, able to host a group of 120 people when closely arranged. This supports the picture of a sizeable private home owned by a relatively prosperous supporter of the disciples where they could meet, pray, and wait for the fulfillment of Jesus' promise.

# Food, Agriculture, and Table Fellowship

Agriculture and food in the Bible are never mere background scenery; they often form the concrete basis for figurative teaching. Understanding daily food habits and table customs sheds light on many passages.

Bread was the staple food. It was so central that "bread" could stand for food in general. Leavened dough was made by mixing a portion of fermented starter with fresh flour and water. This fermenting agent worked its way through the dough invisibly but powerfully. Because of this, leaven could serve as a vivid symbol for pervasive moral influence. When Jesus warned His disciples, "Watch out for the leaven of the Pharisees and Sadducees," they initially thought He spoke of literal bread. Only later did they realize that He spoke of teaching—doctrine and example—that subtly permeated a community (Matthew 16:6, 11–12). The same figure appears when He speaks of "the leaven of Herod," highlighting corrupting political maneuvering (Mark 8:15).

Meals signaled peace, covenant loyalty, status, and acceptance. Understanding ancient table practice clarifies many passages—especially in the ministries of Jesus and Paul.

Milk, especially from goats and sheep, was an important food product, used fresh or soured and sometimes processed into cheese. Jehovah's prohibition, "You shall not boil a young goat in its mother's milk" (Exodus 23:19; 34:26; Deuteronomy 14:21), reflects His concern for the natural order and for basic decency in treatment of animals. Milk exists to nourish the young; to use it as a cooking medium for the very offspring it was meant to sustain turns the Creator's provision on its head. The Law contains several similar protections: a young animal was not to be sacrificed before it had been with its mother for at least seven days; mother and offspring were not to be slaughtered on the same day; a mother bird was not to be taken together with the eggs or chicks in her nest. Such commands trained Israel to respect the balance of creation, even though animals were given for food and sacrifice.

Honey, both wild and domesticated, served as a key sweetener and energizing food. Its richness, pleasant taste, and health value made it a natural vehicle for spiritual analogies. Proverbs calls pleasant, gracious words "a honeycomb, sweetness to the soul and health to the bones," and urges the son to eat honey because it is good, linking that goodness with the pursuit of wisdom (Proverbs 16:24; 24:13–14). The psalmist declares that Jehovah's judgments are "sweeter than honey and drippings of the honeycomb," and confesses, "How sweet are your words to my taste, sweeter than honey to my mouth" (Psalm 19:9–10; 119:103). When Ezekiel eats the scroll symbolizing Jehovah's message, it is "as sweet as honey" in his mouth

(Ezekiel 3:2–3). John has a similar experience with a little scroll that tastes sweet but turns bitter in his stomach (Revelation 10:9–10). The background assumption is simple: honey was a prized, delectable food; therefore, the Word of God, though sometimes leading to difficult assignments, is intrinsically satisfying and life-giving.

Fish were a common food, especially around the Sea of Galilee and along the Mediterranean. Nets, boats, and fish markets were well-known features of daily life. Ecclesiastes compares human vulnerability to that of fish caught in a net and birds trapped in a snare (Ecclesiastes 9:12). Jesus calls His disciples to be "fishers of men," using the familiar image of casting nets and drawing in a catch for an entirely new purpose (Mark 1:17). In a parable about the kingdom, He likens the final separation of the righteous and wicked to fishermen who sort good fish into containers and discard bad ones (Matthew 13:47–50). These figures gain weight when one remembers the physically strenuous, uncertain life of a Galilean fisherman.

Mealtime itself carried covenant and relational meaning. Sharing a meal was a sign of peace, solidarity, and mutual acceptance. Jacob and Laban sealed their agreement with a meal (Genesis 31:54). David honored Mephibosheth by having him eat at the king's table "like one of the king's sons" (2 Samuel 9:7–13). To refuse to eat with someone signaled estrangement or disapproval (1 Samuel 20:34). In many contexts, food was also a gift meant to secure or confirm goodwill, and to accept such a gift obligated one to maintain peace with the giver (Genesis 33:8–16; 1 Samuel 9:6–8; 25:18–35; 1 Kings 14:1–3). When the New Testament speaks of table fellowship between Jewish and Gentile believers, or records controversies about eating together (Acts 11:2–3; Galatians 2:11–12), it presupposes this deep cultural significance of shared meals.

# Purity, Handwashing, and Religious Tradition

The Gospels record controversies about handwashing that puzzle many modern readers. Mark explains that the Pharisees and many Jews "do not eat unless they wash their hands," holding to "the tradition of the elders," and that they also wash cups, pitchers, and vessels (Mark 7:2–4). Matthew records Pharisees confronting Jesus: "Why do your disciples break the tradition of the elders? For they do not wash their hands when they eat bread" (Matthew 15:2).

The issue was not ordinary hygienic washing, which is wise and natural. The controversy centered on an elaborate ritual of ceremonial cleansing that had developed as a fence around the Law. Rabbinic tradition elevated this washing— sometimes involving pouring water in a particular pattern up to the elbows—into a marker of religious seriousness. To eat without such ritual cleansing was treated as a grave offense. Later Jewish tradition harshly condemns those who eat with "unwashed hands," even threatening divine judgment on those who neglect this ritual.

Jesus decisively exposes the problem: these ceremonies are not commanded in the Law but are human traditions elevated to the status of divine requirements. By clinging to them, many Pharisees "leave the commandment of God and hold to the tradition of men," even nullifying God's Word through their practices (Mark 7:8–13). Background knowledge of rabbinic handwashing customs makes clear that Jesus did not oppose cleanliness; He opposed binding human regulations on consciences and using them to judge others while neglecting the heart.

# Postures, Gestures, and Expressions of Emotion

Biblical authors often describe bodily postures and gestures that carry a freight of meaning within their culture. These are not incidental details; they communicate attitudes of worship, respect, grief, or defiance.

Kneeling is frequently associated with prayer. Luke tells us that Jesus withdrew from His disciples "about a stone's throw" and knelt to pray in Gethsemane (Luke 22:41). Solomon knelt when he finished his prayer of dedication for the temple (1 Kings 8:54). Peter, Paul, and other believers likewise kneel in prayer (Acts 9:40; 20:36; 21:5; Ephesians 3:14). Sometimes both knees are in view; other times a single knee may be implied. The essence is humility and earnest dependence.

Bowing could be a gesture of deep respect or, in some contexts, an act of worship. Israelites were able to bow before kings or dignitaries without compromising their loyalty to Jehovah, so long as the act did not imply religious veneration. The tension in the book of Esther arises when Mordecai refuses to bow or pay homage to Haman (Esther 3:2–4).

Haman is identified as an "Agagite," linking him with Amalekite royalty. Amalek was a grandson of Esau, and his descendants, the Amalekites, harassed Israel with brutal ambushes, attacking the weak and stragglers (Genesis 36:12, 15–16; Exodus 17:8–16; Deuteronomy 25:17–19). Jehovah swore to "blot out the memory of Amalek from under heaven" and declared that He would have war with Amalek "from generation to generation." Later, King Saul was commanded to devote Amalek to destruction, but he disobeyed by sparing King Agag and choice spoil (1 Samuel 15). Because of this defiance, Saul lost the kingdom.

In Esther, Mordecai is associated with the house of Saul, and Haman bears a title pointing back to Agag. Their confrontation is a historical echo of the earlier conflict: a descendant of Saul refusing to honor a descendant of Agag. Given Jehovah's explicit sentence against Amalek, Mordecai's refusal to bow is more than personal stubbornness; to him, it would be disloyalty to Jehovah to show public homage to one associated with the ancestral enemy whom God had cursed. Understanding the Amalekite background makes Haman's rage and genocidal plan all the more intelligible.

Another cultural practice that puzzles modern readers is the oath gesture in Genesis 24. Abraham has his senior servant place his hand under Abraham's thigh while swearing to secure a wife for Isaac from Abraham's kin rather than from the Canaanites (Genesis 24:2–4, 9). This was a solemn, intimate way to bind oneself to an oath before Jehovah, likely connected with the patriarch's role as covenant bearer whose descendants would inherit the promise. The gesture underscored the gravity of the vow and the personal responsibility involved.

Expressions of grief and repentance had equally physical forms. When Israel was defeated at Ai, Joshua tore his clothes and fell face-down before the ark of Jehovah until evening, he and the elders placing dust on their heads (Joshua 7:6). Tearing one's garments, wearing coarse sackcloth, shaving the head or beard, throwing dust or ashes on the head, and beating the chest were all visible ways to display inward sorrow, anguish, or repentance. Without knowledge of these customs, such descriptions might seem exaggerated or strange; in context, they are the expected language of intense emotion in the in the ancient Near East and within the covenant community of Israel. When we recognize that these are culturally appropriate signals of agony or repentance, we hear the accounts as their first audience did, and we feel the weight of the moment more fully.

# New Testament Backgrounds and the Roman World

By the time of the New Testament, the people of God lived under a very different set of political and cultural pressures. The world of Jesus and the apostles was shaped by Roman rule, Hellenistic (Greek) culture, and Jewish covenant identity all at once. Every page of the Gospels and Acts assumes that mixed environment.

Roman law, crucifixion, soldiers, roads, taxation, citizenship, and imperial rule. This background clarifies the Gospels, Acts, and the experience of the early church.

Rome imposed imperial control through client kings, governors, taxation, and military presence. The Herodian dynasty ruled parts of Palestine as Roman vassals, blending Jewish lineage with Roman political ambitions. Roman prefects and procurators, such as Pontius Pilate, held ultimate authority for capital cases and public order. Caesar was not just a distant ruler; he was the figure whose image appeared on coins used to pay taxes and whose authority stood behind Roman law.

At the same time, Greek language and culture permeated daily life. Koine Greek served as the common tongue for trade, administration, and literature from Egypt to Syria and beyond. This is why the New Testament is written in Greek, even though many of its speakers used Aramaic among themselves. Greek philosophical terms, rhetorical forms, and civic practices appear in the background of many passages.

Meanwhile, devout Jews were committed to the Law of Moses, to the temple and synagogue, and to the promises of Jehovah to Abraham, Isaac, Jacob, and David. This threefold pressure—imperial power, Greek culture, and covenant identity—shaped questions about loyalty, purity, and hope. When we read the New Testament with that composite background in mind, we better understand why issues such as taxation, circumcision, food laws, and temple worship generated such heated controversy.

# Jewish Religious Institutions in the Time of Jesus

The second temple in Jerusalem was the central symbol of Jewish religious life. It was the place Jehovah chose for His Name, where sacrifices were offered and major festivals observed. Pilgrims from across the Diaspora streamed to Jerusalem for Passover, Pentecost, and the Feast of Booths. The Gospels presuppose this flow of pilgrims and the bustling activity in and around the temple courts.

The priesthood, organized into courses, rotated in service. Priests and Levites conducted sacrifices, maintained sacred vessels, and explained aspects of the Law. The Sanhedrin, a council of chief priests, elders, and scribes, functioned as a high court in religious and some civil matters. When Jesus is interrogated before the high priest and then handed over to Pilate, we see the interface between Jewish religious authority and Roman political power.

Temple rituals, priesthood, synagogues, purity traditions, handwashing, festivals, and religious parties (Pharisees, Sadducees). Without this, much of the Gospels and Acts remains abstract.

Synagogues, meanwhile, had developed as local centers for Scripture reading, prayer, and instruction, both in Palestine and in Jewish communities throughout the Roman world. When Jesus "taught in their synagogues," He was participating in this established pattern of reading from the Law and Prophets, followed by exposition and exhortation (Luke 4:16–21). When Paul travels through Asia Minor and Greece in Acts, he consistently begins his ministry by entering the synagogue each Sabbath to reason from the Scriptures (Acts 17:1–3). Understanding the synagogue as a decentralized but vital institution helps us see why the early

Christian proclamation spread so rapidly: it had a ready-made platform wherever there were Jews and God-fearing Gentiles.

Different Jewish groups also influenced the New Testament scene. The Pharisees emphasized strict adherence to both written Law and oral traditions; the Sadducees were closely tied to the priestly aristocracy and denied resurrection; the Essenes withdrew to more separatist communities; the Zealots favored violent resistance to Rome. The Gospels and Acts mention some of these parties explicitly. Knowing their basic convictions clarifies many discussions and conflicts in the text.

# Roman Power, Citizenship, and Punishment

Roman power expressed itself through military presence, legal structures, citizenship privileges, and brutal punishments designed to deter rebellion.

Taxation was a constant burden and symbol of subjection. When some tried to trap Jesus with the question about paying taxes to Caesar, they appealed to widespread resentment against Roman tribute (Matthew 22:15–22). The denarius with Caesar's image and inscription crystallized the tension between earthly authority and divine ownership. Jesus' response, "Render to Caesar the things that are Caesar's, and to God the things that are God's," makes full sense when we picture the coin stamped with imperial propaganda in the hand of His questioners.

Roman citizenship conferred legal protections and social status. It could be acquired by birth, by manumission, or by purchase at considerable cost. Paul insists on his rights as a Roman citizen to avoid unlawful beating and to secure an appeal to Caesar (Acts 22:25–29; 25:10–12). Without knowledge of Roman law, the significance of these episodes is easily missed. Paul does not merely escape discomfort; he uses his lawful rights to advance the gospel to the heart of the empire.

Crucifixion was a Roman method of execution reserved for slaves, rebels, and the lowest criminals. It was designed to inflict maximum pain, prolonged exposure, and public humiliation. Victims could be scourged beforehand, forced to carry the crossbeam or stake, and then nailed or tied and left to die slowly. The message was clear: Rome crushes resistance and shames its enemies. When the New Testament speaks of "the word of the cross" or of Christ becoming a curse for us by hanging on a tree, it assumes this background of social disgrace and horror (1 Corinthians 1:18; Galatians 3:13).

Jesus' call to "take up his cross" and follow Him (Mark 8:34) is not a vague metaphor for daily difficulties. In the Roman world, carrying a cross meant a condemned man on the way to execution. The call is a summons to absolute self-denial and willingness to face rejection and death for His sake. Historical background sharpens the radical edge of discipleship.

# Daily Life, Households, and Social Relations

New Testament believers lived in a world structured by households, patronage, honor and shame, and slavery.

The basic social unit was the household, headed by a paterfamilias in Roman society or by the senior male in a Jewish family. This household included wife, children, extended kin, servants, and sometimes slaves. It was both an economic and social unit. When Lydia or the Philippian jailer believes and is baptized with "all his household," we are seeing conversion that affects an entire domestic network (Acts 16:14–15, 31–34).

Slavery was widespread and deeply embedded in the ancient economy. Slaves served in households, workshops, farms, and public administration. The New Testament does not present an abstract modern debate about labor; it addresses masters and slaves within that existing structure, calling slaves to serve as to the Lord and masters to remember that they too have a Master in heaven (Ephesians 6:5–9; Colossians 3:22–4:1). Without background knowledge, modern readers may misjudge these instructions; with it, they can see how the gospel planted principles that undermine cruelty, assert the equal worth of believers, and point beyond earthly hierarchies.

Patron-client relationships were also central. Wealthy patrons provided resources, legal assistance, or protection to clients, who in turn owed public honor, service, and loyalty. Public benefactors would sponsor buildings, festivals, or distributions and receive inscriptions praising their generosity. Against this backdrop, Jesus' teaching that leaders must be servants, not lords, directly challenges common expectations (Mark 10:42–45). When Paul refuses financial support in certain contexts to avoid being beholden as a client, or when he insists that the Corinthians stop boasting in human leaders, he is navigating a world where status, patronage, and honor could easily distort the gospel.

Honor and shame formed the currency of social life. Public reputation, family standing, and perceived dignity mattered greatly. This helps explain why confessing Christ openly could lead to exclusion from the synagogue, loss of social position, or even economic hardship. It also sheds light on Paul's repeated insistence that boasting must be in the Lord alone, not in human credentials (2 Corinthians 10:17).

# Geography, Roads, and Travel in Bible Times

Biblical narratives constantly move through specific landscapes: coastal plains, hill country, deserts, river valleys, and seas. Geography is not incidental scenery; it shapes the narrative.

Israel's land bridge position between Africa and Asia meant that major empires marched armies through her territory. The coastal plain and the Jezreel Valley served as invasion corridors. The hill country provided defensible positions but required terracing and cisterns to sustain agriculture and water supplies. The wilderness areas east and south of Judah could be refuges for fugitives but were harsh and demanding.

The journey from Jericho to Jerusalem, for example, involves a steep ascent of more than a thousand meters over a relatively short distance. Jesus' parable of the man going down from Jerusalem to Jericho and falling among robbers gains vividness when we picture a rugged, winding road through lonely ravines where bandits could easily ambush travelers (Luke 10:30–37). Likewise, descriptions of Jesus going "up" to Jerusalem from Galilee or from the Jordan Valley reflect actual topography.

The Roman road system connected cities across the empire. Well-constructed roads, bridges, and sea routes made missionary travel possible on a scale unimaginable in earlier periods. Paul's journeys from Antioch to Cyprus, to Asia Minor, to Macedonia and Greece, and finally toward Rome, all make use of these networks. When Acts speaks of specific harbors, trade routes, and cities, it assumes a reader who recognizes at least some of these names. Understanding distances, travel times, and seasonal dangers (such as winter storms on the Mediterranean) helps explain why certain journeys were delayed or why Paul urged caution before sailing late in the year (Acts 27:9–12).

# Language, Metaphor, and Everyday Objects

The Bible makes extensive use of metaphors drawn from occupations and objects that were common in daily life: shepherding, farming, building, soldiering, athletics, and more. Without a sense of these backgrounds, we risk flattening those images.

Shepherding was a humble but vital occupation in Israel's economy. Sheep required constant guidance, protection from predators, and attentive care. The shepherd knew his flock by sight and voice. When David speaks of Jehovah as his Shepherd, or when Jesus identifies Himself as the Good Shepherd who knows His sheep and lays down His life for them, the analogy rests on this concrete occupational reality (Psalm 23; John 10:1–18). The hired man who flees at danger, the shepherd who calls his own sheep by name, and the rod and staff that comfort are all grounded in actual shepherd practice.

Agricultural imagery pervades Jesus' parables: sowers, seeds, soils, weeds, harvests, vineyards, tenants, fig trees. Knowing the rhythm of planting and harvest, the vulnerability of crops to drought or locusts, the structure of a vineyard lease, or the value of a fig tree informs our reading. When Jesus curses a barren fig tree as a sign of judgment, or when He speaks of the kingdom as a mustard seed growing into a large plant, those figures gain concreteness from familiarity with Palestinian agriculture.

Construction and craftsmanship supply another range of metaphors. Jesus' reference to the man who builds a house on rock rather than sand, or Paul's description of Christ as the cornerstone and believers as living stones, assumes knowledge of building foundations, load-bearing stones, and careful alignment (Matthew 7:24–27; Ephesians 2:19–22; 1 Peter 2:4–6). Armor imagery in Ephesians 6 draws on the equipment of a Roman soldier: belt, breastplate, sandals, shield, helmet, and sword. Understanding the function of each piece enriches the spiritual analogy.

# How Background Study Serves the Historical-Grammatical Method

All these examples point to a central truth: historical and cultural backgrounds are servants of exegesis, not masters of Scripture. The inspired text, as preserved in the Hebrew and Greek, is the final authority. Yet Jehovah chose to inspire that text within real historical situations and cultural forms. When we ask, responsibly and reverently, how the original authors and first readers understood particular words, images, institutions, and events, we are not adding a second layer of authority. We are honoring the way God chose to speak.

The historical-grammatical method takes seriously the grammar of the text and the historical situation it presupposes. Word meanings are shaped by usage; images are shaped by shared experiences; commands are addressed to people living under particular laws, customs, and social structures. Background study helps us avoid reading our assumptions into the text. It guards us from treating the Bible as though it were written in our century, in our political order, or in our denominational debates.

At the same time, we must be careful not to let speculative reconstructions override what Scripture actually says. Archaeology, ancient Near Eastern texts, and Greco-Roman sources are valuable tools, but they are not infallible. They must be weighed carefully and always kept subordinate to the clear teaching of the Word. When responsible background information harmonizes with Scripture and clarifies a passage, it is a gift. When a proposed background contradicts the inspired testimony, the proposal must yield.

# Choosing Reliable Resources for Bible Background Study

Modern believers have access to a remarkable array of tools that previous generations could only have dreamed of. Detailed Bible atlases trace ancient routes and locate cities and regions mentioned in Scripture. Illustrated dictionaries and encyclopedias explain customs, institutions, and archaeological discoveries. Specialized works on manners and customs describe daily life in Old and New Testament times. Background commentaries walk through the text book by book, highlighting historical and cultural details that illuminate specific verses.

Atlases that trace Israel's wilderness wanderings, the tribal allocations in Joshua, the rise and fall of empires, and the missionary journeys of Paul can make the geography of Scripture vivid and concrete. Illustrated dictionaries provide photographs and drawings of artifacts, buildings, inscriptions, and coins, connecting the world of the Bible to visible remains. Works on manners and customs explain topics such as marriage arrangements, inheritance patterns, festivals, warfare, agriculture, and trade.

One-volume background commentaries on the Old and New Testaments can be particularly useful when a reader wants quick orientation to the setting of a passage. They often discuss political rulers, social conditions, religious practices, and local geography in connection with specific chapters.

However, there is a serious caution. Many academic resources are written from perspectives that do not accept the full inerrancy of Scripture or that treat the Bible as a product of purely human religious development. Such works often employ a historical-critical approach, rearranging the text, denying predictive prophecy, and treating supernatural events as late legends. While they may contain useful factual information about archaeology or ancient cultures, their interpretive framework can subtly undermine confidence in the inspired Word.

For that reason, Christians should choose background resources produced by authors who affirm the inspiration and inerrancy of Scripture and who practice the historical-grammatical method rather than skeptical approaches. Publishers and writers committed to a high view of the Bible provide atlases, dictionaries, and background studies that serve faith rather than erode it. There are conservative works on Bible history, archaeology, and manners and customs that are both academically careful and spiritually trustworthy, and believers should prioritize such materials.

Affordable digital editions now put many of these tools within reach of ordinary Bible students. Even with limited finances, a believer can build a modest library: a solid study Bible, a good atlas, a reliable illustrated dictionary, a volume on Bible manners and customs, and a conservative background commentary. These few resources, used alongside the careful reading of Scripture itself, can open up the historical and cultural world of the Bible in remarkable ways.

# Bible Backgrounds and the Modern Reader's Responsibility

We live two to three and a half millennia after most of the events recorded in Scripture. We inhabit different political systems, economic structures, and social patterns. Yet the same God speaks through the same inspired Word. Background study does not create that Word; it helps us, as twenty-first-century readers, cross the gap of time, culture, and geography responsibly.

Every passage of Scripture comes from a particular human author, writing under divine inspiration, to a specific audience, within a concrete historical setting. That author chose words, images, and examples that would communicate clearly to that audience. When we labor to understand their world—its houses and city walls, its foods and festivals, its family structures and legal systems, its empires and local customs—we are taking seriously the reality that Jehovah spoke in history.

Background knowledge will not replace prayer, humility, obedience, or meditation on the text. But it will often transform verses we have read many times into scenes we can picture, relationships we can trace, and commands we can situate properly. The account of Samson carrying Gaza's gate, the fall of Jericho, the friends digging through a roof in Capernaum, the disciples reclining at the table with Jesus, the apostles in an upper room in Jerusalem, Mordecai refusing to bow before an Amalekite, Joshua and the elders throwing dust on their heads, Jesus confronting Pharisaic traditions about handwashing, Paul claiming his rights as a Roman citizen—all these and countless other passages become sharper, richer, and more compelling when read in their proper historical and cultural settings.

In that sense, the study of Bible backgrounds is not an optional hobby for specialists. It is part of loving God with our minds, honoring the way He chose to reveal Himself, and handling His Word accurately. As believers grow in their grasp of the historical and cultural world of Scripture, they are better equipped to grasp the flow of covenant history, to trace the development from promise to fulfillment, and to apply the living Word faithfully in their own time.

# APPENDIX 7 Introduction to Christian Apologetics

**Christian apologetics** [Greek: *apologia*, "verbal defense, speech in defense"] is a field of **Christian theology** that endeavors to offer a reasonable and sensible basis for the **Christian faith**, defending the faith against objections. It is reasoning from the Scriptures, explaining, persuading, proving, and defending, as one instructs in sound doctrine, often having to overturn false reasoning before he can plant the seeds of truth. It can also be earnestly contending for the faith and saving one from losing their faith, as they have begun to doubt. Moreover, it can involve rebuking those who contradict the truth. It is being prepared to make a defense to anyone who asks the Christian evangelist for a reason for the hope that is in him or her. – Jude 1.3, 21-23; 1 Pet 3.15; Acts 17:2-3; Titus 1:9.

# Why the Need for Apologetics?

**1 Timothy 2:3-4** Updated American Standard Version (UASV)

³ This is good, and it is acceptable in the sight of God our Savior, ⁴ who desires all men to be saved and to come to an accurate knowledge¹ of truth.

## Why Should We Be Interested in the Religion of Others?

The world has become a melting pot of people, cultures, values, and many different religions. Religion has the most significant impact on the lives of mankind today. In India, Nepal, Bangladesh, Indonesia (especially in Bali- 84% Hindu), *Hinduism* is practiced. You will often see people doing puja, a prayer ritual performed by Hindus of devotional worship to one or more deities, or to host and honor a guest, or one to spiritually celebrate an event. Millions of Hindus flock each year to the river Ganges to be purified by its waters.

---

¹ The Greek word (ἐπίγνωσις epignōsis) behind the English rendering **accurate knowledge** is a strengthened or intensified form of *gnosis* (*epi,* meaning "additional"), meaning "true," "real," "full," "complete," or "accurate," depending upon the context. Paul and Peter alone use *epignosis*.

In Mexico, Middle America, South America, the Philippines, the United States, and Italy *Catholics* are praying in churches and cathedrals while holding a crucifix or a rosary. The rosary refers to a form of prayer used in the Catholic Church and the string of knots or beads used to count the component prayers offered in devotion to Mary. The nuns and priests are easily identified, as they are distinctive in their black garb.

In Denmark, Estonia, Finland, the central, eastern, and northern parts of Germany, Iceland, Latvia, Norway, Sweden, the United Kingdom, and the eastern, northern, and western parts of Switzerland and the United States, we find *Protestant* lands. There you will discover chapels and churches abound, and on Sunday, churchgoers usually put on their best clothes and congregate to sing hymns and hear sermons, as well as a Bible study class. Many times, the minister, clergy, pastors, or elders are somewhat distinctive in that some wear black suits, or at least a suit, while many churchgoers do not. Jesus Christ and the twelve apostles grew the one Christian faith from a few thousand on Pentecost 33 C.E. to hundreds of thousands throughout the Roman Empire by the beginning of the second century C.E. However, historian Will Durant states: "Faced with the Hostility of a powerful [Roman] government, the church felt the need of unity; it could not safely allow itself to be divided into a hundred feeble parts by every wind of intellect, by disloyal heretics, ecstatic prophets, or brilliant sons. Celsus [an enemy of Christianity] himself had sarcastically observed that Christians were 'split up into ever so many factions, each individual desiring to have his own party.' About 187 [C.E.] Irenaeus listed twenty varieties of Christianity; about 384 [C.E.] Epiphanius counted eighty. At every point, foreign ideas were creeping into Christian belief, and Christian believers were deserting to novel sects." (The Story of Civilization: Part III—Caesar and Christ.) Today, there are over 41,000 different denominations that call themselves Christian. Almost all are not reflective of the form of Christianity that Jesus started, and the apostles grew. Thus, genuine Christianity is obligated to save those Christians who are no longer on the correct path.

In Saudi Arabia, Yemen, Brunei, Qatar, Pakistan, United Arab Emirates, Iraq, Iran, Afghanistan, Sudan, Mauritania, Islamic countries, you can hear the voices of men, the muezzins, who call to call Muslims to prayer from the minaret of a mosque. These Muslim criers make the call from minarets five times each day, summoning the faithful to the *ṣalat,* that is, the ritual prayer of Muslims. All Muslims view the Holy Quran as the Islamic book of Scripture. Under Islamic belief, the Quran was revealed by God and was given to the prophet Muhammad by the angel Gabriel in the seventh century C.E. the Islamic sacred book, believed to be the word of God as dictated to Muhammad by the archangel Gabriel and written down in Arabic. The Quran consists of 114 units of varying lengths, known as Surahs (a chapter or section of the Quran); the first Surah is said as part of the ritual prayer. These touch upon all aspects of human existence, including matters of doctrine, social organization, legislation, and holy war.

In Thailand, Myanmar, Bhutan, and Sri Lanka, we find the monks of *Buddhism,* usually in saffron, black, or red robes, who are viewed as a sign of piety. Ancient temples with the serene Buddha on display are evidence of the antiquity of the Buddhist faith, as some date to sixth-century B.C.E.

In Japan, the *Shinto* religion is practiced in daily life, with family shrines and offerings being made to their ancestors. The Japanese pray for the most mundane things, even success in school examinations.

These are only a few of the major religions that make up billions of people throughout the earth. According to some estimates, there are roughly **4,200 religions** in the world. The word religion is sometimes used interchangeably with "faith" or "belief system," but religion differs from private belief in that it has a public aspect. What can we extrapolate from the variety of religions with billions of devoted adherents? Literally, for thousands of years, mankind has tried to fill its spiritual needs. For thousands of years, man has sought answers to the most troubling questions about life. Why is there so much suffering? Why are we here? How should we live? What are we actually? Why do we grow old, get sick, and eventually die? What does the future hold for mankind? Man has suffered from the trials and burdens of life, doubts about his future, and questions that seem to have no answer. Because man has an inherent spiritual need, religion, in many different ways, has sought to fill that need through God and gods, seeking the blessing from something greater than themselves.

Then again, there are millions of people around the world who profess no religion nor any belief in a god (Atheism), or at least they cannot know for certain if there is some power (God) greater than themselves (Agnostics). However, that obviously does not mean that they are people without religion of principles or ethics, any more than professing a religion means that one does have them. However, one of the definitions of religion in the Merriam-Webster Dictionary is this: "a cause, principle, or system of beliefs held to with ardor and faith." Certainly, atheism fits that definition, and many atheists are quite zealous about their faith system, many being more zealous than much of Christianity. Another source, *The Shorter Oxford English Dictionary*, accepts religion as being "devotion to some principle; strict fidelity or faithfulness; conscientiousness; pious affection or attachment." Therefore, the atheist and the Agnostic have a religious devotion in their lives.

All disciples of Jesus Christ are to be Christian apologetic evangelists. (Matt. 24:14; 29-;19-20; Ac 1:8; 10:42; Jude 1:3, 22-23; 1 Pet. 3:15) If Christians are going to carry out the Great Commission, they need to know something about the background of the world's religions in order to be effective. Parrinder states in *World Religions—From Ancient History to the Present:* "To study different religions need not imply infidelity to one's own faith, but rather it may be enlarged by seeing how other people have sought for reality and have been enriched by their search." When we have at least a basic knowledge of other religions, this leads to understanding and understanding to a tolerance of people with a different viewpoint, which is in no way suggesting that we accept anything unbiblical.

## Why Examine Other Religions?

Many today see their religion as a very personal matter, which they are hesitant about discussing with others. Largely, this is because most are born into their religion because of where they were raised and the parents they had. Sadly, they are usually following the religion of their parents and grandparents with little or no idea about the religion itself. Therefore, religion for many is simply a family tradition. Thus, religion has been chosen for them.

In a sense, many in the world assume that the religion they received at birth is the complete truth. Again, if they were born in Italy or South

America, then, without any choice on their part, they have likely been raised a Catholic. On the other hand, if they were born in India, they were likely born into Hinduism or, if from Punjab, perhaps a Sikh. If their parents are from Pakistan, there is little doubt that they were raised in Islam as Muslims. Then, again, if they were raised in Russia, it is likely that they might be an atheist. – Galatians 1:13-14; Acts 23:6.

Therefore, it seems only wise that they ask if a religion they were born into is automatically the true religion approved by God. If the people of a thousand years ago had the mindset that the religion of my parents was good enough for them, it is good enough for me attitude; many among us would still be following practicing primitive shamanism and ancient fertility cults. It is at least enlightening and mind-broadening for Christians to understand what others believe and how their beliefs originated. And it might also open up opportunities for Christian apologetic evangelists to share the truth of God's Word with them a sure hope for the future. Because of mass immigration over the past few decades, Christians are now sharing neighborhoods with people of many different religious backgrounds. Therefore, When the Christian evangelist understands their viewpoint, it can lead to more meaningful communication and conversation between two people of different faiths. Yes, there is a strong disagreement among many religions, yet this is no reason for hating a person of a different faith or a different viewpoint. – 1 Peter 3:15; 1 John 4:20-21; Revelation 2:6.

The Mosaic Law stated, "You shall not take vengeance, nor bear any grudge against the sons of your people, but you shall love your neighbor as yourself; I am Jehovah." (Lev. 19:17-18) Jesus Christ stated, "But I say to you who hear, love your enemies, do good to those who hate you ... But love your enemies, and do good, and lend, expecting nothing in return, and your reward will be great, and you will be sons of the Most High, for he is kind to the ungrateful and the evil men." (Lu 6:27, 35) In evangelizing Islam, we can let the Muslim know that under the heading "She That Is To Be Examined," the Quran states a similar principle (Surah 60:7, *MMP*): "It may be that Allah will bring about friendship between you and those of them whom you hold as enemies. And Allah is Powerful; and Allah is Forgiving, Merciful." How is it that we are to love our enemy? It means that we are willing to share the Gospel with them, a lifesaving message. While Christians are to be tolerant of others and eagerly evangelizing persons from other religions, this does not mean that it makes no difference what one believes. They are **not just different roads** leading to the same place, as some claim. It is the God of the Bible that is the determiner of what form of worship is acceptable. – Micah 6:8.

The Books of Moses, the first portion of the Holy Bible, is the world's oldest religious book, initially penned under inspiration in the 16th and 15th centuries. On the other hand, the Hindu writings of the Rig-Veda (a collection of hymns) were completed about 900 B.C.E. and do not claim divine inspiration. The Buddhist "Canon of the Three Baskets" dates back to the fifth-century B.C.E. The Quran, claimed to have been transmitted from God through the angel Gabriel, was supposedly given to Muhammad in the seventh century C.E. The Book of Mormon was allegedly given to Joseph Smith in the United States by an angel called Moroni in the 19th century. If any of these other so-called holy books were also divinely inspired, as is claimed by their adherents, they would not contradict the teachings of the Bible, which is the original inspired source.

Many billions in this world are walking through this satanic age of the last days believing that this life is all there is. Others, if they believe in eternal life, the path they have chosen does not lead there at all. Even those who believe that they are doing the will of the Father, Jesus has said," 'I never knew you; depart from me, you workers of lawlessness.'" (Matt. 7:23) Why would Jesus say this? Isn't it enough if your heart is in the right place? No. Many have been doing their will rather than the will of the Father. Therefore, in the eyes of Jesus, they are nothing more "workers of lawlessness." Nevertheless, while there is still time, we can save some who are receptive to the truth. While there is but one Gospel, one biblical truth, there are many ways of delivering that lifesaving message. This one message saves the lives of those who are receptive to it and if we are effective in providing it. However, do not be disheartened, as many more will reject it than accept it. Jesus was the most outstanding teacher of all time, and the apostle Paul was the second greatest. Yet, many hardhearted ones rejected their message.

# One Word—One Gospel

Some church leaders today are nine parts world and one part Christian. They **propagate the idea** that the church is to mold itself to reflect the makeup of its community. They seem to be saying, a church is reflective of its community. The idea is that the church, pastor/leadership should reflect its community. No, it should be that the members of the church, who came out of the community, should reflect the image of God. The goal of genuine Christianity is how we can reintroduce God's Word to the people? We should conform those in the world who are alienated from God so that they take on the mind of Christ, a biblical worldview. Paul wrote, "And do not be conformed to this world, but be transformed by the renewing of your mind, so that you may prove what the will of God is, that which is good and acceptable and perfect." (Romans 12:2) The whole point can be summed up in this; the whole congregation going into the community must share the Gospel, evangelize the community. The congregation must be first trained in evangelizing, communication, reasoning, and teaching so that they can effectively relate the Word of God to the community. Yes, they need to relate to the community and be in the world but be no part of the world.

**Luke 6:40** Updated American Standard Version (UASV)

[40] A disciple is not above his teacher, but everyone when he is fully trained will be like his teacher.

Just how effective was Jesus? How effective were his apostles and early disciples? Jesus' early disciples carried on the work that he had commanded them to accomplish, which ran throughout the Roman Empire, in Asia, Europe, and Africa. (Matt 24:14; 28:18-20; Acts 1:8) At the beginning of the second century, there were over a million Christians and estimated to be between 5-7 million by 300 C.E. In fact, the Christians displaced pagan religion as the official religion by 400 C.E. If an evangelism training program within a church is not ineffective; the one who set up the program is ineffective.

It is quite simple; make a biblical church that is reflective of the New Testament in principle, which has members who are trained in effectively sharing God's Word to all sorts of people in their community, proclaiming, teaching, and making disciples, regardless of the culture one is from.

### A Biblical Church

- The Bible is their foundation in faith, truth, and practice
- Biblical preaching
- The worship is based on Scriptural principles
- The building is designed based on Scriptural principles
- The music chosen is based on biblical principles
- The education is biblical

- The worldview and lifestyle of its members is biblical
- Its evangelism is patterned after the New Testament
- The pastors and servants are chosen based on Scripture
- The structure of leadership is based on Scripture
- Church discipline is based on Scripture
- Organized and governed based on Scripture
- And so on ...

All the while, its members can relate to whoever is in the community. It has an acceptance of cultural aspects if they are not in opposition to the Word of God. This means that they are welcome to engage in any cultural lifestyle that does not violate Scripture. For example, a woman could wear any type of dress that is relevant to her culture, as long as it is modest. There are literally tens of millions of unbelieving North Americans walking around with a receptive heart to the biblical truth, the deeper Gospel. They are low-hanging fruit from the tree of potential disciples; all Christians have to do is pick them. Some will be easy to bring into the fold; some will have to be reasoned with to overcome their firmly entrenched ideas, while some will have to have their criticisms overcome before they begin to believe.

# Christian Apologetics Is a Tool that can Clear Away Any Obstruction to Faith in Jesus Christ

**Preevangelism** is laying a foundation for those who have no knowledge of the Gospel, giving them background information to grasp what they are hearing. The Christian evangelist is preparing their mind and heart to be receptive to the biblical truths. In many ways, this is known as apologetics. In the beginning, we may not be explicitly sharing the Gospel, but instead clearing away anything that might obstruct them from accepting the Gospel. This is called Preevangelism. Sadly, many who have come into the Christian faith did not do so through any kind of investigation into the authenticity and authority of the Bible, the historicity of Jesus Christ, and they lack any deep knowledge of God's Word. They feel as though they have the truth, but they have not been equipped to explain it to others. The following three things are needed, and none of the three can be missing.

(1) Knowledge
(2) Belief
(3) Obedience

To become a spiritually strong, mature Christian, one must ...

(1) obtain an accurate, broad knowledge of Bible truth (1 Timothy 2:3-4),
(2) put faith in the things we have learned (Hebrews 11:6),
(3) repent of your sins (Acts 17:30-31), and
(4) turn around in your course of life. (Acts 3:19);
(5) Then our love for God should move us to dedicate ourselves to Christ. (Matt. 16:24; 22:37)
(6) Finally, baptism (Matt. 28:19-20; Mark 1:9-10; Acts 8:36)

Many Christians believe that they have found true Christianity, but they do not have a correct understanding of the Word of God nor the ability to explain it. If one is missing the knowledge aspect, he cannot maintain his belief in something he has no actual in-depth knowledge of, so this must be corrected right away. Christians who have found themselves believers of the faith but unable to be defenders of the faith are often uncomfortable talking about their faith. They become somewhat defensive if anyone challenges their faith, the Word of God, or the existence of God. This is because they have not acquired enough deep knowledge of God's Word to offer reasonable and rational reasons for Christianity. What will happen many times is that they will **(1)** lock themselves out of any conversation that might lead to an opportunity at sharing their faith, or **(2)** they become contentious, combative, or even hostile, which only alienates the unbeliever even further. This places them in opposition to the very Great Commission Jesus gave them. – Matthew 28:19–20.

Christians are to be in the world while being no part of the world, which does not mean withdrawing from the world and isolating themselves among Christians alone. Christians are to be the salt and the light. (Matt. 5:13-16) Suppose one is new to the Christian faith or has been a Christian for decades. In that case, it is incumbent upon him to take in a deeper knowledge of God's Word to share our doctrinal views, what the authors meant as opposed to what we think, feel, or believe they meant, and acquire the skills needed to effectively share our faith with others. In other words, he needs to have a deep personal Bible study program, prepare for his Christian meetings, and become informed about Christian apologetics and evangelism. When called upon, he has to be able to rise to the challenges of his faith. Have you ever been confronted by an unbeliever who had some challenging questions for you and had to defend your Christian faith? How would you have reacted if challenged with the questions and statements below? Would you have accurate, reasonable, logical answers, or would you become contentious, combative, or even hostile, giving a short response that would persuade no one?

- Jesus never existed.
- Why would an all-powerful, all-loving, all-knowing God allow so much pain and suffering?
- No one can prove God existed.
- How can God, holy, righteous, of love, all-powerful be justified in destroying cities and killing men, women, and young children in Bible times?
- There is no evidence to support Jesus' supposed resurrection from the dead.
- Men wrote the Bible. It is full of errors, contradictions, and mistakes.
- There are no such things as miracles.
- Everyone has their own personal interpretation of the Bible.
- All religions are just different roads leading to the same place.
- Christianity has spilled more blood than most militaries.
- There is no such thing as absolute truth.
- Christianity is based on blind faith.
- Christianity is a laundry list of things to do and not do, meaning that Christians have no freedom or free will.
- Once you become a Christian, being saved by God's gift of grace, it does not matter what you do.

- The New Testament was written long after the events took place and is thus subject to legends being inserted into the text and many mistakes, contradictions, and errors.
- The Bible has been changed or is otherwise not faithful to the original manuscripts.
- The Greek New Testament has over 400,000 scribal errors but only 137,000 words.
- The Bible conflicts with science.
- The Bible promotes slavery.
- The Bible demeans women.
- The Bible is simply out of date and should not be followed.
- The God of the Bible is immoral.

These are just some questions of the types of questions a Christian might face when trying to discuss the Bible, in which they would be obligated to have a ready answer or be willing to go research and find the answer. It is not simply about finding the solution alone, but also how effectively one can deliver that solution. Can he actively listen, reason from the Scriptures, and overturn false reasoning? **Christian apologetics** shows us and others while our Christian faith does not hinge on reason, we are also aware that our Christian faith isn't without rational, reasonable answers either. Our Christian faith is not based on emotions alone, it isn't something we were born into, or simply one out of many religions, and we merely prefer Christianity over the others. **Christian apologetics** seeks to answer the many hundreds of Bible difficulties that exist in the sixty-six books of the Bible. **Bible Difficulties** are **difficulties** that arise because the **Bible** was written in Hebrew, some Aramaic, and Greek over 1,600 years by some forty+ authors, in dozens of different historical settings that require much **Bible** background knowledge. **Christian apologetics** seeks to show that there are no contradictions, errors, or mistakes in the Bible but rather in the originals and an excellent literal translation it is infallible. **Christian apologetics** seeks to remove misconceptions and misunderstandings. **Christian apologetics** aims to provide those with a receptive heart actual evidence for Christianity, the faith, and the inerrant, infallible, authentic, and the accurate Word of God. **Christian apologetics** seeks to demonstrate the deficiencies and flaws of atheism and other religious worldviews that are at odds with the historic Christian faith. **Christian apologetics** offers something far superior in place of every different worldview that has existed or will exist. What do we gain by training ourselves in Christian apologetics? We take on the same boldness that the apostle Paul possessed. We have a built-up hope that dwells in us, and we never have to live out our Christian lives being defensive, contentious, combative, or even hostile because we are always prepared to make a defense to anyone who asks you for a reason. – 1 Peter 3:15.

Some Christians claim that all we need is faith. We do not need to learn apologetics, they say. In fact, they argue that our quest for reasons and logical answers to such things is contrary to faith and even evidences a lack of faith. This wrong mindset is self-defeating within itself because the person spouting such has not even taken the time to have a correct understanding of "faith" (Gr. *pistis*) itself. **Believe, faith, trust in:** (Gr. *pisteuo*) If *pisteuo* is followed by the Greek preposition *eis*, ("into, in, among," accusative case), it is normally rendered "trusting in" or "trust in." (John 3:16, 36; 12:36; 14:1) The grammatical construction of the Greek verb *pisteuo* "believe" followed by the Greek preposition *eis* "into" in the accusative gives us the sense of having faith into Jesus, putting faith in, trusting in Jesus. – Matt. 21:25, 32; 27:42; John 1:7, 12; 2:23–24; 3:15-16, 36; 6:47; 11:25; 12:36; 14:1; 20:31; Acts 16:31; Rom. 4:3.

*A Grammar of New Testament Greek* series, by James Moulton, says, "The importance of the difference between mere belief ... and personal trust."[2] Both these senses can be conveyed using the Greek word *pisteuo*. The context helps us to identify the different definitions of the meaning of *pisteuo*. Then again, we also have other grammatical constructions that convey what the Bible author meant by his use of the word. When *pisteuo* is simply followed by a noun in the dative case, it is merely rendered as "believe," such as the chief priest and elders' response to Jesus at Matthew 21:25, "If we say, 'From heaven,' he will say to us, 'Why then did you not **believe him**?'" However, in Romans 4:3, we have *pisteuo* follow by a

---

[2] James Moulton, A Grammar of New Testament Greek, Vol. 1: Prolegomena (London, England: T & T Clark International, 2006), 68.

noun in the dative in the Updated American Standard Version, yet it is rendered "For what does the Scripture say? "Abraham **put faith in** God, and it was credited to him as righteousness." (The ASV, RSV, ESV, NASB, and others have "Abraham **believed** God")

If *pisteuo* is followed by the Greek preposition *epi*, "on," it can be rendered "believe in" or believe on." At Matthew 27:42, it reads, "we will **believe in** him [i.e., Jesus]." In Acts 16:31, it reads "And they said, **Believe on the Lord** Jesus Christ, and thou shalt be saved ..." (KJV, UASV similarly) What is the difference between "**believing in** Jesus" and "**believing on** Jesus"? **Believing in** Jesus is merely acknowledging that he exists while **believing on** Jesus is to accept absolutely, have no doubt or uncertainty, trust in, put faith in or trust in, and exercise faith in the Lord Jesus Christ. Faith is **not** so much something Christians have, but rather something Christians carry out.

Therefore, *pisteuo* and *pistis* contain a number of senses, all of them encompassing a deliberate, purposeful, engaged trust into Jesus Christ. Our confidence in Jesus Christ is because we have reasons to do so, and actual evidence supports and justifies our faith. It is not an empty belief. In other words, Jesus is not a true historical person, the divine Son of God, because we believe this to be so anymore than it is untrue because an atheist believes it. We start our initial investigation based on some essential insights because trusted persons have told us it is so, and we feel that they understand God's Word. Then, we follow this up by evaluating what we have come to accept as truth. After that, we assess the claims by any opposition against the evidence that we have. It is then that we can exercise faith that is grounded in weighty evidence. We can use apologetics and evangelism to walk those at odds with our Christian faith through the same process. The Bible does not hold back from calling those who accept something without mediating or pondering fools. When we hear the common expression, "you just have to have faith" or "you just have to believe," we will now know that he has not even taken the time to research the term "faith" and has no idea what "faith" is.

**Acts 17:2-4** Updated American Standard Version (UASV)

[2] And according to Paul's custom, he went to them, and for three Sabbaths **reasoned** with them from the Scriptures, [3] **explaining** and **proving** that it was necessary that the Christ had to suffer and rise again from the dead, and saying, "This Jesus whom I am **proclaiming** to you is the Christ." [4] And some of them were **persuaded** and joined Paul and Silas, as did a great many of the devout Greeks and not a few of the leading women.

**Acts 17:10-11** Updated American Standard Version (UASV)

[10] The brothers immediately sent Paul and Silas away by night to Berea, and when they arrived, they went into the synagogue of the Jews. [11] Now these were more noble-minded than those in Thessalonica, who **received the word with all eagerness,**[3] **examining the Scriptures daily to see whether these things were so.**

**Acts 22:1** Updated American Standard Version (UASV)

22 "Brothers and fathers, hear the **defense** that I now make to you."

**Philippians 1:7** Updated American Standard Version (UASV)

[7] It is right for me to feel thus about you all, because I hold you in my heart, for you are all partakers with me of grace, both in my imprisonment and in the **defense** and **confirmation** of the Gospel.

**Philippians 1:16** Updated American Standard Version (UASV)

[16] The latter do it out of love, knowing that I am put here for **the defense of** the Gospel.

**1 Peter 3:15** Updated American Standard Version (UASV)

[15] but sanctify Christ as Lord in your hearts, always being prepared to make a defense[4] to anyone who asks you for a reason for the hope that is in you; yet do it with gentleness and respect;

---

[3] Or with all *readiness of mind*. The Greek word *prothumias* means that one is eager, ready, mentally prepared to engage in some activity.

[4] **Apologetics:** (ἀπολογία apologia) The term literally means "to defend" and is used in the biblical sense to refer to ones who defend the Christian faith, the Bible, and God in speech or written form. The Christian apologist attempts to prove that the Christian faith, the Bible, and God are reasonable, logical, necessary, and right. – Ac 25:16; 2 Cor. 7:11; Phil. 1:7, 16; 2 Tim. 4:16; 1 Pet. 3:15.

**Jude 3** Updated American Standard Version (UASV)

³ Beloved, while I was making every effort to write you about our common salvation, I found it necessary to write to you appealing that you **contend earnestly for the faith** that was once for all delivered to the holy ones.

The objective of Christian apologetics is to persuade to save lives, not to win arguments. We might win a given argument, but our tone and demeanor in doing so may very well push a person away from the faith. All Christians are to proclaim the Word of God, teach, and make disciples, and Christian apologetics is one way in which we do so. God could very easily and quickly expose Himself to every human as He did with the apostle Paul, but He chose to use us, imperfect humans, to make Him known to the world. This is a privilege, not a burden. We are to do this with gentleness and respect (1 Pet. 3:15), seasoning our words with salt so that you may know how you ought to answer each person. (Col. 4:6) We need to remember, it is the Holy Spirit that saves people. We are fortunate enough to play a role in the process. As we inform, the Holy Spirit is acting upon the hearts of those receptive to Bible truth. Christian apologetics can be carried out by evangelizing the community house to house, in the public square, when waiting at the doctor's office, traveling on public transportation, phone, and social media. Most are begun by starting spontaneous conversations, so Christians need to always be prepared to make a defense to anyone who asks them for a reason.

• *Basic Evangelism* is planting seeds of truth and watering any seeds that have been planted. [In the basic sense of this word (euaggelistes), this would involve all Christians.] In some cases, it may be that one Christian planted the seed, which was initially rejected, so he was left in a good way because the planter did not try to force the truth down his throat. However, later he faces something in life that moves him to reconsider those seeds and another Christian waters what had already been planted by the first Christian. This evangelism can be carried out in all available methods: informal, house-to-house, street, phone, internet, and the like. The amount of time invested in the evangelism work is up to each Christian to decide for themselves.

• *Making Disciples* is having any role in the process of getting an unbeliever from his unbelief state to the point of accepting Christ as his Savior. Once the unbeliever has become a believer, he is still developed by the one who brought him into the faith until he has become spiritually mature and strong. Any Christian could potentially carry this one person through all of the developmental stages. On the other hand, it may be that several have some parts. It is like a person specializing in a certain aspect of a job, but all are aware of the other aspects if they are called on to carry out that phase. Again, each Christian must decide for themselves what role they are to have and how much of a role, but should be prepared to fill any role if needed.

• *Part-Time or Full-Time Evangelist* sees this as their calling and chooses to be very involved as an evangelist in their local church and community. They may work part-time to supplement their work as an evangelist. They may be married with children, but they realize their gift is in the field of evangelism. If it were the wife, the husband would work toward supporting her work as an evangelist and vice-versa. If it were a single person, they would supplement their work by being employed part-time, but also the church would also help. This person is well trained in every aspect of bringing one to Christ.

• *Congregation Evangelists* should be very involved in evangelizing their communities and helping the church members play their role at the basic levels of evangelism. There is nothing to say that one church could not have many who take on part-time or full-time evangelism within the congregation, which would and should be cultivated.[5]

---

[5] https://christianpublishinghouse.co/apologetics/

# APPENDIX 8 Introduction to Christian Evangelism

## The Meaning and Importance of Christian Evangelism

Christian evangelism is the proclamation of the good news about Jesus Christ with the purpose of calling people to repentance, faith, baptism, and a lifelong path of discipleship. It is not merely religious conversation or personal testimony, though those may be included. Evangelism is a deliberate communication of a specific message grounded in Scripture: that Jehovah, the Creator of heaven and earth, has acted decisively in history through His Son Jesus Christ to rescue fallen humans from sin and death and to bring them into His Kingdom.

Evangelism is central to the life and mission of the church. It is not an optional ministry for a select few specialists, but a responsibility that belongs to all true followers of Christ. Jesus' final instructions before His ascension make this unmistakably clear:

"All authority in heaven and on earth has been given to Me. Go therefore and make disciples of all nations, baptizing them in the name of the Father and of the Son and of the Holy Spirit, teaching them to observe all that I have commanded you." (Matthew 28:18–20)

In this commission, Jesus does not tell the apostles merely to gather decisions or professions. He orders them to make disciples, to baptize, and to teach ongoing obedience. Evangelism therefore cannot be restricted to a momentary appeal; it is the entry point into a lifelong journey of following Christ.

# The Biblical Foundation of Evangelism

### Jehovah's Saving Purpose In Scripture

From Genesis to Revelation, Scripture reveals Jehovah as a God who speaks, calls, and gathers a people for Himself. After the entrance of sin and death into the world (Genesis 3; Romans 5:12), Jehovah's response is not to abandon His creation but to initiate a redemptive plan. He calls Abraham, promising that "in you all the families of the earth shall be blessed" (Genesis 12:3). This is the root of the universal scope of evangelism. The blessing promised to Abraham reaches "all the families of the earth" as the gospel goes to all nations.

The Mosaic covenant, given centuries later, functions as a temporary tutor, exposing sin and clarifying Jehovah's holiness, yet never providing the ultimate solution to the human problem. As the apostle Paul explains, "the law was our guardian until Christ came" (Galatians 3:24). The law reveals the seriousness of sin and the impossibility of earning righteousness by human effort. This prepares the way for the New Covenant in Christ, in which forgiveness and new life are granted through His sacrificial death and resurrection.

Evangelism, therefore, is not a human invention or a church program added later. It is the direct outworking of Jehovah's long-promised plan of salvation, centered in the New Covenant inaugurated by Jesus' blood (Luke 22:20). To proclaim the gospel is to stand in continuity with the Abrahamic promise, to declare the fulfillment of the Law and the Prophets in Christ, and to call all peoples to the obedience of faith.

## Jesus Christ As the Model Evangelist

Jesus Himself is the supreme example of evangelism carried out in truth and love. He preached the Kingdom of God, exposed sin without compromise, showed compassion to the broken, and called people to turn and follow Him.

He announced, "The time is fulfilled, and the kingdom of God is at hand; repent and believe in the gospel" (Mark 1:15). His message was not vague spirituality or moral uplift. It was a concrete announcement that Jehovah's promised reign was breaking into history through His own ministry, and that the appropriate response was repentance and faith.

Jesus spoke differently in different situations while never changing His message. To the rich young ruler, He exposed the man's attachment to wealth. To Nicodemus, He explained the necessity of being born again from above (John 3). To the Samaritan woman, He confronted her sin compassionately and revealed Himself as the Messiah (John 4). Evangelism today must reflect this balance: the unchanging core message presented wisely and sensitively to real people in real situations.

## The Apostolic Pattern

After Jesus' resurrection and ascension, the apostles proclaimed the gospel with clarity, urgency, and confidence in the power of the Word of God. On the day of Pentecost, Peter's sermon centers on Jesus' death, resurrection, and exaltation, and calls the listeners to repent and be baptized in His name for the forgiveness of sins (Acts 2:22–38). Evangelism here includes a clear explanation of who Jesus is, what He has done, the guilt of those who rejected Him, and the gracious invitation to respond.

Throughout Acts, evangelism is consistently Word-centered, Christ-centered, and Kingdom-focused. The message confronts idolatry among Jews and Gentiles, exposes the reality of coming judgment, and announces the resurrected Christ as Lord and Judge (Acts 17:30–31). The response required is repentance and faith, followed by baptism and incorporation into the community of believers.

# The Message of Evangelism: The Biblical Gospel

## The Nature of God

Evangelism begins with Jehovah. He is the Creator, holy, righteous, and loving. He is not a remote force or an impersonal energy, but the living God who speaks and acts in history. Evangelism must communicate that He alone has the right to define truth, goodness, and human purpose. Without this foundation, the gospel is reduced to a therapeutic message that merely meets felt needs instead of addressing the reality of sin and accountability before a holy God.

## The Human Condition

According to Scripture, humans are created in the image of God, dignified and accountable. Yet all have sinned (Romans 3:23), and death spread to all humans because all sinned (Romans 5:12). Humanity's problem is not that people are good but misinformed; the problem is that people freely choose sin, are enslaved by it, and face death and judgment as a result.

"Flesh" in the New Testament describes humans in their mortal weakness, subject to corruption and death. It does not teach that humans possess an evil substance, but that our present condition is frail, inclined to sin, and unable to attain righteousness apart from God's grace. Evangelism must be honest about guilt and the seriousness of sin. Without law there is no knowledge of sin; without sin, the cross becomes unnecessary.

The Bible does not teach an inherently immortal soul that survives consciously after death by its own nature. Humans are living souls; when they die, they return to gravedom (Sheol/Hades). The hope held out is not disembodied survival but resurrection. This truth sharpens the urgency of evangelism. Without Christ, humans face eventual resurrection to judgment and eternal destruction (Gehenna), not eternal life apart from Jehovah.

## The Person and Work of Christ

The heart of evangelism is the historical person and work of Jesus Christ. He is the eternal Son of God who took on true humanity, lived a sinless life, and willingly gave Himself as a ransom for many (Mark 10:45). He bore our sins in His body on the tree (1 Peter 2:24), shedding His blood as the once-for-all sacrifice that satisfies the demands of divine justice and opens the way for forgiveness.

His resurrection in 33 C.E. is the decisive vindication of His identity and mission. Evangelism must proclaim that Jesus is alive, that He has triumphed over sin and death, and that He will return to rule and judge. This is not a myth or symbol but a concrete historical event and a future certainty. Premillennial hope affirms that Christ will return before His thousand-year reign, during which He will rule the nations and bring Jehovah's purposes to completion.

## The Call to Repentance, Faith, and Baptism

The proper response to the gospel consists of repentance, faith, and baptism, leading into a life of obedient discipleship.

Repentance is a decisive turning away from sin and self-rule toward God. It is not mere sorrow or regret, but a change of mind and heart toward sin and toward Christ. Faith is personal reliance on Jesus as Lord and Savior, trusting His sacrifice and resurrection alone for forgiveness and life, not our works or religious merits.

Baptism by immersion is the biblically mandated act that publicly identifies a believer with Christ's death, burial, and resurrection (Romans 6:3–4). It is not performed on infants who cannot repent or believe. It does not function as a magical ritual that works automatically, but as an obedient response commanded by Christ and practiced by the apostles. The New Testament pattern unites faith, repentance, and baptism closely, with baptism marking the visible entrance into the community of believers.

Salvation in Scripture is not treated as a static label attached to a person once and for all upon a momentary decision. It is a path of ongoing faith and obedience, a journey of being saved, continuing in the faith, and enduring to the end (Hebrews 3:14; Colossians 1:23). Evangelism must therefore avoid promising a false security divorced from a life of repentance and obedience.

## The Hope of The Kingdom

Evangelism announces not only forgiveness of sins but also the positive hope of the Kingdom of God. Those who belong to Christ receive the gift of eternal life, not as something naturally possessed, but as a gracious gift from God. A select number of holy ones will rule with Christ in heaven, while the rest of the righteous will inherit eternal life on a restored earth, free from sin, suffering, and death.

This hope is grounded in Christ's resurrection and promised return. Evangelism must therefore present the Christian hope as resurrection and renewal, not as escape into an immaterial realm. The future reign of Christ in His millennial Kingdom gives weight and urgency to present proclamation.

# The Motives for Evangelism

## Obedience To Christ's Command

The most basic motive for evangelism is obedience. The risen Christ commands His followers to make disciples of all nations. To call Him Lord while ignoring His clear instructions is inconsistent. Love for Christ is expressed in keeping His commandments (John 14:15). Evangelism is one of those commandments.

## Love For God's Glory

Evangelism arises from concern that Jehovah be honored as God. Idolatry robs Him of the honor that belongs to Him alone. When believers proclaim the gospel and people turn from idols to serve the living and true God, Jehovah's name is magnified. Evangelism is therefore not man-centered flattery; it is God-centered proclamation that calls people to give to Him the glory due His name.

## Love For Neighbor

If the gospel is true, then those without Christ face resurrection to judgment and eternal destruction rather than life. Love refuses to remain silent while others rush toward such an outcome. The second greatest commandment, to love one's neighbor as oneself, compels believers to speak. Genuine love seeks the highest good of others, which includes their reconciliation to God through Christ.

## Confidence In The Power of the Word

Evangelism is sustained by confidence that Jehovah uses His Word to accomplish His saving purposes. The Holy Spirit works through the inspired Scriptures, not through private mystical experiences or modern extra-biblical revelations. The gospel is "the power of God for salvation to everyone who believes" (Romans 1:16). Evangelism therefore relies on Scripture proclaimed and explained, trusting that God will use His Word to convict, awaken, and draw people to Himself.

# The Scope and Contexts of Evangelism

## Personal Evangelism

Every believer has spheres of influence: family, friends, neighbors, co-workers, classmates. Personal evangelism involves intentional conversation and witness within these relationships. It includes living with integrity and kindness so that one's life does not contradict the message, but it never stops at silent example. So-called "lifestyle evangelism" that never speaks the gospel is not biblical evangelism. Faith comes by hearing the Word of Christ (Romans 10:17), not by merely observing the moral life of a Christian.

Personal evangelism grows from regular prayer for opportunities, a readiness to speak, and a willingness to be patient as people wrestle with truth. It does not pressure or manipulate, but it refuses to hide Christ out of fear of rejection.

## Congregational Evangelism

Local congregations act together in evangelism by teaching sound doctrine, equipping believers to share their faith, and organizing activities that extend the gospel into their communities. Public preaching, Bible studies, home groups, literature distribution, and structured outreach efforts all belong here.

Sound congregational evangelism is anchored in expository preaching, careful teaching, and meaningful membership. Those who respond to the gospel should be gathered into a local body where they receive instruction, encouragement, discipline, and opportunities to serve. Evangelism cut off from the local congregation produces isolated individuals rather than disciples who grow in community.

Congregational leadership must follow biblical patterns. Men qualified according to Scripture lead as elders and deacons; women serve in many significant ways but are not appointed as pastors or deacons. This created order does not hinder evangelism; it protects doctrinal fidelity and ensures that the message proclaimed is consistent with Scripture.

## Global Evangelism and Mission

The Great Commission extends to "all nations." Evangelism includes cross-cultural mission, translation of Scripture, training of teachers, and the planting of congregations among peoples who have little or no access to the gospel.

Mission work must avoid importing cultural preferences as if they were biblical mandates. The universal elements are the message of Christ, the call to repentance and faith, immersion in baptism, and the formation of congregations with qualified male leadership and mutual accountability among the holy ones. Cultural forms of music, dress, and architecture may vary, but the gospel itself does not.

## Methods Of Evangelism: Principles And Dangers

### Faithfulness to the Message

The first requirement in evangelistic method is fidelity to the biblical gospel. No method can compensate for a distorted message. The temptation to soften or adjust the message to make it more appealing must be resisted. Removing repentance, downplaying sin, or obscuring the exclusivity of

Christ may produce outward responses, but it does not produce genuine disciples.

Evangelism must plainly confess that Jesus is the only way to the Father (John 14:6), that there is salvation in no one else (Acts 4:12), and that trusting any mixture of Christ plus works or rituals undermines the grace of God.

## Clarity And Simplicity

The gospel message, while profound, can be expressed in clear terms. Jehovah, the holy Creator, made humans for Himself. All have sinned and face death and judgment. Jesus Christ, God's Son, lived without sin, died on the cross for our sins, and rose from the dead. He calls all people to turn from sin, to believe in Him, and to confess Him as Lord. Those who respond in repentance and faith, and who are baptized and continue in obedience, receive forgiveness and the gift of eternal life.

This core message should not be buried under complex philosophical arguments. There is a proper place for apologetics that defend the faith and remove misunderstandings, especially in skeptical contexts. Yet these defenses must serve the proclamation of the gospel, not replace it.

## Integrity and Honesty

Evangelism must be carried out with complete honesty. High-pressure tactics, emotional manipulation, and deceptive promises contradict the character of the God whose message we carry. Believers must not promise material prosperity, health, or earthly success as automatic results of conversion. Instead, they must speak truthfully: following Christ may bring hardship and opposition in this present world, but it leads to eternal life and future glory.

## Avoiding Confusion with Social Activism

Social engagement, mercy ministries, and care for the needy are important expressions of love and obedience. Yet they are not identical with evangelism. Feeding the hungry, advocating justice, or improving education can create favorable conditions for evangelism and may adorn the gospel, but unless the message of Christ's death and resurrection and the call to repentance and faith are clearly communicated, evangelism has not occurred.

The "social gospel," which reduces Christianity to moral improvement and social reform, empties the cross of its meaning. True evangelism may motivate social concern, but it cannot be replaced by it.

## Avoiding Ritualism and Sacramentalism

Another danger is to replace evangelism with ritual participation. Some traditions treat baptism or communion as automatically conveying grace regardless of personal repentance and faith. Biblical evangelism refuses to treat any ritual, however sacred, as a substitute for proclamation and heart response.

Baptism is essential as an obedient response to the gospel, but only as the outward expression of genuine faith and repentance. Without personal trust in Christ, immersion becomes a mere washing of the body rather than the appeal of a good conscience toward God (1 Peter 3:21).

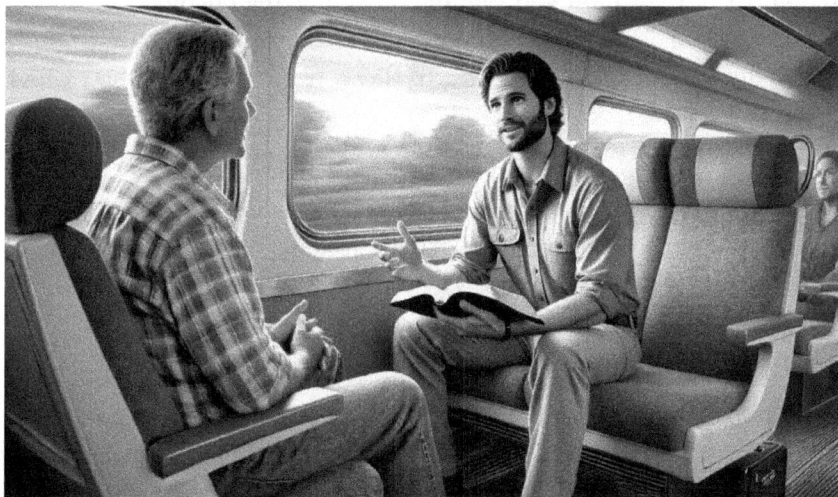

# Evangelism, the Holy Spirit, And the Word

The Holy Spirit is fully God and is active in the work of evangelism. However, His work is not to grant new, extra-biblical revelations or to produce mystical experiences that bypass Scripture. His role is to empower the proclamation of the Word He inspired, to convict the world concerning sin, righteousness, and judgment, and to open hearts to respond.

The Spirit does not indwell believers in a way that gives them ongoing private revelations or inner voices competing with Scripture. Instead, believers are led by the Spirit as they submit to the inspired Word, renew their minds, and obey the commands of Christ. Evangelism, therefore, is carried out not by chasing ecstatic experiences, but by faithful reliance on Scripture and prayer, trusting that the Spirit uses the Word to accomplish Jehovah's purposes.

# Evangelism and the Path of Discipleship

Evangelism and discipleship are distinct but inseparable. Evangelism is the initial proclamation and call; discipleship is the ongoing instruction, formation, and obedience that follow. The Great Commission unites both: make disciples, baptize, and teach them to observe all that Christ commanded.

Because salvation is a journey rather than a one-time label, evangelism must be oriented toward the long path of following Christ. Those who respond to the gospel must be taught to read Scripture, to pray, to participate faithfully in the life of a local congregation, to put to death sinful practices, and to grow in Christlike character.

Evangelism that merely collects names or tallies "decisions" but fails to connect people with ongoing discipleship undermines the very goal Christ gave. Biblical evangelism expects and calls for perseverance, recognizing that only those who continue in the faith grounded and steadfast will be presented holy and blameless before Him.

# Practical Beginnings in Evangelism for Believers

A believer who desires to begin sharing the gospel often faces fear, uncertainty, or a sense of inadequacy. Scripture does not demand that every believer become a public preacher, but it does call each one to be a witness, ready to give a reason for the hope that is in them (1 Peter 3:15).

Growth in evangelism begins with deeper grounding in Scripture. The more a believer understands the storyline of the Bible, the nature of God, the seriousness of sin, the work of Christ, and the hope of the Kingdom, the more naturally the gospel will flow into conversation.

Prayer is central. Believers can pray for specific individuals, for boldness, for clarity, and for opportunities to speak. They can ask Jehovah to open doors for the Word and to soften hearts. This is not a mystical shortcut but a humble acknowledgement that only God can grant spiritual life.

Developing simple ways to express the gospel is helpful. A believer might learn to explain in a few minutes who God is, what sin is, who Jesus is, what He did, and how one must respond. Then, as conversations allow, this simple outline can be expanded and clarified.

Believers should also cultivate lives that commend the gospel. Integrity, kindness, patience, purity, and humility do not replace verbal proclamation, but they give credibility to it. When those around them see consistency between message and life, they are more inclined to listen.

# Living a Life Shaped by Evangelism

Christian evangelism is not an occasional project; it is a way of life shaped by the reality of who God is, what He has done in Christ, and where history is moving under His sovereign rule. The certainty of Christ's return and His millennial reign fills the present with eternal significance. Every conversation, every relationship, and every decision can be viewed through the lens of Jehovah's saving purpose in the gospel.

A life shaped by evangelism is marked by reverence for Scripture, confidence in the power of the Word, love for God's glory, compassion for the lost, and steady obedience to Christ's command to make disciples. It refuses to reduce the gospel to human opinion, social activism, religious ritual, or emotional experience. Instead, it proclaims Jesus Christ crucified, risen, and coming again, and calls all people everywhere to repent, believe, be baptized, and walk the lifelong path of discipleship that leads to eternal life.

# APPENDIX 9 Bible Difficulties Explained

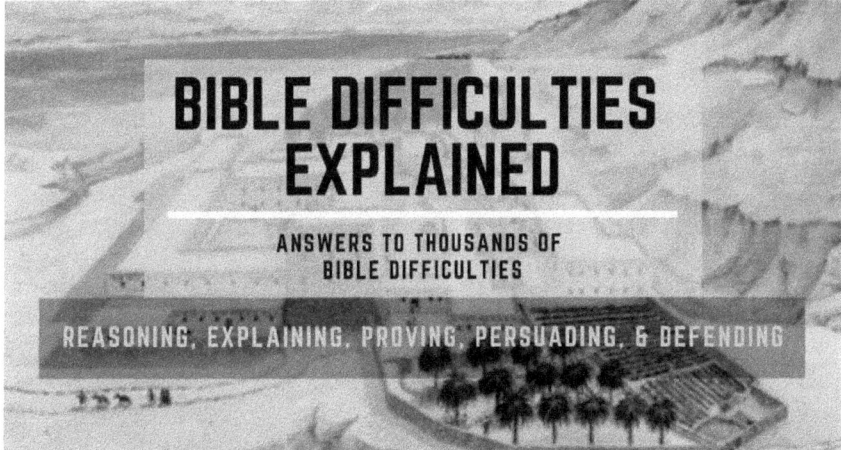

## Introduction to Bible Difficulties

In short, there are no contradictions, errors, or mistakes in the Bible, but there are Bible difficulties. Basically, **Bible Difficulties** are **difficulties** that arise because the **Bible** was written in Hebrew, some Aramaic, and Greek over 1,600 years by some forty+ authors, in dozens of different historical settings that require much **Bible** background knowledge. The above is not enough to satisfy a doubting or an unbeliever; you need a basic understanding of what they are, how to explain them, how to approach them, procedures in dealing with them, and how you should view them, as well as some examples.

IT SEEMS THAT the charge that the Bible contradicts itself has been made more and more in the last 30 years. Generally, those making such claims merely repeat what they have heard because most have not even read the Bible, let alone done an in-depth study of it. I do not wish, however, to set aside all concerns as though they have no merit. There are many who raise legitimate questions that seem, on the surface anyway, to be about well-founded contradiction. Sadly, these issues have caused many to lose their faith in God's Word, the Bible. The purpose of this article is to help its readers to be able to defend the Bible against Bible critics (1 Pet. 3:15), to contend for the faith (Jude 1:3) and help those who have begun to doubt. – Jude 1:22-23.

## Understanding The Nature of Bible Difficulties

Bible difficulties arise when a passage initially appears contradictory, unclear, or in tension with another section of Scripture. These challenges do not undermine the inspiration or inerrancy of the biblical text. Instead, they invite deeper examination using sound interpretive principles. Because all Scripture is breathed by God and conveyed through human authors who wrote under the direction of the Holy Spirit (2 Peter 1:21), the Scriptures reflect divine coherence. Apparent conflicts often stem from translation issues, textual variants, historical misunderstandings, or incorrect assumptions brought to the text. A disciplined approach grounded in the Historical-Grammatical method allows each difficulty to be evaluated in its immediate context, in its historical setting, and in harmony with the total canonical witness.

Bible difficulties should never be interpreted as evidence of flaws within the divine message. Rather, they highlight the importance of careful interpretation. The biblical writers lived in real cultures, used ordinary language conventions, and communicated with purpose. Understanding idioms, figures of speech, chronology, geography, and covenantal history eliminates many perceived tensions. When interpreted accurately, the Scriptures demonstrate a remarkable unity that testifies to their divine origin and preservation. The Hebrew Old Testament and the Greek New Testament critical texts reflect this precision, displaying an accuracy of approximately 99.99% when compared to the original writings.

## The Historical-Grammatical Method as the Foundation

The most reliable approach to understanding Bible difficulties is the Historical-Grammatical method. This method seeks authorial intent within divine inspiration, respecting grammar, syntax, vocabulary, and historical context. Unlike the Historical-Critical method, which imposes modern skepticism and philosophical presuppositions upon the text, the Historical-Grammatical approach reads Scripture objectively according to how language operates.

Historical context clarifies customs, geography, chronology, and political circumstances. For example, understanding Judean kingship patterns, Roman governance, or ancient Near Eastern legal structures illuminates passages that otherwise appear obscure. Grammatical analysis ensures that verb tenses, participles, prepositions, and narrative sequencing are interpreted accurately. Covenant context is equally essential, as Scripture unfolds progressively through the Abrahamic promise (2091 B.C.E.), the temporary role of the Mosaic Law (Exodus 1446 B.C.E.), and the fulfillment of the New Covenant in Christ (33 C.E.). Difficulties that seem doctrinal or theological are frequently clarified when placed back into their covenantal setting.

This method avoids eisegesis and preserves the reliability of Scripture by approaching the text with humility, recognizing that misunderstandings arise not from the Word but from human limitation. It also respects distinctions such as narrative versus law, poetry versus prophecy, and literal statements versus figures of speech. Through this lens, perceived contradictions often vanish.

## Textual Accuracy and Preservation

A significant portion of Bible difficulties relates to textual variants. Because Scripture was copied manually for centuries, scribal variations naturally arose. However, these variants are overwhelmingly minor—differences in spelling, word order, or similar non-substantive features. They do not affect doctrine or historical claims. Through textual criticism, conservative scholars have evaluated thousands of Hebrew and Greek manuscripts, confirming the remarkable accuracy of the preserved text.

The Hebrew Masoretic Text, supported by earlier textual witnesses such as the Dead Sea Scrolls, reflects a stable tradition. The Greek New Testament, reconstructed from over 5,800 manuscripts, provides a highly reliable textual base. While scribal variants exist, the original readings can be identified with an extremely high degree of certainty. The text Christians possess today faithfully conveys the message originally inspired by Jehovah.

Understanding these realities helps explain why some Bible difficulties appear in footnotes or translation differences. A textual variant may introduce a question, but when analyzed accurately, the integrity of Scripture remains intact. The variants themselves become evidence of careful preservation and scholarly scrutiny rather than evidence of corruption.

## Literal Chronology and Historical Coherence

Chronology plays a vital role in resolving Bible difficulties. When biblical events are dated according to Scripture's internal framework rather than modern critical reconstructions, the narrative reveals a consistent historical line. Anchor dates include Noah's Flood (2348 B.C.E.), Abraham's covenant (2091 B.C.E.), Jacob entering Egypt (1876 B.C.E.), the Exodus (1446 B.C.E.), the Conquest of Canaan (1406 B.C.E.), the Temple construction by Solomon (966 B.C.E.), Jesus' birth (c. 2 B.C.E.), His ministry beginning in 29 C.E., His execution on Nisan 14, 33 C.E., and the writing of the New Testament between 41–98 C.E.

Many Bible difficulties arise when interpreters impose alternate chronologies derived from skeptical academic theories. Because such reconstructions ignore the internal biblical markers, they create artificial tensions. When the internal biblical chronology is honored, synchronisms between Kings and Chronicles align, the prophetic books fit their intended historical settings, and the Gospels maintain their coherence as historical biographies of Jesus.

Chronology is especially valuable in reconciling narratives that appear parallel but may refer to different events or stages of an event. Understanding the timing allows readers to recognize progressive revelation, sequential orders, and the unique emphases of individual authors.

## The Role of Covenant Progression

Covenantal development is essential for interpreting Scripture coherently. The Abrahamic covenant established the foundation of God's redemptive plan, promising a nation, a land, and blessings to all families of the earth. The Mosaic covenant was temporary, serving as a guardian until Christ. The New Covenant, inaugurated through Jesus' sacrificial death, fulfilled the earlier covenants without invalidating their promises. This progression clarifies many difficulties by explaining why certain laws, rituals, or practices held authority for ancient Israel but are no longer binding.

Understanding the role of the Mosaic Law eliminates supposed contradictions related to ceremonial requirements, genealogical inheritance, judicial regulations, or priestly functions. Jesus fulfilled the Law, and the New Covenant reveals the permanence of His sacrificial atonement. Bible difficulties involving moral commands, Sabbath regulations, or food restrictions are resolved when each passage is understood in its covenantal placement.

Covenant context also clarifies passages that refer to future restoration, the Messiah's rule, and Jehovah's promises to Abraham's descendants. Because promise and fulfillment operate within historical frameworks, many difficulties dissolve when covenant boundaries are recognized.

## Genre And Literary Features

A crucial but often overlooked element in resolving Bible difficulties is recognizing literary genre. Scripture includes narrative, law, poetry, wisdom, prophecy, letters, and apocalyptic literature. Each genre uses distinctive features that affect interpretation. Figures of speech, poetic parallelism, hyperbole, rhetorical questions, and symbolic vision language must be understood according to genre rather than interpreted woodenly.

For example, Hebrew poetry often uses parallelism to reinforce an idea rather than introduce separate or contradictory statements. Similarly, apocalyptic visions—such as those found in Daniel or Revelation—use symbols to convey literal truths but in visionary form. Correctly identifying these features prevents the reader from forcing the text into unintended meanings. Bible difficulties related to exaggerated language, anthropomorphism, or symbolic imagery are resolved by applying the principles of genre analysis.

Narrative perspective is also relevant. When two accounts describe the same event from different angles or focus on different details, the variation does not indicate contradiction. Instead, it demonstrates complementary testimony, similar to multiple witnesses recounting the same real event. The Gospels, for example, often present different emphases tailored to their intended audiences and purposes.

## Contextual Cohesion Across Scripture

Because all Scripture originates from one divine Author working through chosen human writers, the Bible possesses unity across sixty-six books. Difficulties that appear to conflict with this unity typically arise when verses are removed from context. Sound interpretation requires examining the immediate context, the broader chapter or section, the book as a whole, and ultimately the canonical context.

The principle that Scripture interprets Scripture ensures clarity. A passage that is ambiguous is illuminated by clearer related texts. A statement that appears contradictory is reconciled by examining all relevant passages. Doctrines such as the nature of man, the meaning of death, resurrection hope, the identity of Jesus, the role of faith and obedience, and the purpose of baptism are clarified when the full biblical witness is considered.

Context also prevents misapplication. Commands given to Israel under the Mosaic covenant cannot be imposed directly upon Christians under the New Covenant. Prophetic warnings directed at specific nations in antiquity cannot be universalized without considering their original setting. Many difficulties disappear when the interpreter respects the flow and unity of Scripture.

## Harmonization as a Scholarly Discipline

Harmonization is not forced manipulation of the text; it is a scholarly acknowledgment that Scripture is coherent and that different accounts can be reconciled when contextual factors are understood. This method is especially important in the study of the Gospels and historical books such as Samuel, Kings, and Chronicles. Differences in wording, sequencing, or emphasis reflect diverse perspectives rather than contradictions.

Harmonization also requires recognizing legitimate textual variants while maintaining confidence in the preserved text. When manuscripts differ, scholars evaluate internal and external evidence to determine the most original reading. This process reinforces the credibility of the Scriptures, ensuring accurate interpretation and eliminating manufactured difficulties.

Chronological harmonization, geographical clarification, and cultural understanding are additional tools that provide clarity. Bible difficulties often dissolve when these factors are applied correctly.

## Doctrinal Clarity and Difficult Passages

Some difficulties appear theological rather than textual. These often involve topics such as the nature of Christ, human mortality, resurrection, judgment, salvation, baptism, the Holy Spirit, the Kingdom, or the role of God's sovereignty and human responsibility. Such difficulties require careful comparison of passages, attention to definitions, and recognition that Scripture presents truth progressively.

Doctrinal clarity emerges when interpretations align with the entire biblical witness. For example:

- Humanity does not possess an immortal soul; individuals are souls who die, awaiting resurrection.
- Eternal life is a gift given by God through Christ.
- Gehenna represents final destruction, not eternal conscious torment.
- Salvation is a path that requires faith, obedience, repentance, and perseverance.
- Baptism is immersion for committed believers.
- The Holy Spirit guides through the inspired Word rather than through emotional or mystical experiences.
- Christ will return prior to the Millennial reign.
- A limited number will rule with Christ in Heaven while the rest of the righteous inherit eternal life on earth.

When doctrinal passages are interpreted consistently with these biblical teachings, difficulties that appear doctrinally contradictory are resolved.

## Moral And Ethical Difficulties

Some readers struggle with moral commands, judgments, or narratives involving warfare, polygamy, or human imperfection. These concerns must be evaluated within the context of human sinfulness, ancient cultural norms, divine justice, and the progressive unfolding of revelation. Jehovah's judgments are righteous, His patience is immense, and His dealings with humanity always reflect His holiness.

Moral difficulties often arise when modern assumptions or standards are retroactively imposed upon ancient contexts. Understanding historical setting, ancient Near Eastern legal norms, and Israel's unique covenant role clarifies why certain actions were permitted, tolerated, or judged. Scripture records human failures honestly, providing no justification for sin but demonstrating Jehovah's dealings with imperfect humanity.

## The Unifying Testimony of Scripture

Bible difficulties ultimately highlight Scripture's unity rather than undermine it. The consistent message of redemption, covenant faithfulness, divine justice, and Kingdom hope connects every portion of the Bible. The narrative reveals the devastating effects of sin, humanity's need for a Savior, and the triumph of Christ's sacrificial atonement.

From Genesis to Revelation, Scripture maintains a coherent message. Difficulties invite deeper study, sharpen interpretive skill, and reinforce the believer's confidence in the inspired Word. As each difficulty is examined using sound methods, the Bible's precision becomes even more evident. The Scriptures are an inexhaustible well of truth, preserving Jehovah's revelation with unparalleled accuracy.

## Using This Volume to Address Difficulties

This work is designed to address Bible difficulties comprehensively. Each article approaches a specific question by providing context, linguistic analysis, historical background, covenantal placement, and cross-referencing. The goal is not merely to resolve individual problems but to equip readers with the tools to interpret Scripture accurately.

By applying the Historical-Grammatical method, respecting textual accuracy, and maintaining confidence in the preserved Scriptures, readers will find that Bible difficulties are not obstacles but opportunities to behold the depth and richness of the inspired Word.

# Inerrancy: Can the Bible Be Trusted?

## Foundational Principles of Inspiration and Inerrancy

A correct understanding of inerrancy begins with the recognition that the Scriptures originated under the superintending guidance of the Holy Spirit, Who carried men along so that their writings conveyed the exact meaning intended by God. The writers were not passive secretaries; they used their vocabulary, grammar, and literary skill. Yet, under divine influence, they never selected a word or phrase that misrepresented the intended meaning. This is why the Greek text affirms with precision: "All Scripture is inspired by God" (2 Timothy 3:16 UASV) and "men carried along by the Holy Spirit spoke from God" (2 Peter 1:21 UASV).

Full inerrancy means the original autographs contain no errors—whether in history, theology, ethics, or any affirmations they make. Scripture reports phenomena in human-observational language, such as the "sun rising," which reflects common perception rather than asserting an astronomical model. This is not error but communication grounded in everyday language. Full inerrancy does not require technical precision where such precision serves no purpose within the author's intent. Instead, it requires absolute truthfulness in everything the biblical authors affirm.

By contrast, limited inerrancy claims that Scripture is reliable in matters of faith but may contain historical or geographical mistakes. Such a position contradicts the internal claims of Scripture, the testimony of Jesus regarding Scripture's authority, and the apostolic conviction that all teachings of the biblical authors are grounded in God's truthful revelation.

If the Bible were merely a human product, it would share the limitations of human wisdom and uncertainty. But if inspired by God, the Scriptures reflect His perfect integrity, and the message they deliver is trustworthy. The entire redemptive purpose of God depends upon the reliability of His Word. Without inerrancy, doctrines—salvation, resurrection hope, the reliability of Jehovah's covenants—would stand on unstable ground.

Therefore, before addressing alleged difficulties such as the numerical question between Numbers 25:9 and 1 Corinthians 10:8, we must first establish the framework by which such issues should be evaluated.

## Why Some Passages Appear to Conflict

The Bible contains 31,173 verses written across approximately 1,600 years, by about forty authors, during multiple covenants, cultural settings, and political climates. Shepherds, kings, fishermen, tax collectors, prophets, physicians, and governors were used to produce Jehovah's revelation. Therefore, if one reads casually, differences of emphasis, perspective, idiom, rounding of numbers, and telescoping of events appear as "contradictions" to the untrained eye.

The vast majority of alleged contradictions evaporate under responsible exegesis using the historical-grammatical method. This involves understanding the grammar, syntax, lexical usage, covenantal context, historical setting, and the theological purpose of the author. Scripture must interpret Scripture. The meanings of words must be drawn from the Hebrew and Greek languages used by the inspired authors, not imported from later philosophical ideas.

The critic's argument is often formed as a simplistic syllogism:

- God does not err.

- The Bible claims to be the Word of God.

- The Bible appears to contain errors. Therefore, it is not the Word of God.

This argument collapses if the "appearing" of error is due to misinterpretation, insufficient understanding of textual variants, lack of familiarity with ancient Near Eastern literary conventions, or the critic's failure to read the text according to its grammatical and historical context.

The Scriptures have withstood millennia of examination, persecution, copying, translation, and intense public scrutiny. If they contained genuine contradictions that undermined their message, critics would have exposed them long ago, and the Christian faith would have collapsed. Instead, Scripture continues to stand as the most printed, most translated, most studied, and most resilient book in human history.

## The Nature of Alleged Contradictions: A Case Study On Numbers 25:9 And 1 Corinthians 10:8

Numbers 25:9 states that 24,000 died in the plague associated with Israel's immorality with Moabite women. Paul, writing in 1 Corinthians 10:8, says that 23,000 fell "in one day." The important exegetical detail is Paul's phrase "in one day." Numbers records the complete death toll of the entire event; Paul emphasizes the number who died immediately on that single day. The remaining thousand perished in the aftermath, consistent with the full plague described in Numbers.

Thus, there is no contradiction. A single essential observation resolves the difficulty.

This demonstrates a larger truth: superficial reading produces superficial accusations. Accurate exegesis resolves them.

## Understanding Inspiration, Transmission, and Textual Accuracy

Textual inerrancy applies to the autographs—the original scrolls penned by Moses, David, Isaiah, Luke, Paul, and others. These originals, written under divine inspiration, were free from error. Jehovah did not choose to preserve the autographs themselves, but He ensured the preservation of their content through tens of thousands of manuscripts.

Copyists were not inspired. Therefore, natural copying errors—misspellings, skipped lines, minor variations—entered the manuscript tradition. For 1,400 years of hand-copying, these accumulated. However, textual criticism, especially from the fourteenth century onward, restored the text with remarkable precision. The Hebrew and Greek critical texts available now reflect the originals accurately to 99.99%.

Thus, modern literal translations (such as the UASV) are mirror-accurate renderings of the original content. The existence of transmission variants does not undermine inerrancy; rather, it demonstrates Jehovah's providence in preserving His Word through an abundance of manuscripts, enabling scholars to reconstruct the original readings with extraordinary confidence.

Properly understood, textual criticism protects inerrancy—it does not challenge it.

### Approaching Alleged Problems with a Right Methodology

Paul instructed Timothy:

"Practice these things, be absorbed in them... Pay close attention to yourself and your teaching" (1 Timothy 4:15–16 UASV).

This means Christians must pursue disciplined study. Surface reading is insufficient. Deep engagement with the text strengthens faith and equips believers for apologetics. When confronted with an alleged biblical error, one should respond with honesty and humility. If one does not know the answer immediately, it is appropriate to acknowledge this and commit to study. However, one must not respond with doubt, uncertainty, or concession that errors must exist. Instead, affirm confidence that Scripture has stood against every criticism for centuries and that careful examination will yield an answer.

Paul also wrote:

"The weapons of our warfare are not of the flesh but powerful to God for destroying strongholds" (2 Corinthians 10:4 UASV).

Believers destroy speculations not by emotional argumentation but by rigorous reasoning from Scripture. Every thought must be taken captive to the obedience of Christ. This intellectual discipline is strengthened by continual study.

## The Apologetic Task: Handling Criticism With Gentleness And Precision

Peter commands Christians to "always be prepared to make a defense" (1 Peter 3:15 UASV). The term *apologia* refers to a legal defense— structured, reasoned, evidence-based argumentation. Christians must be able to articulate why Scripture is trustworthy and why accusations of error misunderstand the text.

However, the manner of defense matters. Paul instructs:

"A slave of the Lord... needs to be kind to all, qualified to teach, showing restraint when wronged, with gentleness correcting those who are in opposition" (2 Timothy 2:24–25 UASV).

The purpose of apologetics is not victory in debate but the hope that God may bring opponents to repentance and accurate knowledge. This accurate knowledge, *epignōsis*, refers to full, exact knowledge—deep comprehension of the truth.

Thus, apologetics is both an intellectual and spiritual discipline. It requires the ability to dismantle false arguments and to do so in a manner that reflects the character of Christ.

## Why The Bible Cannot Contain Contradictions

### 1. The Character of God

Scripture reflects the character of Jehovah, Who does not lie or contradict Himself. If He inspired Scripture, it necessarily reflects His truthfulness.

### 2. The Testimony of Jesus

Jesus treated Scripture as authoritative, unbreakable, and historically accurate. He grounded His arguments on individual words of the Old Testament. If Scripture contained errors, Jesus' trust in Scripture would be misplaced—an impossibility.

### 3. The Consistency of the Biblical Narrative

Across 1,600 years, 66 books, multiple cultures, languages, and authors, Scripture maintains perfect doctrinal and historical unity. Such harmony cannot occur naturally across so vast a literary corpus.

### 4. The Precision of Fulfilled Prophecy

Prophecy fulfilled precisely and historically demonstrates divine inspiration. A flawed or inconsistent document would not produce such fulfillment.

## Why Critics Misinterpret Scripture

### 1. Reading Ancient Texts Through Modern Assumptions

Critics often impose modern expectations upon ancient literature. Ancient Near Eastern narrative technique, covenantal presentation, and Hebrew idioms must be understood on their own terms.

### 2. Ignoring Genre

The Bible contains law, narrative, prophecy, wisdom literature, and epistles. Each must be read according to its genre. Misreading genre leads to false accusations.

### 3. Lacking Knowledge Of Ancient Conventions

Number rounding, telescoping of genealogies, and selective narration were standard literary practices. These are not errors.

### 4. Elevated Skepticism

Some critics begin with the presupposition that the Bible must err. Their conclusions reflect their starting assumptions rather than textual reality.

## How Bible Students Resolve Difficulties

### 1. Identify Context

Historical, grammatical, and covenantal context must be studied carefully.

### 2. Examine The Original Languages

Hebrew and Greek often clarify difficulties. Word meaning, tense, aspect, and syntax may resolve the issue immediately.

### 3. Compare All Parallel Texts

Scripture interprets Scripture. Many questions resolve through cross-referencing.

### 4. Consider Textual Variants

Occasionally, differences arise from copyist alterations, not from the original text.

### 5. Recognize Perspective

Two authors may describe the same event from different vantage points without contradiction.

## Examples of Additional Resolved Difficulties

(For length, only major explanations are provided without summaries.)

### The Census Figures In Samuel And Chronicles

The difference between the number of fighting men in 2 Samuel 24:9 and 1 Chronicles 21:5 arises because Samuel includes only certain categories of soldiers, whereas Chronicles includes additional divisions. The chronicler frequently provides fuller administrative detail.

### Who Killed Goliath?

1 Samuel 17 accurately records David killing Goliath. 2 Samuel 21:19 mentions Elhanan killing "Goliath," but the correct reading (preserved in reliable manuscripts and reflected in parallel Chronicles) identifies the slain man as the brother of Goliath. A copyist omission of "brother of" in one manuscript tradition accounts for the difference.

### Judas' Death

Matthew 27:5 describes Judas hanging himself. Acts 1:18 describes the aftermath when his body fell and burst open. These are not contradictory but consecutive events.

### The Women at the Tomb

Differences in listing which women visited the tomb reflect selection, not contradiction. No Gospel claims to list every woman present.

## The Role of Chronology In Supporting Inerrancy

Accurate understanding of historical chronology—such as the dating of the Exodus (1446 B.C.E.), the entry of Jacob into Egypt (1876 B.C.E.), Solomon's temple construction (966 B.C.E.), Jesus' execution (33 C.E. Nisan 14), Paul's missionary travels (beginning c. 47–48 C.E.)— demonstrates the internal coherence of Scripture. These dates align with archaeological, linguistic, and extrabiblical evidence that confirms rather than undermines Scripture's reliability.

Chronology also demonstrates covenantal continuity. Jehovah's promises unfold progressively through the Abrahamic covenant (2091 B.C.E.), the Mosaic covenant, and the New Covenant inaugurated through Christ. The ages, genealogies, and timelines all function coherently, demonstrating purposeful structure rather than mythological invention.

## Why Inerrancy Matters Today

Inerrancy safeguards the authority of Scripture. If Scripture errs, theology collapses. If Scripture is trustworthy, then its teachings regarding salvation, moral transformation, resurrection hope, and Jehovah's future purposes—particularly the premillennial return of Christ and restoration of the earth for the redeemed—stand secure.

Because humans do not possess immortal souls and eternal life is a gift granted through resurrection, the reliability of Scripture becomes foundational. Our knowledge of the future Kingdom, the 1,000-year reign of Christ, judgment, and restored creation depends entirely upon the truthfulness of the Word.

Christians are called to immerse themselves in Scripture, defend its integrity, and abide by its teachings as part of their salvation journey. Apologetics is not optional; it is an expression of loyalty to the God Who has spoken.

# Inerrancy: Practical Principles to Overcoming Bible Difficulties

## Introduction: The Necessity of Sound Principles When Approaching Alleged Discrepancies

The Bible is the inspired, inerrant, and infallible Word of God. Because Scripture was written through human authors moved by the Holy Spirit (2 Pet. 1:21), it reflects authorial intent, grammatical precision, covenantal development, and historical reality. Yet, due to differences in perspective, writing style, cultural background, literary form, and the limitations of human readers, many passages initially appear difficult or even contradictory. These difficulties do not stem from imperfection in divine revelation but from the imperfect understanding of those interpreting it.

The following principles demonstrate how careful exegesis, the Historical-Grammatical method, contextual analysis, and logical evaluation dissolve alleged problems, allowing the student of Scripture to see that the unified voice of God's Word stands without contradiction.

## Different Points of View

Scripture at times presents two accurate descriptions of the same geographical location or situation based on different vantage points. When the reader recognizes each writer's physical perspective and historical setting, the difficulty disappears.

### Example: "This Side of the Jordan" vs. "The Other Side of the Jordan"

Numbers 35:14 (UASV)

**14** *You shall give three cities across the Jordan and three cities you shall give in the land of Canaan; they will be cities of refuge.*

Joshua 22:4 (UASV)

**4** *And now Jehovah your God has given rest to your brothers, as he spoke to them; therefore turn now and go to your tents, to the land of your possession, which Moses the servant of Jehovah gave you beyond the Jordan.*

Moses wrote before Israel crossed the Jordan, making the east bank "this side." Joshua wrote after Israel crossed, making the same area "the other side." Both writers describe the identical region accurately according to their own physical location at the time of writing. No contradiction exists. The key is recognizing changing perspectives within redemptive history.

## A Careful Reading

Many supposed contradictions evaporate when the student simply slows down and examines the details of each passage. Narrative sequences, territorial borders, military events, and partial conquests often require patient reading.

### Example: Jerusalem and the Tribes of Benjamin And Judah

A series of passages mention Benjamin, Judah, and the Jebusites in relation to Jerusalem:

- Joshua 18:28 – Jerusalem listed among Benjamin's inheritance

- Judges 1:21 – Benjamin failed to drive out the Jebusites

- Joshua 15:63 – Judah also could not drive them out

- Judges 1:8–9 – Judah captured and burned the city

- 2 Samuel 5:5–9 – David captured Jerusalem centuries later

The key observation is that Jerusalem's boundary line ran between Benjamin and Judah. The fortified Jebusite stronghold sat strategically across the tribal border. Benjamin could not remove them. Judah temporarily captured and burned parts of the city, yet did not fully secure the stronghold. The Jebusites regrouped and fortified their position until David conquered the stronghold of Zion long afterward.

Thus, each passage describes a different stage in the ongoing struggle against the Jebusites. Different events do not conflict; they complement one another when examined together.

## Intended Meaning of the Writer

God's inspired authors used precise language when necessary, approximate numerical references when appropriate, and paraphrase when helpful. Recognizing genre, authorial purpose, and the norms of ancient communication clarifies meaning.

## Rounded Numbers and Approximation

Acts 2:41 (UASV)

**41** *So those who received his word were baptized, and there were added that day about three thousand souls.*

"About three thousand" is an ordinary, accurate rounding. Scripture does not mislead by employing estimations, just as modern historians report approximate figures when exactness is unnecessary.

### Paraphrase

Acts 7:2–3 (UASV)

Stephen paraphrases Jehovah's call to Abraham. Checking Genesis 12:1 reveals similar content phrased differently. Scripture often paraphrases earlier revelation without requiring word-for-word equivalence.

### Human Perspective in Descriptions

Numbers 34:15 (UASV)

**15** *The two and a half tribes have received their inheritance beyond the Jordan opposite Jericho, eastward toward the sunrising.*

This represents the standard human vantage point of sunrise in the east. Likewise:

- "four corners of the earth"

- "four winds"

- "ends of the earth"

These are everyday expressions describing directions or extremities, not cosmological claims.

## Unexplained Does Not Mean Unexplainable

With 31,173 verses written by approximately 40 authors over 1,600 years, it is unsurprising that a small percentage of passages pose interpretive challenges. The vast majority are fully explainable, and the remaining few are not due to error in Scripture but due to the limitations of current knowledge. Progress in archaeology, ancient Near Eastern studies, historical geography, and linguistic analysis continually resolves formerly difficult texts.

One must avoid assuming that absence of external data equates to error in Scripture. History repeatedly vindicates the biblical text.

## Guilty Until Proven Innocent: The Critic's Error

Critics often apply a prejudicial standard to Scripture that they would never apply to classical literature or historical inscriptions. They assume error until outside evidence proves otherwise. This approach has been refuted countless times.

### Example: Belshazzar In Daniel 5

Daniel 5:1 (UASV)

*1 Belshazzar the king made a great feast for a thousand of his nobles...*

For centuries critics argued that Belshazzar never existed. Yet Babylonian tablets discovered in 1854 revealed that King Nabonidus entrusted kingship to his eldest son, Bel-sar-ussur (Belshazzar), making him coregent. Daniel was historically accurate long before archaeology confirmed it.

This underscores a vital principle: Scripture deserves the presumption of truthfulness rather than the unwarranted suspicion critics impose upon it.

## Ignoring Literary Styles

The Bible employs various forms of literature: narrative, legal instruction, prophetic oracles, poetry, wisdom, parables, and symbolic apocalyptic visions. Confusing figurative language with literal description inevitably produces false accusations.

### Example: Hyperbole In Matthew 24:35

Matthew 24:35 (UASV)

*35 Heaven and earth will pass away, but my words will not pass away.*

Jesus used emphatic hyperbole to stress the reliability of His words. His Jewish audience, familiar with the Hebrew Scriptures, understood this as rhetorical emphasis, not a prediction that the physical world would cease to exist. Recognizing the type of speech dissolves the supposed contradiction.

## Two Accounts of the Same Incident

Multiple eyewitnesses of the same event naturally emphasize different details. Ancient Mediterranean culture also frequently used representatives to act and speak on behalf of others. When these realities are recognized, the harmony of the narratives becomes evident.

### Example: The Centurion and the Elders

Matthew 8:5 (UASV)

**5** *When he had entered Capernaum, a centurion came forward to him...*

Luke 7:2–3 (UASV)

**2–3** The centurion sent older men of the Jews to speak to Jesus.

Matthew condenses the narrative, attributing the approach to the centurion himself because the elders represented him and carried his authority. Luke provides fuller detail. In first-century culture, a representative's words were considered the direct speech of the one represented. There is no contradiction—only complementary perspectives.

## Man's Fallible Interpretations

The text of Scripture is infallible; human interpretations are not. Misunderstandings arise from reading into the text, ignoring context, importing traditions, or interpreting through modern philosophical lenses. Recognizing the danger of imposing modern assumptions on ancient documents helps preserve the original meaning intended by God and the human authors.

## The Autograph Alone Is Inspired And Inerrant

The original writings (autographs) were flawless. Though copies were made by human scribes over centuries, the science of textual criticism has restored the biblical text to a degree of accuracy unparalleled by any ancient work. The Hebrew and Greek texts available today reflect the autographs with approximately 99.99% accuracy.

### Example: The Second Cainan in Luke 3

Luke 3:36 includes a "Cainan" not present in the Hebrew text or early extrabiblical genealogical traditions. This reflects a copyist insertion drawn from a later form of the Greek Septuagint. Because early manuscripts of Genesis and the genealogies lack this name, scholars recognize it as a transmissional anomaly.

The presence of such rare scribal variants does not undermine inerrancy because inerrancy applies to the autographs, and textual criticism allows us to reconstruct them with extraordinary precision. The negligible number of variants does not affect any doctrine or major historical point.

## Look At the Context

Context determines meaning. Words, sentences, and concepts must be interpreted according to their literary, historical, and covenantal setting. When a passage is extracted from its context, distortion occurs.

### Example: Faith, Works, And Salvation

Ephesians 2:8–9 (UASV)

**8–9** *For by grace you have been saved through faith... not from works...*

James 2:26 (UASV)

**26** *faith apart from works is dead.*

Paul confronts Jewish Christians who wrongly believed that works of the Mosaic Law established righteousness. He insists that salvation is a gift, not the result of law-keeping. James addresses nominal believers whose "faith" was mere profession without righteous conduct. Paul refutes legalism; James refutes empty claim. Both uphold that genuine faith produces action consistent with loyalty to Christ.

Because each author addresses a distinct problem, their teachings harmonize perfectly when contextualized.

### The Unity and Reliability Of Scripture

The Bible contains no contradictions. When examined through the proper lenses—varying perspectives, authorial intent, literary forms, context, established textual integrity, and basic logic—alleged difficulties fade. Human limitations, not divine revelation, generate confusion. The believer who approaches Scripture with humility, diligence, and confidence in its divine origin discovers its complete harmony.

# Inerrancy: Are There Contradictions?

### Foundational Considerations for Addressing Apparent Contradictions

When confronting Bible difficulties, the critic often begins with a philosophical assumption rather than an exegetical investigation. When someone approaches Scripture believing it is a merely human composition, fallible and inconsistent, every tension becomes a contradiction and every complexity becomes an error. The conservative evangelical interpreter, however, operates from the conviction that Scripture is the inspired and infallible Word of God, a record preserved with extraordinary accuracy in the Hebrew and Greek critical texts. Therefore, the task is not to force harmonization, but to seek the most coherent, contextually grounded explanation within the historical-covenantal setting revealed by God. Because Scripture interprets Scripture, the careful examination of parallel texts, linguistic patterns, and the progressive nature of revelation consistently dissolves claims of contradiction.

The following article examines several well-known objections raised by critics, presenting the critic's claim, the relevant biblical text as provided, and an exegetically grounded response reflecting a conservative and historically informed hermeneutic.

## Where Did Cain Obtain His Wife?

### The Critic's Objection

Genesis records that Adam and Eve had Cain and Abel, after which Cain killed Abel. The critic argues that since only three people appear to exist at this point, the question "Where did Cain get his wife?" exposes a flaw in the historical record.

### The Text of Difficulty

### Genesis 4:17 (UASV)

"Cain had sexual relations with his wife and she conceived and gave birth to Enoch; and he built a city, and called the name of the city Enoch, after the name of his son, Enoch."

### Answer to the Critic

The genealogies in Genesis are selective, not exhaustive. After describing the birth of Seth, Genesis states that Adam "became father to sons and daughters" (Genesis 5:4). Adam lived 930 years, providing vast opportunity for a large human population to emerge from his immediate descendants. Cain therefore either married a sister or, depending on chronology, a niece. Early human genetic integrity permitted close-kin marriage without biological consequences. As human imperfection increased after the rebellion of Adam, genetic instability accumulated, and lifespans diminished—from Adam's 930 years to Shem's 600, Arpachshad's 438, and Abraham's 175. By the time of the Mosaic Law, close-kin marriage was prohibited (Leviticus 18:9) because accumulated genetic defects made such unions dangerous. Nothing in the Genesis account contains a contradiction; the critic's difficulty arises from assuming the absence of descendants not explicitly listed in early genealogical summaries.

## Did God Harden Pharaoh's Heart?

### The Critic's Objection

If God hardened Pharaoh's heart, then Pharaoh cannot be responsible for his decisions. The critic views this as undermining moral accountability and exposing inconsistency in God's dealings.

### The Text of Difficulty

### Exodus 4:21 (UASV)

"Jehovah said to Moses, 'When you go and return to Egypt see that you perform before Pharaoh all the wonders which I have put in your hand; but I will harden his heart so that he will not let the people go.'"

### Answer to the Critic

The statement in Exodus 4:21 is prophetic, not causal. God reveals what Pharaoh will do in response to the signs and judgments, not what Pharaoh is irresistibly compelled to do. Hebrew idiom frequently attributes to God what He merely permits. The broader narrative emphasizes Pharaoh's agency: Pharaoh hardens his own heart repeatedly (e.g., Exodus 8:15; 8:32; 9:34). Exodus records nineteen references to the hardening of Pharaoh's heart; Jehovah is the explicit subject only once (10:1). The remainder emphasize Pharaoh's responsibility or describe his heart as becoming hardened through his own obstinacy.

God's actions—plagues, signs, warnings—expose Pharaoh's rebellion, but do not produce it. When God reveals truth and a wicked individual chooses rebellion, the outcome is described as God "hardening" that person, meaning He allowed the individual's character to manifest fully. This is consistent with the biblical portrayal of human freedom under divine foreknowledge. Pharaoh's moral culpability is therefore intact, and Exodus presents a coherent historical and theological narrative.

## Was The Bronze Serpent A Violation of the Second Commandment?

### The Critic's Objection

The second commandment forbids carved images. Yet Moses made a bronze serpent at Jehovah's direction. The critic argues that this violates the commandment itself.

### The Text of Difficulty

### Numbers 21:9 (UASV)

"And Moses made a bronze serpent and set it on the standard; and it came about, that if a serpent bit any man, when he looked to the bronze serpent, he lived."

### Answer to the Critic

A carved image becomes an idol only when it becomes an object of worship or veneration. The bronze serpent was a sign, not a god; it conveyed God's provision of healing, not an alternative deity. The second commandment forbids constructing images for worship, not images used for symbolic or instructional purposes.

Centuries later, Israel did transform this symbol into an object of veneration, at which point Hezekiah destroyed it:

**2 Kings 18:4** records that the Israelites "had made offerings to it," and therefore it was broken in pieces.

The serpent did not violate the commandment; Israel's later misuse of it did. God's people were often permitted objects that pointed to divine truths—ark cherubim, priestly garments, memorial stones—none of which violated the commandment because they were neither worshiped nor treated as divine.

## Does Deuteronomy Contradict Itself Concerning the Poor?

### The Critic's Objection

Deuteronomy 15:4 states that there will be no poor in Israel, but verse 11 states that the poor will never cease to exist.

### The Texts of Difficulty

### Deuteronomy 15:4 (UASV)

"However, there will be no poor among you, since Jehovah will surely bless you in the land which Jehovah your God is giving you as an inheritance to possess,"

### NET (for the critic's quotation)

"There will never cease to be some poor people in the land..."

### Answer to the Critic

Verse 4 expresses what *should* occur within the covenant community when the Israelites obey God's commands. If they follow Jehovah's instruction concerning generosity, debt release, and care for their brethren, no Israelite should remain destitute because the community would lift up anyone who fell into hardship.

Verse 11 acknowledges the reality of a fallen world: poverty will always appear because of sickness, poor harvests, economic misfortune, injury, or other hardships in an imperfect society. The Israelites were therefore commanded to respond with generosity.

There is no contradiction; verse 4 addresses Israel's responsibility within the covenant, while verse 11 acknowledges the ongoing presence of need requiring continued obedience.

# Did Joshua Take All the Land or Leave Much Unconquered?

## The Critic's Objection

Joshua 11:23 states Joshua took the whole land, yet Joshua 13:1 states that much remained to be possessed. The critic asserts that both statements cannot be true.

## The Texts of Difficulty

### Joshua 11:23 (UASV)

"So Joshua took the whole land, according to all that Jehovah had spoken to Moses..."

### Joshua 13:1 (UASV)

"You are old and advanced in years, and there remains yet very much land to possess."

## Answer to the Critic

Israel's conquest unfolded in two phases:

### 1. National Conquest Under Joshua

The coalition armies of Canaan were broken, their kings defeated, and their military power dismantled. This fulfilled the national objective.

### 2. Tribal Allotment and Local Occupation

Each tribe was responsible for fully occupying its allotted territory and removing remaining enclaves.

Joshua 11:23 speaks of the first phase: the military superiority of the Canaanites was crushed. Joshua 13:1 refers to the second: many local strongholds remained for individual tribes to address. Joshua did everything commissioned to him; the tribes did not complete theirs.

Because the remaining Canaanites posed no existential threat, the statement that "the land had rest from war" (Joshua 11:23; cf. 21:44) remains true. The critic's objection fails because it misunderstands the structure of the conquest.

## Has Anyone Seen God?

### The Critic's Objection

John 1:18 states that no one has seen God. Yet Exodus 24:10 says Moses and the elders "saw the God of Israel," and Exodus 33:20 says no one can see God and live. The critic claims this is a direct contradiction.

### The Texts of Difficulty

### John 1:18 (UASV)

"No one has seen God at any time; the only begotten God who is in the bosom of the Father, that one has made him fully known."

### Exodus 24:10 (UASV)

"and they saw the God of Israel..."

### Exodus 33:20 (UASV)

"You cannot see my face, for no man can see me and live!"

### Answer to the Critic

Scripture affirms repeatedly that Jehovah is invisible and cannot be beheld directly by human eyes. Moses could not see His "face" (Exodus 33:20). Christ is "the image of the invisible God" (Colossians 1:15) and the "exact representation of His nature" (Hebrews 1:3). Human beings therefore encounter God through manifestations that reveal His presence without disclosing His essence.

The appearances described in Exodus involve manifestations of divine glory, often through angelic representatives who carry God's authority. Scripture frequently speaks of encountering God when the encounter is mediated by one of His angels:

- **Exodus 3:2**—"the angel of the Lord appeared," yet verse 6 identifies the speaker as God.

- **Acts 7:53**, **Galatians 3:19**, and **Hebrews 2:2** reveal that the Law was delivered by angels.

- **Luke 2:9** associates "the glory of the Lord" with the appearance of an angel.

When Exodus 24:10 states that the elders "saw the God of Israel," they beheld the appearance of His glory through an angelic representative, not His unmediated essence. Exodus 33:22–23 clarifies this when God tells Moses he will see His "back," meaning a mediated manifestation.

Similarly, Jacob wrestled with a "man" who was clearly an angelic representative (Genesis 32:24–30). Manoah and his wife encountered an angel and said, "We have seen God" (Judges 13:3–22). Ancient Israelites commonly spoke of encountering God when they encountered His messenger.

John 1:18 therefore stands in complete harmony with the Exodus accounts: no human has ever seen God Himself, though many have seen His representative manifestations.

# BIBLE DIFFICULTIES
## INERRANCY: ARE THERE MISTAKES?

# Inerrancy: Are There Mistakes?

## Addressing Alleged Mistakes

While many alleged contradictions in Scripture have been refuted through sound exegetical and historical analysis, critics persist in asserting that the Bible contains mistakes. Such accusations often stem from either a superficial reading of the text, a failure to harmonize passages within their contexts, or a misunderstanding of the literary and linguistic conventions of the biblical world. This article will examine several often-cited cases of supposed error and demonstrate that they are nothing of the sort when carefully examined using the Historical-Grammatical method and a high view of Scripture's inerrancy.

## Judas' Death: Hanging or Falling Headlong?

### Matthew 27:5 (UASV):

*"And he threw the pieces of silver into the temple and departed; and he went away and hanged himself."*

### Acts 1:18 (UASV):

*"(Now this man acquired a field with the price of his wickedness, and falling headlong, he burst open in the middle and all his intestines gushed out."*

### Answer:

This alleged contradiction arises only when one insists that both verses are giving identical details rather than complementary ones. In reality, Matthew recounts *how* Judas committed suicide—by hanging himself—while Luke in Acts reports the *result* of that suicide.

What likely occurred is that Judas, in his despair, hanged himself on a tree located near a cliff edge. Whether due to the branch breaking, the rope snapping, or the body being left to decay until it fell, the end result is what Luke describes: the body fell and burst open. Thus, Luke's record complements Matthew's by supplying further detail, not conflicting information. There is no contradiction—only two perspectives of the same tragic event.

## Plague Numbers: 23,000 or 24,000?

### Numbers 25:9 (UASV):

*"The ones who died in the plague were twenty-four thousand."*

### 1 Corinthians 10:8 (UASV):

*"Neither let us commit sexual immorality, as some of them committed sexual immorality, only to fall, twenty-three thousand of them in one day."*

**Answer:**
Paul, writing under inspiration, refers to *those who died in one day*—23,000. Moses, by contrast, refers to the *total* number who died as a result of the plague—24,000. The discrepancy is only apparent if one fails to observe the time frame specified in 1 Corinthians.

Moreover, Moses' account includes "the chiefs of the people" who were slain by judges prior to the outbreak of the plague (Numbers 25:4–5). This could account for the extra 1,000 individuals mentioned. Paul is precise in noting that the 23,000 died "in one day," while Moses provides a complete tally of all those who perished in the event. Both are correct within their stated scope.

## Joseph's Burial: In Abraham's or Jacob's Tomb?

### Acts 7:15–16 (UASV):

*"And Jacob went down to Egypt and died, he and our fathers. And they were brought back to Shechem and buried in the tomb that Abraham had bought for a sum of silver from the sons of Hamor in Shechem."*

### Genesis 33:19 (UASV):

*"And he bought the piece of land where he had pitched his tent from the hand of the sons of Hamor, Shechem's father, for one hundred qesitahs."*

### Joshua 24:32 (UASV):

*"As for the bones of Joseph, which the sons of Israel brought up from Egypt, they buried them at Shechem, in the piece of land that Jacob bought from the sons of Hamor the father of Shechem for one hundred qesitahs."*

**Answer:**

Critics argue that Acts 7:16 attributes to Abraham a land purchase in Shechem that Genesis attributes to Jacob. However, there are reasonable explanations consistent with biblical inerrancy:

1. **Oral Tradition Not Preserved in Genesis:** Stephen may have been referencing an event preserved in reliable oral tradition not recorded in Genesis. Genesis 12:6–7 states that Abraham's first stop in Canaan was Shechem, where he built an altar and received the promise from Jehovah. It is reasonable to suggest that Abraham may have secured that land, and later generations, having left the area, required Jacob to repurchase it due to lapsing local recognition of prior ownership.

2. **Representative Attribution:** In biblical thought, a descendant could be viewed as a representative of the patriarch. Thus, Jacob's purchase may have been considered an extension of Abraham's

217

claim to the land. This form of attribution is consistent with ancient Near Eastern practices.

3. **Textual Explanation:** Some scholars have noted a potential syntactical construction in Acts 7:16 where the Greek allows for the interpretation that the tomb and the purchase are not being attributed directly to Abraham in the absolute sense but that Shechem is simply the site where a tomb was, connected genealogically to Abraham's lineage.

4. **Proleptic Use of "Tomb":** The word *mnema* (tomb) used in Acts could refer to the land that later *became* a tomb. Abraham bought land in Hebron (Machpelah), but it is not called a "tomb" until its later use. Similarly, the tract of land in Shechem could have been considered Abraham's by ancestral claim and later became a tomb for Joseph.

Thus, Acts 7:16 presents no contradiction but reflects common Jewish interpretive traditions and linguistic flexibility.

## David's Census: Moved by God or Satan?

### 2 Samuel 24:1 (UASV):

*"Now again the anger of Jehovah burned against Israel, and it incited David against them to say, 'Go, number Israel and Judah.'"*

### 1 Chronicles 21:1 (UASV):

*"Then Satan stood up against Israel and moved David to number Israel."*

### Answer:

The two texts reflect different aspects of causality. 2 Samuel attributes the census to the wrath of Jehovah—He *allowed* the census as a disciplinary measure against Israel's sin. 1 Chronicles identifies Satan (or a resister) as the immediate agent provoking David to commit the act.

This is consistent with the broader Scriptural principle that God permits evil within His sovereign plan without being the author of it. Just as God permitted Satan to test Job (Job 1:12), so He allowed Satan to tempt David, not because He endorsed the act, but as a judgment upon Israel.

The language of divine causation in 2 Samuel is permissive, not deterministic. Scripture often expresses God's permission of an action as though He directly caused it. For example, Jehovah "hardened Pharaoh's heart" (Exodus 4:21), but the context reveals that Pharaoh's heart was already resistant, and God merely allowed the hardening to persist for His purposes.

In the case of David's census, Jehovah's anger was already kindled against Israel, likely due to widespread national sin. He thus permitted Satan to act, and David, failing to rely on Jehovah, gave in to the temptation. The parallel accounts are not contradictory—they simply emphasize different agents involved in the event.

The alleged mistakes examined above are nothing more than misunderstandings or superficial readings of the text. When approached with a proper hermeneutic that respects authorial intent, grammatical context, and covenantal continuity, these so-called errors dissolve under the light of faithful exegesis. The Bible remains wholly inspired and inerrant in all that it affirms. Each example—whether concerning historical events, numerical data, or theological implications—demonstrates the internal consistency and truthfulness of Scripture.

# Inerrancy: Are There Scientific Errors?

## Scripture's Authority and the Question of Scientific Accuracy

The question of whether the Bible contains scientific errors has been raised throughout history by skeptics, critics, and those influenced by naturalistic assumptions. Yet the Scriptures are the inspired, inerrant, and infallible Word of God, conveyed through divinely guided human authors who wrote with precision and clarity according to the Historical-Grammatical method. As 2 Peter 1:21 affirms, these men "spoke from God as they were carried along by the Holy Spirit." The issue is therefore not whether Scripture fails, but whether interpreters misunderstand the text, impose foreign expectations onto its wording, or ignore the context, genre, or authorial intent under divine inspiration.

The Bible is not a scientific textbook. It does not use modern technical terminology, nor does it attempt to explain natural phenomena through the lens of twenty-first-century research. Rather, it communicates truth accurately and coherently to its intended audience while describing reality in common observational language, the same way people speak today when referencing sunrise, sunset, or the movement of the heavens. Scientific precision and phenomenological expression are not mutually exclusive. When Scripture touches on matters involving the natural world, it consistently aligns with accurate scientific concepts—often long before human discovery.

Science itself cannot answer ultimate questions of origin, purpose, design, morality, or destiny. It can examine created processes, but it cannot account for the existence of those processes. Scientific inquiry repeatedly reveals astonishing levels of order, complexity, precision, and interdependence—realities that testify to the infinite intelligence and power of the Creator. The apostle Paul makes this unmistakably clear: "For his invisible attributes, namely, his eternal power and divine nature, have been clearly perceived, ever since the creation of the world, in the things that have been made." (Romans 1:20, UASV) Astronomy, cosmology, biology, neurology, genetics, and physics all reveal layers of complexity that comport naturally with the biblical worldview.

The issue, then, is never that Scripture contradicts science. The conflict arises when human interpretations of either Scripture or scientific data are flawed.

## Historical Case Study: Galileo, Misinterpretation, and Misplaced Authority

The conflict surrounding Galileo is frequently misrepresented as a battle between the Bible and science. In reality, it was a confrontation between scientific evidence and ecclesiastical tradition. The Catholic Church had adopted a geocentric cosmology derived from pagan Greek philosophical views, especially those of Aristotle and Ptolemy. Ptolemy (b. c. 85 C.E.) had argued that the earth was the center of the cosmos, and this model became entrenched in church dogma—not because Scripture teaches it, but because church authorities imposed it.

Galileo's observations demonstrated that the earth revolves around the sun. Instead of reexamining their interpretation of Scripture, Catholic authorities insisted Galileo's findings were heretical. He was forced to recant, and only centuries later (in 1992) did the Church officially acknowledge its error.

The Bible itself never teaches geocentrism. No verse states that the sun orbits the earth. The controversy arose solely because the Church conflated its own tradition with divine revelation. It treated pagan cosmology as if it were inspired.

This event illustrates a crucial principle: Scripture does not err, but interpreters often do. Galileo himself wrote, "Even though Scripture cannot err, its interpreters and expositors can." The issue was not with the biblical text, but with a faulty hermeneutic that ignored genre, context, and authorial intent.

## The Historical-Grammatical Framework: Understanding Scriptural Language

Biblical authors communicated in normal human language, using observational terminology understandable to their readers. This is fully compatible with accuracy. Modern meteorologists still speak of "sunrise" and "sunset," though they know the earth rotates. Scientific precision and phenomenological description coexist without contradiction.

Scripture also employs poetry, metaphor, hyperbole, personification, and parallelism—all legitimate features of human language. The presence of figurative expressions does not diminish truthfulness; it enriches communication. The key is identifying the genre and interpreting accordingly.

The Historical-Grammatical method recognizes:

1. **Authorial intent under divine inspiration.**

2. **The linguistic conventions of Hebrew and Greek.**

3. **Normal rules of grammar and syntax.**

4. **The historical and covenantal context.**

5. **The difference between literal description and figurative imagery.**

With this foundation established, we now examine specific passages often misunderstood as scientifically inaccurate. In each case, Scripture demonstrates precision when rightly interpreted.

### Isaiah 40:22: The Circle of the Earth

#### Isaiah 40:22 (UASV)

*22 It is he who sits above the circle of the earth, and its inhabitants are like grasshoppers; who stretches out the heavens like a curtain, and spreads them like a tent to dwell in.*

Isaiah wrote around the eighth century B.C.E., long before formal astronomical discovery. Yet he accurately referred to the earth as a "circle," a term consistent with a spherical shape. The Hebrew word *chugh* conveys roundness or sphericity. Isaiah was not delivering a technical astronomical treatise, but the language is fully compatible with modern understanding.

Furthermore, Isaiah describes the heavens as being "stretched out." This expression is remarkably consistent with the expanding universe model, which modern cosmology has confirmed. The prophet's observation stands in striking harmony with scientific discovery, though he wrote in pre-scientific times.

The remarkable accuracy of the text cannot be attributed to human speculation; it reflects divine revelation. The choice of vocabulary fits perfectly with what later generations would observe from space.

## Job 26:7: The Earth Hanging on Nothing

### Job 26:7 (UASV)

*7 He stretches out the north over empty space and hangs the earth on nothing.*

Many ancient cultures imagined the earth resting on pillars, animals, or deities. Yet the book of Job—written centuries before classical Greek philosophy—states that the earth "hangs on nothing." This perfectly matches gravitational reality. Moses, who compiled the book of Job, recorded this truth long before the Greek astronomer Eratosthenes (c. 276–194 B.C.E.) estimated the earth's circumference.

There is no naturalistic explanation for how Job could have known this apart from divine revelation. The text is scientifically accurate in a way unique for its time.

## Joshua 10:13: Did the Sun Stand Still?

### Joshua 10:13 (UASV)

*13 And the sun stood still, and the moon stopped, until the nation avenged themselves of their enemies...*

Critics frequently cite this verse to claim that the Bible teaches geocentrism. Yet this account uses observational language, just as modern people speak of sunrise and sunset. The miracle involved an extraordinary extension of daylight for Israel's battle.

Two considerations preserve inerrancy:

1. **Scripture describes the event phenomenologically.** It reports what observers saw, not the mechanics behind it.

2. **Jehovah, who created all physical laws, can alter natural processes.** If He chose to modify the earth's rotation or produce extended light through refraction, atmospheric conditions, or another mechanism, the result would appear exactly as described.

Nothing in the account asserts incorrect scientific principles. Instead, it affirms God's sovereign intervention.

## 2 Kings 20:8–11: The Shadow Moving Backward

In Hezekiah's day, Jehovah provided a sign involving the shadow on the steps of Ahaz moving backward. This phenomenon involved an extraordinary manipulation of light or time-scale perception. Again, Scripture does not explain the mechanism, nor is it required to do so. The text reports the observed result accurately.

Intervention by the Creator does not undermine scientific order; it demonstrates His authority over the laws He established.

## Judges 5:20: Did the Stars Fight?

### Judges 5:20 (UASV)

*20 From heaven the stars fought, from their courses they fought against Sisera.*

This verse appears in a poetic victory song. Poetry employs imagery to communicate theological truth—in this case, that Jehovah intervened decisively for Israel. Judges 4 (prose) provides the historical narrative, while Judges 5 (poetry) conveys emotional and theological depth.

The phrase "the stars fought" is not scientific description but poetic language indicating divine involvement. Hebrew poetry frequently uses cosmological imagery to portray God's power. The context requires figurative interpretation, not literal astronomical combat.

## Phenomenological Language and Scientific Accuracy

The Bible uses normal human speech describing phenomena as they appear. This does not compromise factual accuracy. People today still describe the sun rising or setting though they understand the earth's rotation. Scripture uses such expressions without affirming geocentric cosmology.

Key examples:

- The "foundations of the earth" refer to stability (Psalm 104:5).

- "Winds" are described by direction or effect, not meteorological categorization.

- The "ends of the earth" refer to extremities, not flat geography.

These expressions conform to ancient Near Eastern communication, not to error. The inerrant Scriptures convey truth in language suited to their readership.

## Creation and the Nature of Scientific Inquiry

Genesis describes creation in six "days," which represent extended periods. The account is orderly, coherent, and compatible with known scientific principles. Genesis does not employ mythological language. It avoids pagan cosmologies involving cosmic battles, sexualized deities, or the materialization of gods. Instead, it presents Jehovah as the sovereign Creator who brings all things into existence through His command.

Scientific investigation repeatedly confirms design, fine-tuning, and complexity inconsistent with random emergence:

- The precise constants of physics

- The anthropic balance of the cosmos

- Genetic information encoded with astonishing sophistication

- Cellular machinery exhibiting engineering-level complexity

- Ecological interdependence

- Mathematical structure embedded in the natural world

These realities support a biblical worldview grounded in divine wisdom.

## Misinterpretation as the Source of Alleged Errors

Historically, supposed contradictions between science and Scripture stem from misreadings of the text. Critics often:

1. Demand modern scientific vocabulary from ancient authors.

2. Ignore genre distinctions.

3. Misunderstand phenomenological descriptions.

4. Assume ancient people were incapable of accurate observation.

5. Impose naturalistic assumptions on the biblical record.

When these errors are removed, Scripture stands consistent, coherent, and scientifically aligned whenever it addresses the natural world.

## Scientific Consistency Across the Canon

Throughout the Bible, one finds numerous phrases that harmonize with scientific realities:

- Water cycle descriptions (Ecclesiastes 1:7)

- Sea paths (Psalm 8:8)

- Fixed stars and distinct constellations (Job 38:31–33)

- Life existing in "kinds" rather than evolutionary transmutation (Genesis 1)

- Human biology described with remarkable insight (Psalm 139:13–16)

- Gravitational and orbital stability implied in creation language

None of these passages contain scientific errors. Instead, they show an awareness that surpasses the cosmological myths of neighboring cultures.

### Scripture Stands Without Error

The Bible contains no scientific mistakes. What critics perceive as errors are either misunderstandings of observational language, failures to recognize genre, or attempts to impose modern scientific categories on ancient expressions. When interpreted using the Historical-Grammatical method, every passage harmonizes with established scientific principles or legitimately employs figurative language.

The Word of God is trustworthy, accurate, and fully reliable. Scientific discoveries continually confirm, rather than contradict, the truths of Scripture. As Hebrews 3:4 states, "every house is built by someone, but the builder of all things is God." Creation itself testifies to His genius, His sovereignty, and His power.

# Procedures for Handling Biblical Difficulties

### Absolute Conviction in the Inerrancy of Scripture

The foundational prerequisite for addressing any biblical difficulty is unwavering conviction in the inerrancy of Scripture as originally penned by the inspired writers (2 Peter 1:20–21; 2 Timothy 3:16–17). This conviction is not based on blind faith but on the massive weight of textual evidence, internal consistency, historical accuracy, and fulfilled prophecy that collectively testify to the Bible's divine origin. The original autographs were without error; what we possess today, due to the extraordinary preservation of thousands of manuscripts, is a text that is 99.99% accurate and faithful to those originals. Therefore, any apparent contradiction or difficulty must be viewed within this framework of reverent trust and scholarly diligence.

## Grammatical-Historical Exegesis: The Method of Resolution

A biblical difficulty cannot be understood—or resolved—apart from the proper interpretive method. The Historical-Grammatical method, not the Historical-Critical, is the only legitimate approach. It begins with understanding the *author's intended meaning* under divine inspiration. This demands attention to:

- **Immediate Literary Context:** One must not isolate a verse or phrase from its surrounding verses or literary unit. Determine where the author begins and ends his point. This clarifies ambiguity and prevents misreading.

- **Historical Background:** Knowing the cultural, geographical, and temporal setting in which a text was written enhances one's grasp of its meaning. For example, understanding first-century Jewish customs can elucidate much in the Gospels.

- **Lexical Study:** Investigate key words using conservative lexicons to uncover nuance. What did the original Hebrew or Greek term convey in that time and context?

- **Parallel Passages**: Scripture must interpret Scripture. Look for other inspired writings addressing the same issue for clarity.

- **Genre Awareness**: Recognize whether the passage is narrative, prophecy, poetry, apocalyptic, parable, or didactic prose. Figures of speech like hyperbole or metaphor must not be mistaken for literal declarations (e.g., Psalm 91:4—Jehovah will not literally have feathers).

## Honest and Courageous Engagement with Difficulties

### 1. Honestly

The conservative Bible student must *never dodge or obscure* legitimate questions. Suppressing them is intellectually dishonest and pastorally harmful. If one cannot yet provide an answer, it is better to confess ignorance than to force an artificial or weak explanation. Zeal without knowledge can do more damage than open opposition. Historical experience confirms that many alleged contradictions have been overturned by advances in archaeology, linguistics, or manuscript discoveries.

### 2. Humbly

No interpreter has omniscience. Many difficulties are not due to flaws in the text but limitations in our knowledge. A humble interpreter acknowledges the finiteness of human understanding and the infinite wisdom of God (Deuteronomy 29:29; Isaiah 55:8–9). A perceived contradiction is not proof of error, but a challenge to dig deeper.

### 3. Determinedly

Treat each difficulty as a challenge to mature faith and sharpen understanding. Some issues may require hours or days of careful work. A shallow approach will yield shallow results. Diligent and prayerful study, often accompanied by comparing multiple conservative commentaries, dictionaries, or Greek-Hebrew tools, will reward the patient investigator.

### 4. Fearlessly

Do not fear so-called "problem texts." The Bible has withstood hostile scrutiny for nearly two millennia—from pagan emperors to Enlightenment skeptics to modern liberal theologians. Every generation of critics believes it has uncovered something new—only for their arguments to fall before the weight of rigorous scholarship and manuscript evidence. The Bible remains the most scrutinized and yet the most vindicated text in human history. Jehovah has preserved His Word (Psalm 119:89; Isaiah 40:8).

### 5. Patiently

Some problems resist immediate answers. The wise student will catalog the question, continue studying, and return to it later with fresh insight. Over time, familiarity with the whole counsel of God can often bring a solution that once seemed elusive.

## Scriptural and Prayerful Solutions

### 1. Scripturally

The most powerful interpretive tool is the Bible itself. Cross-referencing difficult passages with related ones often dissolves the perceived tension. Scripture is internally harmonious when understood in context. For example, Paul's emphasis on justification by faith in Romans does not contradict James' emphasis on a faith that works (James 2:14–26). They address different audiences and problems, not different gospels.

### 2. Prayerfully

Interpreting Scripture is not merely an academic endeavor; it is a spiritual discipline. Jehovah gives understanding to the humble seeker (Psalm 119:18; Proverbs 2:1–6). Through prayer, the interpreter aligns himself with the Author of Scripture and gains insight into what the natural man cannot discern (1 Corinthians 2:14).

## Evaluating the Nature of the Difficulty

### 1. Apparent Contradiction or Misunderstood Genre?

Many so-called contradictions vanish when genre and literary devices are rightly understood. For example, Matthew 5:29–30 (regarding cutting off the hand or plucking out the eye) is clearly hyperbolic, emphasizing the radical seriousness of sin—not instructing literal mutilation.

## 2. Numerical or Chronological Differences

Scripture often uses rounded numbers or estimates in casual discourse, which is entirely appropriate. When 1 Kings 7:26 says Solomon's sea held "2,000 baths" and 2 Chronicles 4:5 says "3,000 baths," it may reflect capacity versus actual content, or a copyist variance that does not affect doctrine or practice.

## 3. Transmission Errors

In extremely rare cases (constituting less than 0.01% of the text), transmission or scribal errors have occurred. These are usually obvious and identifiable by textual comparison across manuscripts and do not affect any doctrine. For example, 1 Samuel 13:1 presents a textual challenge likely due to a dropped numeral in early transmission, but this impacts no doctrine and is easily addressed with manuscript evidence and contextual analysis.

## 4. Harmonization of Parallel Accounts

Gospel differences, for example, in the number of angels at the tomb (Matthew 28:2; Mark 16:5; Luke 24:4; John 20:12), are reconcilable. One writer may focus on the one speaking or central figure. Absence of detail is not contradiction. Harmonization respects the fact that each Gospel writer selected details for theological and narrative purposes under divine inspiration.

## Value of Conservative Scholarly Tools

Use of trusted resources—such as conservative Bible dictionaries, lexicons (e.g., HALOT, BDAG), encyclopedias, and commentaries by faithful scholars—is encouraged. Authors such as Edward D. Andrews, Gleason Archer, and Norman Geisler offer excellent conservative insights on difficult texts without capitulating to liberal methodology.

Avoid tools that promote Higher Criticism, deny Mosaic authorship, question supernatural events, or treat Scripture as mythological or evolutionary in theology. Uphold the unity, divine authorship, and redemptive focus of the 66 canonical books.

## Confidence in the Textual Foundation

The integrity of the biblical text is unmatched in the ancient world. With over 5,898 Greek New Testament manuscripts and thousands more in Latin, Syriac, and other languages, and with Old Testament texts such as the Dead Sea Scrolls confirming remarkable accuracy going back centuries before Christ, the Bible's preservation is a divine marvel. No other ancient work comes remotely close to this level of textual support.

## Concluding Admonitions for the Faithful Student

- **Face difficulties head-on**, with intellectual honesty and doctrinal fidelity.

- **Never allow a question to undermine confidence** in the whole.

- **Recognize your limitations**, and submit to the Word as authoritative and sufficient.

- **Commit to diligent study**, aided by prayer and wise counsel.

- **Trust the God who inspired the Scriptures** to also illumine your understanding as you submit to His will.

# APPENDIX 10 The Divine Name in the Hebrew Scriptures

## Jehovah, There Was No "J"?

### Widely Held False Belief That There Was No "J" In Hebrew

The belief that there was no "J" sound in ancient Hebrew has led to misconceptions about the pronunciation of the Tetragrammaton and other Hebrew words. This article delves into the linguistic and historical evidence supporting the existence of the "J" sound in ancient Hebrew, particularly in the context of the Tetragrammaton.

### The Sephardic and Ashkenazi Pronunciations of Hebrew

1. **Differences in Phonetics**: The Sephardic Jews, unlike their Ashkenazi counterparts, have retained pronunciations closer to ancient Hebrew. This includes the "J" sound for the Hebrew letter ׳ (Yod).

2. **Impact on Modern Hebrew**: The State of Israel and modern Hebrew linguistics have largely adopted the Sephardic pronunciation, which is believed to be more reflective of ancient Hebrew phonetics.

## The Jod in Ancient Hebrew

1. **Jod's Historical Pronunciation**: Ancient Hebrew's ' (Jod or Yod) has been represented with a "J" sound, as evidenced in the Sephardic tradition. This contradicts the common belief of its absence in ancient Hebrew. We prefer the use of 'Jod,' but for convenience's sake, we will mainly use 'Yod' in this article.

2. **Classification as a Palatal**: The Hebrew letter ' is classified as a palatal, capable of producing the "J" sound, among others. This classification is supported by Sephardic grammarians and historical linguistics.

## Tyndale's Transliteration and the Tetragrammaton

1. **Tyndale's Hebrew Sources**: When William Tyndale transliterated the Tetragrammaton as "Jehovah," he followed the Sephardic phonetic system. His translation reflects the then-accepted scholarly understanding of Hebrew pronunciation.

2. **Jehovah in Historical Context**: The use of "Jehovah" dates back to at least the 8th century CE. This pronunciation has been preserved in significant biblical translations, including the American Standard Version.

The Ashkenazic Influence and Modern Misconceptions

1. **Shift in Pronunciation**: The Ashkenazic tradition, which emerged in European contexts, altered the pronunciation of ' (Jod) to a "Y" sound. This change has influenced modern perceptions of Hebrew pronunciation.

2. **Linguistic Evolution**: The evolution of languages and the divergence in Jewish communities have contributed to the

widespread belief in the non-existence of the "J" sound in ancient Hebrew.

The Authenticity of the Sephardic Pronunciation

1. **Endorsement by Scholars**: Historical linguists and scholars, including Gesenius, have acknowledged the Sephardic pronunciation as more closely aligned with ancient Hebrew.

2. **Reuchlin's Influence**: Reuchlin, a leading authority in Hebrew studies during the Renaissance, affirmed the Sephardic pronunciation, influencing subsequent scholars and translators like Tyndale.

# Debunking the Myth: Was There a 'J' Sound in Ancient Hebrew?

## Comparative Semitic Linguistics

Research in the field of comparative Semitic linguistics can offer insights into the evolution of sounds in related languages. Ancient Hebrew, being part of the Semitic language family, shares characteristics with languages like Aramaic, Arabic, and Akkadian. Investigating how the 'J' sound is represented in these languages could provide clues about its presence or absence in ancient Hebrew.

In comparative Semitic linguistics, concrete evidence from related languages such as Aramaic, Arabic, and Akkadian can provide insights into the presence of the 'J' sound in ancient Hebrew:

1. **Aramaic**: Aramaic, closely related to Hebrew, historically used the letter Daleth (ד) to represent a sound similar to the modern 'J' in some dialects. This indicates that a 'J'-like sound was not unfamiliar in the linguistic environment close to ancient Hebrew. However, the direct correspondence of this sound to the Hebrew Yod (י) is not evident in Aramaic.

2. **Arabic**: Classical Arabic has the letter Jim (ج), which is pronounced as a 'J' sound in most dialects. This sound has been consistent in

Arabic, a language known for preserving many archaic Semitic phonetic features. The presence of this sound in Arabic, a Semitic language, suggests the possibility of its existence in related languages, including ancient Hebrew.

3. **Akkadian**: Akkadian, one of the earliest Semitic languages, utilized cuneiform script which did not directly correspond to the Hebrew alphabet. The representation of a 'J' sound in Akkadian is not as straightforward, but the language did have a diversity of phonetic sounds. However, there is no direct evidence of a 'J' sound similar to that in modern English.

4. **Phonetic Shifts**: Historical linguistics shows that phonetic shifts are common in language evolution. For instance, the Hebrew Yod (ʾ) initially may have had a broader range of sounds that narrowed over time. While the exact nature of this sound in ancient Hebrew is still debated, the variation in its pronunciation in related Semitic languages suggests that a 'J'-like sound could have been plausible in certain linguistic contexts.

5. **Transliteration Practices**: Ancient transliterations of Hebrew names into Greek and Latin do not consistently support the presence of a 'J' sound. For example, in the Septuagint (Greek translation of the Hebrew Bible), Hebrew names with Yod (ʾ) are often transliterated with an 'I' sound (as in Iesous for Yeshua). This indicates that the Greek speakers perceived the Yod more like an 'I' than a 'J.'

6. **Linguistic Reconstruction**: Linguistic reconstruction of Proto-Semitic, the common ancestor of Semitic languages, suggests that the sound represented by Yod (ʾ) in Hebrew could have had different realizations in different branches of the Semitic family. While a 'J' sound is plausible, it is not definitively evidenced in the earliest reconstructable stages of the language.

In summary, while the presence of a 'J' sound in related Semitic languages like Arabic suggests its possibility in ancient Hebrew, direct evidence from historical linguistic sources, such as transliterations and phonetic reconstructions, does not conclusively confirm its presence in ancient Hebrew. The evolution of Semitic phonetics and the variety of realizations of similar sounds in related languages provide a complex and multifaceted picture of ancient Hebrew phonology.

## Ancient Hebrew Inscriptions

Archaeological findings, including inscriptions and ancient manuscripts, can provide direct evidence of pronunciation. For instance, the Moabite Stone (Mesha Stele) and the Siloam Inscription, which date back to the first millennium BCE, might offer clues about the phonetics of the period.

In exploring the existence of a 'J' sound in Biblical Hebrew and Paleo-Hebrew, particularly in supporting "Jehovah" as the correct pronunciation of the Tetragrammaton, we can look at specific archaeological findings and ancient manuscripts:

1.  **Moabite Stone (Mesha Stele):** Dating back to the 9th century BCE, the Moabite Stone features the Moabite language, which is closely related to Hebrew. The Moabite language, like early Hebrew, used the letter ' (Yod). However, the stele does not provide direct evidence for the pronunciation of ' as 'J'. The Moabite language is believed to have similarities with Hebrew, but direct transliterations indicating a 'J' sound in the Moabite language have not been conclusively identified in the stone's inscriptions.

2.  **Siloam Inscription:** The Siloam Inscription, dating from the 8th century BCE, is written in ancient Hebrew. It provides valuable insights into the language's phonetics during this period. The inscription includes the letter ' (Yod), but similar to the Moabite Stone, it does not offer explicit evidence of the 'J' sound. The script is consonantal, and without vowels, it's challenging to determine the exact pronunciation of ' in this context.

3.  **Lachish Letters:** The Lachish Letters, a set of ostraca (pottery shards) written in ancient Hebrew and dating to the 6th century BCE, include the use of ' (Yod). However, these inscriptions also

lack vowel markings, making it difficult to determine if the 'J' sound was used.

4. **Gezer Calendar**: The Gezer Calendar, dated to the 10th century BCE, is one of the earliest examples of Hebrew script. It is an agricultural calendar that includes the letter ʼ (Yod). Like other ancient inscriptions, it does not provide vowel indications, leaving the exact pronunciation of ʼ ambiguous.

5. **Comparative Analysis with Other Semitic Languages**: Inscriptions in related Semitic languages, such as Phoenician and Ugaritic, which share the alphabetic script with ancient Hebrew, include characters similar to ʼ (Yod). However, these inscriptions also do not give a definitive indication of a 'J' sound as they are primarily consonantal scripts without explicit vowel notations.

In conclusion, while these ancient Hebrew inscriptions are crucial for understanding the script and language of the period, they do not provide concrete evidence of the 'J' sound for the pronunciation of ʼ (Yod) in the context of the Tetragrammaton or other Hebrew words. The absence of vowel indicators in these inscriptions means that the exact pronunciation, particularly whether it included a 'J' sound, remains a topic of scholarly debate and interpretation based on indirect linguistic and historical evidence.

## Etymology of Biblical Names

The etymology and pronunciation of biblical names that include the letter ʼ (Yod) in Hebrew can provide evidence. For example, examining how these names were transliterated into other ancient languages like Greek and Latin could indicate how the sound was perceived and pronounced.

To explore the presence of a 'J' sound in Biblical Hebrew and Paleo-Hebrew, particularly in relation to the pronunciation of "Jehovah," we can analyze the etymology and pronunciation of biblical names containing the letter ʼ (Yod) and how these names were transliterated into other ancient languages like Greek and Latin:

1. **Transliteration into Greek:** In the Septuagint, the ancient Greek translation of the Hebrew Bible, Hebrew names containing ' (Yod) were often transliterated with an initial 'I' sound (represented by the Greek iota, I). For instance, the Hebrew name יהושע (Yehoshua) was transliterated as Ἰησοῦς (Iesous). This suggests that the Greek translators perceived the ' (Yod) as having a sound closer to 'I' than to 'J.'

2. **Transliteration into Latin:** Similarly, when these Hebrew names were transliterated into Latin, the initial ' (Yod) was often represented by 'I,' as in the case of Iesus (Jesus) from Ἰησοῦς (Iesous). This again points to an 'I' sound rather than a 'J' sound.

3. **Evolution of the 'J' Sound in Latin:** It is important to note that the 'J' sound as we know it today in English and some other modern languages did not exist in classical Latin. The letter 'J' was originally a variant of 'I,' and its pronunciation as 'J' developed in later Latin during the medieval period. This indicates that the 'J' sound was not used in the transliteration of Hebrew names into early Latin.

4. **Names in the Dead Sea Scrolls:** The Dead Sea Scrolls, which include texts in Hebrew, Aramaic, and Greek, provide additional sources for examining transliteration practices. However, these texts predominantly use the Hebrew script and thus do not offer direct evidence for the 'J' sound in transliterations.

5. **Phonetic Shifts Over Time:** The way that ' (Yod) was transliterated into Greek and Latin suggests that its pronunciation in Biblical and Paleo-Hebrew was closer to an 'I' sound. The shift to a 'J' sound in the pronunciation of Hebrew names and words like "Jehovah" seems to be a later development, influenced by changes in the phonetics of European languages, rather than a reflection of ancient Hebrew pronunciation

The use of "I" in Latin to represent what evolved into the "J" sound in later languages, including English, is similar to Tyndale's usage in his English translation.

In classical Latin, the letter "I" was used both as a vowel (like the English 'i' in "machine") and as a consonant (similar to the English 'y' in "yes"). Over time, especially during the Middle Ages, the consonantal "I" (also called "I" consonant or "jot") started being pronounced more like the modern English 'j' sound in certain positions, particularly at the beginning of words. This phonetic shift was part of the evolution of the Romance languages from Latin.

When Raymundus Martini used the spelling "Yohoua" in the 13th century, it reflected the pronunciation norms of his time and linguistic background. Similarly, when Tyndale transliterated the Tetragrammaton as "Jehovah" in the 16th century, the "I" in his sources was understood as having a consonantal sound, aligning with the evolving pronunciation of "J" in Early Modern English. This development in English paralleled the evolution of the "I" consonant into a distinct "J" sound in other European languages, including the transition in Latin.

Therefore, the use of "I" in these historical Latin sources and in Tyndale's English was indeed indicative of a sound that was shifting towards or had become similar to the modern "J" sound. This linguistic transition reflects the broader evolution of European languages in the post-classical and medieval periods.

In summary, the etymology and transliteration of biblical names containing ' (Yod) into Greek and Latin suggest that this letter was originally pronounced more like an 'I' than a 'J' in Biblical and Paleo-Hebrew. The pronunciation of "Jehovah" with a 'J' sound appears to be a later development, not grounded in the original pronunciation of the Hebrew Tetragrammaton.

### Early Greek and Latin Transcriptions of Hebrew Texts

The way Hebrew words, especially the Tetragrammaton, were transcribed in early Greek and Latin texts could shed light on their original pronunciation. This includes works by early Church Fathers and translations like the Septuagint.

In examining the early Greek and Latin transcriptions of Hebrew texts, particularly the Tetragrammaton, we find evidence that can provide insights into the original pronunciation of the Hebrew name of God, often rendered as "Jehovah":

1. **Septuagint Translations:** The Septuagint, a Greek translation of the Hebrew Scriptures, completed by the 2nd century BCE, does not directly transcribe the Tetragrammaton (JHVH) into Greek letters. Instead, it consistently substitutes it with "Κύριος" (Kyrios), meaning "Lord." This practice indicates the reverence for the name but does not shed light on its phonetic pronunciation in Hebrew. (See LXXP. Fouad Inv. 266 Excursion below)

2. **Early Greek Transcriptions:** Some of the earliest Greek transcriptions of Hebrew texts, including fragments of the Septuagint and other manuscripts, avoid representing the Tetragrammaton with Greek characters, again typically using "Κύριος." This lack of direct transcription makes it challenging to ascertain the original pronunciation from these Greek sources.

3. **Latin Transcriptions:** In Latin translations of the Hebrew Scriptures, such as the Vulgate (completed in the 4th century CE), the Tetragrammaton is often transcribed as "Dominus" (Lord), similar to the Greek practice. However, Jerome, the translator of the Vulgate, was aware of the pronunciation of the Tetragrammaton, which he transliterated as "Iehova" in his other writings. This reflects the Latin usage of 'I' for the 'J' sound.

4. **Writings of Early Church Fathers:** Some early Church Fathers, including Jerome, mention the Tetragrammaton in their writings. Jerome, who had access to Jewish scholars and texts, used "Iehova" in Latin, indicating the 'J' sound as used in the Latin of his time.

5. **No Direct Greek Equivalents:** The Greek language, at the time of the Septuagint's translation, did not have a direct equivalent for the 'J' sound. The Greek alphabet and phonetics did not include this sound, which explains why the Tetragrammaton was not transliterated phonetically into Greek.

In conclusion, while the early Greek transcriptions do not provide direct evidence of the 'J' sound due to the phonetic limitations of Greek, the Latin transcriptions, particularly by scholars like Jerome who had a deep understanding of Hebrew, suggest that a 'J'-like sound (represented by 'I' in Latin) was recognized in the pronunciation of the Tetragrammaton during the early centuries CE. This aligns with the later English pronunciation "Jehovah" that emerged with the development of modern English phonetics.

# Jehovah, There Was No "J" Until 500 Years Ago?

### Was Jehovah's Name Altered by the Creation of the Letter "J"?

### The Historical Development of the Letter "J"

The issue of the letter "J" and its pronunciation has often been at the heart of debates surrounding the correct spelling and pronunciation of the divine name, represented by the Hebrew letters יהוה (JHVH). The argument centers on whether "Jehovah" is a legitimate representation of the tetragrammaton or if the form "Yahweh" should be regarded as more accurate. Critics of the name "Jehovah" often point to the fact that the letter "J" is a relatively modern addition to the alphabet and argue that this discredits the use of "Jehovah" as a faithful transliteration of JHVH.

To begin with, it is important to recognize that the first symbol representing both the "i" and "j" sound appeared around 800 C.E. This symbol was created by French monks who adapted Roman alphabetic practices. The sound represented by this symbol was a voiced palatal approximant, which today corresponds to the "y" sound in English. Over time, as language evolved, this symbol began to be used in various forms throughout Europe, eventually arriving in Saxon England in 1066, brought by William the Conqueror. Therefore, the first symbol representing the "j" sound entered the English-speaking world over 900 years ago, well before William Tyndale transliterated the tetragrammaton as "Iehouah."

The lowercase "j," as it is used today, was developed around 1200 C.E. by adding a tail to the bottom of the lowercase "i." This was done to distinguish the "i" sound from the "j" sound. However, the capital "J," as we now use it, did not emerge until much later, near the end of the 16th century. Thus, during the time of Tyndale (early 16th century), the "j" sound was represented by the letter "i" when placed before a vowel. For instance, "Iehouah" was pronounced with a consonantal "j" sound, even though it began with the letter "I."

## Tyndale's Contribution and the Name "Jehovah"

William Tyndale's translation of the Pentateuch in 1530 is one of the earliest known instances of the divine name JHVH being rendered as "Iehouah." This was a transliteration based on the vowel points of Adonai, which were inserted into the consonants of the tetragrammaton by Masoretic scribes. Tyndale's choice of "Iehouah" was not an invention of a new name but rather an attempt to make the sacred name accessible to English speakers in a manner that reflected its Hebrew origins. Since the capital "J" had not yet been invented, the name began with "I," which was understood by English speakers to represent the "j" sound.

For example, in Exodus 6:3, Tyndale writes, "And I appeared unto Abraham, unto Isaac, and unto Jacob, by the name of God Almighty, but by my name Iehouah was I not known to them." The name "Iehouah" in Tyndale's day represented the same pronunciation that "Jehovah" later would, even though the spelling of the divine name evolved over time as the English language continued to develop.

During this period, other letters were also in flux. The letters "u" and "v" were used interchangeably, much like "i" and "j." For instance, Tyndale's translation uses "v" as a vowel in some words and as a consonant in others. This reflects the fluid nature of English orthography in the 16th century.

It is important to understand that while the spelling of names and words in English has evolved significantly, the sounds these letters represent have often remained consistent. The sounds that correspond to the English letters "J," "U," and "V" existed long before the letters themselves were standardized. This means that while the letter "J" is a relatively recent addition to the English alphabet, the sound it represents was present in the spoken language well before the invention of the letter itself.

## The Argument Against "Yahweh"

Scholars who support the pronunciation "Yahweh" often argue that the name "Jehovah" is a mistranslation or a misrepresentation of the divine name JHVH. They assert that because the letter "J" did not exist in ancient Hebrew, "Jehovah" must be incorrect, and "Yahweh" is the only proper way to pronounce the name of God.

However, this argument overlooks a key detail: the spelling "Yahweh" also relies on English letters that did not exist in ancient times. For instance, the letter "W," which is central to the spelling of "Yahweh," was not invented until several centuries after the letter "J." The letter "W" emerged around the 13th century, long after the Hebrew Scriptures were written. Additionally, the vowel "A" and the letter "H" used in "Yahweh" were standardized into their modern forms even later.

This creates an inconsistency in the argument of those who reject "Jehovah" on the basis of the letter "J." If the argument is based on the premise that "Jehovah" is incorrect because the letter "J" did not exist in ancient Hebrew, then "Yahweh" must also be disqualified by the same reasoning, as it uses letters that likewise did not exist at the time the Hebrew Scriptures were written. Both names—Jehovah and Yahweh—are ultimately transliterations, using English letters to represent Hebrew sounds.

## Language Evolution and Pronunciation

It is important to remember that the letters we use to represent the sounds of a name are simply symbols. Over the centuries, languages have evolved, and the symbols used to represent sounds have changed. This is particularly true of English, where the alphabet has undergone numerous revisions, especially during the Middle Ages and the early modern period. The development of new letters, such as "J," does not negate the validity of the sounds they represent. The sounds existed long before the letters were standardized.

For example, the "j" sound in "Jehovah" was represented by the letter "i" before the letter "j" was officially introduced into the English alphabet. This demonstrates that even though the symbols used to represent sounds may change over time, the sounds themselves remain constant. Therefore, the argument that "Jehovah" is incorrect because the letter "J" did not exist is fundamentally flawed.

The same principle applies to the name "Yahshua," a variant spelling of "Joshua," used by certain groups to refer to Jesus Christ. Those who insist on the use of "Yahshua" instead of "Jesus" often base their argument on the idea that the letter "J" did not exist in ancient Hebrew. However, this reasoning fails to account for the fact that the letters "s" and "u" used in "Yahshua" were also later developments in English orthography. This inconsistency reveals a bias in the critique against "Jehovah."

## The Legitimacy of "Jehovah" in Scripture

It is important to note that "Jehovah" has been used as a valid representation of the divine name JHVH in multiple translations of the Bible, including William Tyndale's translations in 1526, 1530, and 1534. The King James Version (KJV) of 1611, one of the most widely read English translations, also uses "Jehovah" to represent the tetragrammaton in several places, including Exodus 6:3 and Psalm 83:18.

The American Standard Version (ASV) of 1901, another respected English translation, consistently uses "Jehovah" throughout the Old Testament. These translations reflect the long-standing tradition of using "Jehovah" to represent the divine name in English-speaking Christian communities.

Critics of the name "Jehovah" often claim that it is a recent invention, but historical evidence shows that it has been in use for several centuries. Furthermore, the principle of transliteration—rendering the sounds of one language into the alphabet of another—supports the legitimacy of "Jehovah" as an acceptable representation of JHVH in English. Just as "Jesus" is a legitimate transliteration of the Hebrew name "Yeshua," so too is "Jehovah" a valid transliteration of JHVH.

The debate surrounding the divine name, whether it should be "Jehovah" or "Yahweh," ultimately rests on issues of transliteration and linguistic evolution. The key takeaway is that while the letters used to represent sounds have changed over time, the sounds themselves have remained consistent. Both "Jehovah" and "Yahweh" are transliterations of the Hebrew name JHVH, using the English alphabet to represent Hebrew sounds. The argument that "Jehovah" is incorrect because the letter "J" did not exist is flawed, as the same reasoning would disqualify the spelling "Yahweh" as well.

The specific letters and pronunciation of the divine name JHVH **do matter** because they reflect the sacredness and identity of the one true God. The name "Jehovah" has been used as a legitimate representation of JHVH for centuries, and it is crucial to recognize its importance in accurately conveying God's revealed name. Translations like those of Tyndale, the King James Version, and the American Standard Version faithfully preserve "Jehovah" as the divine name, showing deep respect for the sacredness of God's personal name in English. This representation matters because it is tied directly to how God is identified and called upon in scripture, and altering or disregarding it undermines the reverence and accuracy that such translations strive to uphold.

# Jehovah, Pointed with the Vowel Markings of Adonai?

## The Background of Vowel Pointing and the Hebrew Text

The divine name JHVH (יהוה) appears 6,823 times in the Masoretic Text, the authoritative Hebrew text of the Old Testament. This includes 6,518 occurrences where the name is marked to be pronounced as יְהֹוָה (J'hōh-vāh) and 305 occurrences where it is marked to be pronounced as יֱהֹוִה (Jehōh-vih). The Masoretes, Levites tasked with preserving the Hebrew Scriptures, undertook the important task of pointing the text with vowel markers to ensure proper pronunciation. Yet, some scholars argue that these vowel markings were not original to the divine name but borrowed from the title Adonai (אֲדֹנָי), meaning "Lord," to prevent the misuse of the name of God.

Scholars who prefer the pronunciation "Yahweh" generally argue that the Masoretic vowel points do not reflect the true original pronunciation of

JHVH. Instead, they claim the points were added deliberately to indicate that Adonai should be read in place of JHVH when the text was publicly read. As a result, the form "Jehovah," which follows the vowel markings of the Masoretic Text, is sometimes dismissed as a hybrid or inaccurate form, allegedly a creation from a combination of JHVH's consonants and Adonai's vowels.

The claim that the name "Jehovah" is the result of mixing the vowels of Adonai with JHVH's consonants is widespread in academic literature. For instance, John R. Kohlenberger III states in *The NIV Interlinear Hebrew-English Old Testament* that the name Jehovah was invented by a 16th-century scholar named Galatinus, who supposedly created this form by combining the consonants of JHVH with the vowels of Adonai. But is this assertion correct? Can we find historical evidence supporting the view that the name Jehovah is a fabrication?

## The Use of Jehovah Before Galatinus

The claim that Galatinus invented the name Jehovah is not supported by historical evidence. Jehovah (or similar forms) appears in records dating back centuries before Galatinus. The name was used by Christian scholars and theologians well before the 16th century. As far back as the medieval period, forms resembling Jehovah were commonly employed in writings about the divine name. In fact, early Christian scholars used the form Jehovah based on the vowel markings they observed in the Hebrew manuscripts available to them.

It is important to recognize that the Masoretes were devout preservers of the Hebrew text, not innovators or manipulators of it. Their task was not to create new readings but to record the oral tradition faithfully, ensuring that future generations would pronounce the text correctly. As Wurthwein notes, the work of the Masoretes began in the fifth century C.E. and involved standardizing the Hebrew text with vowel points to safeguard against mispronunciation or misinterpretation. The Masoretes operated under a strict sense of responsibility to the text. They had inherited the ancient tradition of Hebrew pronunciation from the priests and Levites who transmitted it orally over many centuries.

Wurthwein explains that the Masoretes developed vowel points to clarify pronunciation for readers who did not have access to oral instruction. Before this, the Hebrew text consisted only of consonants, which made accurate reading difficult. The introduction of vowel points provided a reliable guide for reading and interpreting the text. However, contrary to claims by some modern scholars, there is no evidence that the Masoretes engaged in deliberate tampering with the divine name.

## The Accuracy of the Masoretic Text

The Masoretes' work reflects a deep reverence for the sacredness of the text. These Levites, unlike the rabbis who focused on the Talmud, aimed to preserve the Hebrew Scriptures without alteration. They rejected rabbinical traditions that sought to obscure the divine name. The Masoretes were not advocates of hiding JHVH's name or replacing it with Adonai. Had they attempted to alter the text in such a manner, historical records would have documented the outcry from the scholarly community at that time. However, there is no such protest found in any historical sources. On the contrary, the Masoretes' vowel system is lauded for its accuracy.

Among the Masoretic schools, the Ben Asher and Ben Naphtali schools are the most prominent. Although they differed slightly in pronunciation and accents, their vowel pointing system is almost identical. This consistency across different schools further attests to the authenticity and reliability of the vowel system developed by the Masoretes.

By the time the Ben Asher family completed its work in the tenth century C.E., the Masoretic Text had become the authoritative standard for the Hebrew Scriptures. It was from this text that later scholars learned the pronunciation Jehovah. The earliest printed Hebrew Bibles, including the Soncino and Brescia Bibles, relied on the Ben Asher Masoretic Text. When early Protestant translators like William Tyndale rendered JHVH as Jehovah, they were following the vowel markings found in this standard text.

## Did the Masoretes Borrow from Adonai?

The theory that the vowel points under JHVH were borrowed from Adonai to signal readers to substitute the word "Lord" when pronouncing the name is a popular one, but it is not based on any clear historical evidence. The Masoretes' goal was to preserve, not obscure, the pronunciation of the text. While some rabbis did promote the reading of Adonai in place of JHVH, the Masoretes themselves were Levites, not rabbis, and had no interest in promoting Talmudic traditions.

The Talmudists, whose writings were influenced by mystical and esoteric traditions, did attempt to hide the name of God. Some Talmudic rabbis taught that JHVH was too sacred to be pronounced and should be replaced with Adonai when read aloud. This practice eventually influenced later Jewish communities, leading to the widespread substitution of Adonai for JHVH in synagogue readings. However, this was not a practice supported by the Masoretes. In fact, the Masoretes inserted vowel points into JHVH, not to hide the name, but to preserve its pronunciation. Their work was intended to ensure that future generations could continue to pronounce the name of God as it was revealed in the Scriptures.

## The Role of the Levites and the Oral Tradition

One key fact often overlooked in debates about the pronunciation of JHVH is the role of the Levites in transmitting the Hebrew text. The Levites were entrusted with teaching and preserving the Law (Deuteronomy 31:9-13). This responsibility included accurately passing down the pronunciation of the divine name. From the time of Moses, the Levites were the guardians of the Law, which they transmitted both in writing and through oral tradition. As time went on, the need for a written system of vowels arose, especially as the Hebrew language changed, and the Levites fulfilled this need by developing vowel points that reflected the pronunciation they had received from their ancestors.

Scripture provides evidence of the Levites' dedication to preserving the Law. In Nehemiah 8:8, it is recorded that the Levites "read from the book, from the Law of God, clearly, and they gave the sense, so that the people understood the reading." This verse demonstrates that the Levites were responsible for ensuring that the people correctly understood and pronounced the Scriptures. This task was not taken lightly, and the Masoretes, as descendants of the Levitical tradition, continued this sacred responsibility by accurately recording the pronunciation of JHVH.

The suggestion that the Masoretes would have borrowed vowel points from Adonai to obscure the divine name is inconsistent with their role as preservers of the text. The Masoretes were deeply committed to safeguarding the integrity of the Scriptures, and their vowel points reflect the traditional pronunciation of JHVH, as passed down from the Levites to future generations.

## The Name Jehovah in Christian History

The use of Jehovah in Christian history dates back many centuries. Early Christian writers, influenced by the Hebrew text, used the form Jehovah to refer to the God of Israel. These writers, relying on the Masoretic Text, viewed Jehovah as the correct pronunciation of the divine name.

Even after the Protestant Reformation, when scholars began to engage more deeply with the Hebrew text, the name Jehovah remained in widespread use. Protestant reformers such as William Tyndale and John Calvin adopted the pronunciation Jehovah based on their study of the Hebrew Scriptures. Calvin, in his commentary on the Psalms, used the form Jehovah, as did many other Christian scholars of his time. This was not a result of borrowing from Adonai but a reflection of the Hebrew vowel points found in the Masoretic Text.

## Is "Yahweh" More Accurate?

The preference for "Yahweh" over "Jehovah" is a relatively modern trend that emerged in academic circles during the 19th and 20th centuries. Scholars who support "Yahweh" often argue that this form is closer to the original pronunciation of JHVH. However, there is little historical evidence to support the idea that Yahweh is the original pronunciation. The pronunciation Jehovah is rooted in centuries of usage and is supported by the structure of the Hebrew language as reflected in the Masoretic Text.

Semitic philology provides evidence that the vowel points used by the Masoretes accurately reflect the traditional pronunciation of Hebrew words, including the divine name. As Waltke explains in his *Introduction to Biblical Hebrew Syntax*, the Tiberian vowel system (developed by the Masoretes) corresponds to ancient Hebrew grammar and phonology. The vowel points used with JHVH fit the traditional structure of Hebrew words and are consistent with the pronunciation patterns of the language.

Waltke argues that it would be impossible for the Masoretes to have faked the vowel points for JHVH without violating the basic rules of Semitic philology. A deliberate mispointing of the divine name would stand out as an anomaly in the text, but no such anomalies are present. Instead, the vowel points inserted by the Masoretes represent a reliable tradition of pronunciation passed down through the generations.

The claim that the name Jehovah is a hybrid form created by borrowing the vowels of Adonai is not supported by historical or linguistic evidence. The Masoretes, in their role as preservers of the Hebrew Scriptures, pointed JHVH to be pronounced Jehovah, following the oral tradition they had inherited from their Levitical ancestors. This pronunciation was widely used by Christian scholars long before Galatinus, and it continues to be supported by the structure of the Hebrew language.

Rather than obscuring the name of God, the Masoretes sought to preserve it for future generations. The vowel points they added to the Hebrew text reflect the traditional pronunciation of JHVH, which was known and used by both priests and common people alike. The name Jehovah is not a fabrication but the true pronunciation of the divine name as recorded in the Masoretic Text.

# Jehovah, Tetragrammaton?

## Is the Father's Personal Name Important?

The Bible frequently mentions God's personal name, revealing its significance and its relationship to His identity. The name Jehovah, represented in the Hebrew text as יהוה (JHVH or YHWH), appears 6,828 times, starting in Genesis 2:4, where it is first introduced in the phrase, "These are the generations of the heavens and the earth when they were created, in the day that Jehovah God made the earth and the heavens." (UASV). The frequency of this name's usage alone underscores the importance that God Himself places on being known by His personal name. The removal of Jehovah's name from modern translations has serious theological implications that affect our understanding of who God is and how we are to relate to Him.

## What Is the Significance of God's Name?

God's personal name is a reflection of His nature and His relationship with His people. The name Jehovah is often connected with His covenantal relationship with Israel. For instance, in Exodus 6:3, God declares, "And I appeared unto Abraham, unto Isaac, and unto Jacob, by the name of God Almighty, but by my name Jehovah I was not known to them." This verse reveals that while the patriarchs knew God, they had not yet experienced the full significance of His name Jehovah. This would unfold as God redeemed Israel from Egypt and fulfilled His covenant promises to them.

Moreover, Jehovah is not merely a title or a designation; it is a name filled with meaning. It comes from the Hebrew root word meaning "to be" or "to become." This relates directly to God's statement to Moses at the burning bush: "I AM WHO I AM" (Exodus 3:14). Jehovah, therefore, signifies the one who causes to become, the one who brings things into existence according to His will. He is the one who fulfills His promises, and His name is a constant reminder of His sovereign power and faithfulness. The Bible highlights the protective and salvific power of Jehovah's name, as we see in Proverbs 18:10: "The name of Jehovah is a strong tower; the righteous runs into it and is safe."

## The Deletion of Jehovah's Name from Modern Translations

One of the most troubling developments in biblical translation history is the removal of God's personal name in favor of titles such as "Lord" or "God." This practice can be traced back to the Jewish tradition of avoiding the pronunciation of the divine name out of reverence. However, this tradition did not originate with God's command but arose from human custom. Over time, this led to the replacement of Jehovah's name with titles like Adonai (Lord) in Jewish and Christian texts, particularly in translations like the Septuagint and the Latin Vulgate. In these texts, the Tetragrammaton (JHVH) was substituted, contributing to the gradual erasure of Jehovah's name from common usage.

Most modern translations have followed this pattern. The English Standard Version (ESV), for example, renders God's personal name as "Lord" in most instances. This practice obscures the personal aspect of God's name, reducing it to a mere title and weakening the sense of intimacy that comes with knowing God's name. The Holman Christian Standard Bible (HCSB) and the Lexham English Bible (LEB) do use Yahweh in some places, but even they fail to fully restore God's name throughout the Old Testament, opting instead to follow the tradition of substituting "LORD" or "GOD" in most occurrences of the Tetragrammaton.

## Scriptural Commands to Honor God's Name

Scripture is clear that God's name is to be revered and proclaimed. Jehovah Himself emphasizes the importance of His name in passages such as Isaiah 42:8: "I am Jehovah, that is my name; and my glory will I not give to another, neither my praise unto graven images." The name Jehovah signifies God's unique identity as the only true God, distinct from the idols and false gods worshiped by the surrounding nations.

The Psalms are replete with calls to praise Jehovah's name: "Let them praise the name of Jehovah, for his name alone is exalted; his glory is above earth and heaven" (Psalm 148:13). The command to honor and proclaim God's name is not just a suggestion; it is a crucial aspect of biblical worship. As Christians, we are called to "walk in the name of Jehovah our God forever and ever" (Micah 4:5). The removal of Jehovah's name from modern translations undermines this fundamental biblical principle and hinders believers from fully understanding the richness of God's self-revelation.

## The Restoration of Jehovah's Name in Modern Translations

Despite the widespread removal of Jehovah's name from many Bible translations, efforts have been made to restore it. One notable example is William Tyndale, who included Jehovah's name in his English translation of the Pentateuch in 1530. Tyndale understood the importance of retaining God's personal name and even explained to his readers that whenever they saw "LORD" in all capital letters, it represented the divine name Jehovah.

The 1901 American Standard Version (ASV) also restored Jehovah's name in over 6,000 instances, recognizing that it was inappropriate to replace the divine name with mere titles. The translators of the ASV declared: "A Jewish superstition, which regarded the Divine Name as too sacred to be uttered, ought no longer to dominate in the English or any other version of the Old Testament." This stance highlights the necessity of preserving the name that God has revealed to us in Scripture.

The UASV continues this tradition of faithfully restoring Jehovah's name, recognizing that the name is not a human invention but a divine self-revelation. God wants His people to know His name, to call upon Him in prayer, and to trust in the meaning and power that His name embodies.

## The Theological and Relational Implications of Using God's Name

Using God's personal name, Jehovah, has profound theological and relational implications. First, it reminds us of the personal relationship that God desires to have with His people. In Exodus 34:5-6, Jehovah descends in a cloud and proclaims His name to Moses, emphasizing His character: "Jehovah, Jehovah, a God merciful and gracious, slow to anger, and abundant in loving-kindness and truth." The repetition of the name highlights its importance and its connection to God's covenantal faithfulness.

Knowing God by His personal name also enhances our understanding of His promises. In the case of Moses and the Israelites, Jehovah promised to become whatever was needed to bring them out of slavery and into the Promised Land. This is a powerful expression of God's role as a deliverer and protector. God's name is tied to His actions in history, and to erase that name from the Bible is to diminish the full scope of His saving work.

Moreover, using Jehovah's name in prayer and worship acknowledges God's sovereignty and distinctiveness. The Bible is filled with warnings against the worship of false gods and idols. As Psalm 115:4-6 points out, idols have "mouths, but cannot speak; eyes, but cannot see; ears, but cannot hear." In contrast, Jehovah is the living God who interacts with His people, answers prayers, and fulfills His promises. To remove His name from the Bible is to reduce the personal connection that believers can have with their Creator.

## Why Is the Removal of Jehovah's Name a Problem?

The removal of Jehovah's name from most Bible translations is more than a simple issue of pronunciation or translation choices. It reflects a broader trend of diminishing the personal and relational aspect of God's revelation. The Bible is not merely a collection of theological concepts; it is a revelation of a personal God who desires a relationship with His creation. The name Jehovah is integral to understanding that relationship.

When modern translators choose to replace Jehovah's name with titles like "LORD" or "God," they make a theological decision that affects how readers perceive God. Titles can convey authority and power, but they do not carry the same personal intimacy that comes with a name. Imagine addressing a close friend or family member by their title rather than their name. It would create a sense of distance and formality, rather than closeness and familiarity.

Furthermore, the removal of Jehovah's name can lead to confusion about who God is. In a world filled with false gods and competing religious systems, the Bible clearly distinguishes Jehovah as the only true God. In passages like 1 Kings 18, where Elijah confronts the prophets of Baal, the distinction between Jehovah and Baal is made clear through the use of God's personal name. Elijah's prayer to Jehovah results in fire coming down from heaven, proving that Jehovah is the one true God (1 Kings 18:38-39). If Elijah had prayed to a generic "Lord," the distinction between the true God and the false gods would have been obscured.

## The Example of Jesus and the Apostles

Jesus and the apostles also recognized the importance of God's name. Jesus taught His disciples to pray, "Our Father who is in heaven, hallowed be your name" (Matthew 6:9). This statement emphasizes the sanctity of God's name and the need to honor it in prayer. Jesus' use of the word "Father" in this context highlights the personal relationship that believers are called to have with God, but it does not negate the importance of knowing and using God's personal name, Jehovah.

In fact, the apostles quoted Old Testament passages that referenced Jehovah and applied them to their teachings. For example, in Acts 2:21, Peter quotes Joel 2:32, saying, "Everyone who calls upon the name of Jehovah will be saved." Similarly, in Romans 10:13, Paul cites the same verse from Joel, reinforcing the importance of calling on Jehovah's name for salvation. These New Testament references to the divine name show that the apostles understood the significance of Jehovah's name and its role in God's plan of salvation.

## The Consequences of Ignoring God's Name

Ignoring or removing Jehovah's name from the Bible has far-reaching consequences. It not only diminishes the personal nature of God's revelation but also affects how believers relate to Him in worship and prayer. When we remove God's name, we risk turning Him into an abstract concept rather than a personal being who desires to be known by His people.

Furthermore, the removal of Jehovah's name can lead to theological confusion. If God's name is not used, it becomes easier for people to conflate the God of the Bible with the gods of other religions. This is especially concerning in an age of increasing religious pluralism and interfaith dialogue. The Bible is clear that Jehovah is distinct from all other gods, and His name serves as a marker of that distinction. In Deuteronomy 6:4, we read, "Hear, O Israel: Jehovah our God, Jehovah is one." This verse not only affirms the oneness of God but also emphasizes His unique identity as Jehovah.

# Jehovah, Was Invented?

### Understanding the Scholars Who Prefer Yahweh Movement's Claims

The question of whether "Jehovah" is a legitimate pronunciation of the divine name has become a source of debate, particularly among those involved in the Sacred Name movement. Advocates of this movement assert that "Jehovah" is a relatively recent invention, introduced by a Catholic scholar named Galatinus in the 1500s. Scholars who prefer Yahweh emphasize the importance of using what they believe to be the "correct" pronunciation of God's name, often advocating for "Yahweh" instead. According to them, "Jehovah" was unknown in biblical times, and it was Galatinus who supposedly concocted the form as a hybrid, combining the consonants from the Tetragrammaton (JHVH) with vowels from the title "Adonai."

This line of reasoning is supported by certain scholars and publications that argue against the use of the name "Jehovah." For example, one publication cites Joseph Rotherham's *The Emphasized Bible*, where he wrote: "The pronunciation Jehovah was unknown until 1520, when it was introduced by Galatinus." Critics of the name Jehovah often quote sources such as *The Jewish Encyclopedia*, which claims: "The reading Jehovah is a comparatively recent invention. Jehovah is generally held to have been the invention of Pope Leo the 10th's confessor, Peter Galatin (De Arcanis Catholic Veritates 1518)."

However, upon closer examination, historical evidence reveals that the name "Jehovah" was in use long before Galatinus. The claim that Jehovah was an invention is based on misunderstanding and confusion between various historical figures and sources. This article will systematically address the origin and legitimacy of the name Jehovah, tracing its history, analyzing the role of Galatinus, and demonstrating that the name was well-known and used centuries before his time.

## Was the Name Jehovah Known Before Galatinus?

One of the key arguments presented by those who oppose the use of the name Jehovah is the assertion that it was unknown before Galatinus introduced it in the early 16th century. However, historical evidence clearly demonstrates that the name Jehovah was in use long before Galatinus wrote *De Arcanis Catholicae Veritatis* in 1516. Several records, dating back to the 10th century C.E., confirm the presence and use of this pronunciation.

For instance, the form "Jehovah" appears in the works of the 14th-century theologian Porchetus Salvagus. Porchetus' *Victoria Porcheti adversus impios Hebraeos* was written in 1303 and contains the form "Jehovah" long before Galatinus. This record alone invalidates the claim that the name was invented in the 1500s. Further, Raymond Martin, in his work *Pugio Fidei* (written around 1270), also uses the form Jehovah. These instances predate Galatinus by several centuries and prove that the name was known and used by scholars well before the 16th century.

Additionally, various Hebrew texts and translations employed the name Jehovah. The Masoretes, Levites responsible for preserving the Hebrew Scriptures, developed the vowel-pointing system in the early Middle Ages, around the 5th to 10th centuries C.E. The Tetragrammaton, JHVH, was vowel-pointed by the Masoretes as "Jehovah" in the Ben Asher texts, the most authoritative versions of the Hebrew Scriptures. This alone demonstrates that the pronunciation Jehovah was not a recent innovation but a legitimate form that had been used for centuries.

The 13th-century work *Pugio Fidei*, written by Raymond Martin, contains numerous instances of the name Jehovah, establishing a clear precedent for its usage long before the Reformation era. If Galatinus had invented the name Jehovah, there would be no reason to find it in earlier works by Jewish and Christian scholars.

## The Role of Galatinus: Was He the Inventor of Jehovah?

To understand how the myth about the invention of the name Jehovah by Galatinus developed, it is necessary to examine the role of Pietro Colonna Galatino (Latinized as Galatinus) in the history of theology. Galatinus was a Catholic scholar who lived in the early 16th century and served as the confessor to Pope Leo X. In 1516, he authored *De Arcanis Catholicae Veritatis*, a theological work that sought to demonstrate the validity of Christian teachings using Jewish sources, including the Kabbalah.

Sacred-namers claim that Galatinus invented the form Jehovah by combining the consonants of JHVH with the vowels of Adonai. Yet, this assertion is demonstrably false when we consider that the name Jehovah was already in use by numerous scholars centuries before Galatinus. Galatinus did use the name Jehovah in his work, but he did not invent it. Instead, he employed a form of the divine name that was already well-known and accepted by many scholars of his day, both Catholic and Protestant.

One source of confusion stems from the writings of the Dutch theologian Johann Clemens, also known as Drusius or Van Der Driesche. Drusius lived from 1550 to 1616 and was a contemporary of Galatinus. He was the first to attribute the introduction of the name Jehovah to Galatinus, though this claim was based on a misunderstanding. Drusius himself had earlier discovered the name Jehovah in the works of Porchetus and others, but later retracted this fact, perhaps due to pressure or other external influences. His misattribution has since been repeated in scholarly works, contributing to the perpetuation of the myth that Galatinus invented the name Jehovah.

### Did Fagius Support the Name Jehovah?

Another figure who played a role in the history of the name Jehovah is Paulus Fagius (1504-1549), a Protestant scholar and Hebraist. Fagius, whose real name was Paul Buechelin, was a professor of Hebrew who studied under the famous Jewish scholar Elijah Levita. Fagius was well-versed in the Hebrew language and taught it at prestigious universities such as Strasbourg and Cambridge.

Fagius supported the use of the name Jehovah, based on the Hebrew Scriptures and the vowel-pointing system of the Masoretes. His understanding of the Hebrew language, along with his scholarship in Jewish sources, provided him with the knowledge necessary to endorse the pronunciation Jehovah. Fagius translated several Hebrew texts into Latin and edited works like the *Tishbi* and the *Meturgeman*, making significant contributions to the field of biblical studies. He recognized Jehovah as a legitimate rendering of the divine name and promoted its use in his writings.

Contrary to the claims made by those who oppose the name Jehovah, Fagius was not part of a Catholic conspiracy to promote a "false" name. He was a Protestant scholar who based his conclusions on careful study of the Hebrew texts, not on a desire to propagate a hybrid form of the divine name. His endorsement of Jehovah adds further weight to the argument that this name is both legitimate and rooted in historical scholarship.

## The Influence of Higher Criticism on the Name Jehovah

The myth that Jehovah was an invented name gained traction in the 17th and 18th centuries, largely due to the rise of higher criticism in biblical studies. Higher criticism, which seeks to analyze the origins and composition of biblical texts, often introduces skepticism and casts doubt on traditional understandings of Scripture. One of the effects of higher criticism was to challenge the authenticity of the Masoretic Text and the vowel-pointing system it employed.

Ludovicus Capellus, a French Huguenot theologian and Hebrew scholar, was one of the figures who contributed to this trend. In his work *Critica Sacra* (1650), Capellus argued that the Masoretic Text was defective and that other ancient manuscripts should be preferred. His work laid the foundation for later scholars to challenge the integrity of the Masoretic Text, including the pronunciation of the divine name as Jehovah. Capellus rejected Jehovah on the grounds that it was based on what he considered to be faulty vowel points in the Masoretic tradition.

Capellus' work was influential in spreading the idea that Jehovah was a hybrid form, and his conclusions were adopted by many later scholars. Over time, his views became part of the critical apparatus used by higher critics to undermine the reliability of the Hebrew text. However, Capellus' conclusions were not based on objective scholarship but rather on his preference for other manuscripts that he believed were superior to the Masoretic Text.

## Drusius and the Spread of the Myth

Johann Clemens Drusius (1550-1616), another influential scholar, played a critical role in spreading the myth that Jehovah was invented by Galatinus. Drusius was a Protestant scholar who, like Capellus, was influenced by the rising trend of higher criticism. He questioned the legitimacy of the name Jehovah and was among the first to claim that Galatinus had invented it.

Despite Drusius' scholarly reputation, his conclusions regarding Jehovah were flawed. As noted earlier, Drusius himself had discovered the name Jehovah in the works of Porchetus, but he later ignored this fact and promoted the idea that the name was a recent invention. His work in the *Critici Sacri* series, a multi-volume collection of biblical commentaries, further spread the false notion that Jehovah was an invented name.

Drusius' conclusions were picked up by later scholars, including Louis Cappel and the compilers of the *Critici Sacri*, who helped solidify the myth that Jehovah was a recent creation. These works became widely accepted in academic circles, and the myth that Jehovah was invented continued to spread.

## Bottcher and the Oxford Gesenius

In the 19th century, the myth that Jehovah was invented in the 16th century reached its peak with the publication of Wilhelm Bottcher's works. Bottcher, a German scholar, stated in 1866 that "the pronunciation of Jehovah was unknown until 1520, when it was introduced by Galatinus." Bottcher's conclusions were not based on original research but were derived from earlier works such as those of Drusius and Capellus. He simply repeated the claims that had already been made by these scholars, contributing to the perpetuation of the myth.

The *Oxford Gesenius*, published between 1892 and 1900, also propagated the idea that Jehovah was a modern invention. Edited by scholars such as Brown, Driver, and Briggs, the *Oxford Gesenius* included the same flawed reasoning found in earlier works, asserting that the pronunciation of Jehovah was unknown before the 16th century. This publication, along with the work of Bottcher, became a key source for those who opposed the use of the name Jehovah.

## The Jewish Encyclopedia and Rotherham's Influence

In the early 20th century, the myth continued to gain traction with the publication of *The Jewish Encyclopedia* (1907) and Joseph Bryant Rotherham's *Emphasized Bible* (1902). Both works repeated the claim that Jehovah was a hybrid form invented by Galatinus in the 1500s. Rotherham, in particular, was influential among sacred-namers, as his translation emphasized the importance of using what he believed to be the correct name of God.

However, Rotherham's conclusions were based on earlier scholarship that had already been shown to be flawed. He relied on sources like Bottcher and the *Oxford Gesenius*, which themselves were influenced by higher criticism and the faulty conclusions of Drusius and Capellus. As a result, Rotherham's work further entrenched the myth that Jehovah was a modern invention.

*The Jewish Encyclopedia* also contributed to the confusion by conflating the names of two scholars, Paulus Fagius and Johann Clemens Drusius. The encyclopedia stated that Fagius and Drusius were responsible for propagating the use of Jehovah, when in fact these were two separate individuals with differing views on the matter. The incorrect attribution of Fagius' support for Jehovah to Drusius only added to the misunderstanding surrounding the name.

## The Masoretic Tradition and the Legitimacy of Jehovah

The historical and linguistic evidence supports the conclusion that Jehovah is a legitimate rendering of the divine name, based on the Masoretic tradition. The Masoretes, who were responsible for preserving the Hebrew Scriptures, developed the vowel-pointing system that allowed the correct pronunciation of Hebrew words to be transmitted accurately. The name Jehovah, as it appears in the Masoretic Text, is the result of this careful preservation.

The vowel points inserted by the Masoretes reflect an ancient tradition of pronunciation that had been passed down through generations. The claim that these vowel points were deliberately altered to obscure the true pronunciation of God's name is not supported by any historical evidence. In fact, the Masoretes were known for their meticulous attention to detail and their desire to preserve the Hebrew text as accurately as possible.

The pronunciation Jehovah, far from being a modern invention, is rooted in this ancient tradition. The Masoretic Text, finalized around 980 C.E., consistently points the divine name as Jehovah. This form of the name was known and used by scholars long before Galatinus, and it continues to be supported by the structure of the Hebrew language itself.

## Final Reflections on the Name Jehovah

The historical and linguistic evidence overwhelmingly supports the legitimacy of the name Jehovah. The myth that it was a modern invention, introduced by Galatinus in the 16th century, has been thoroughly debunked by a careful examination of the available sources. From the Masoretic Text to the works of scholars like Raymond Martin and Porchetus Salvagus, the name Jehovah has been known and used for centuries.

Despite the claims of sacred-namers and critics, Jehovah remains a valid and historically attested pronunciation of the divine name. The careful preservation of the Hebrew Scriptures by the Masoretes, along with the testimony of early Christian and Jewish scholars, affirms that Jehovah is not a fabrication but a true representation of God's name as it appears in the Hebrew text.